Jewish Latin America
Ilan Stavans, series editor

KING DAVID'S HARP

KING DAVID'S HARP

*Autobiographical Essays
by Jewish Latin American Writers*

Edited with an Introduction by
STEPHEN A. SADOW

University of New Mexico Press
Albuquerque

First edition
Library of Congress Cataloging-in-Publication Data
King David's harp : autobiographical essays by Jewish Latin American writers / edited
with an introduction by Stephen A. Sadow.
    p.   cm. — (Jewish Latin America)
Includes bibliographical references.
ISBN 0-8263-1847-9 (cloth : alk. paper). — ISBN 0-8263-2087-2 (paper : alk. paper)
  1. Jewish authors—Latin America—Biography. I. Sadow, Stephen A., 1946– .
II. Series.
PQ7081.3.K56 1999
860.9'8924'098—dc21
[B]   99–28486
                                              CIP

Marjorie Agosín. "Through a Field of Stars, I Remember." Published by permission of the author.

Marcos Aguinis. "Boredom Is the Worst of the Sins." Published by permission of the author.

Ruth Behar. "Juban América." *Poetics Today* 16:1 (Spring 1995): 151–70. Copyright © 1995. Porter Institute for Poetics and Semiotics. Reprinted by permission of Duke University Press.

Ariel Dorfman. From *Going North, Looking South*. Copyright © 1997 by Ariel Dorfman. Reprinted by permission of The Wylie Agency, Inc.

Ricardo Feierstein. From *Contraexilio y mestizaje*. Buenos Aires: Milá, 1997. Published by permission of the author.

Alicia Freilich de Segal. "Memories of a Criolla Zionist." Published by permission of the author.

Alberto Gerchunoff. Adapted from "Mi autobiografía." Every attempt has been made to locate the publisher of the original Spanish version.

Margo Glantz. "Family Trees." From *The Family Tree*. London: Serpent's Tale, 1991. Published by permission of the author.

Isaac Goldemberg. "Life in Installments." Published by permission of the author. Previously published by Gale's Contemporary Authors Autobiographical Series.

José Kozer. "Natural Instincts." Published by permission of the author. Previously published by Gale's Contemporary Authors Autobiographical Series.

Alcina Lubitch Domecq. "Résumé Raisonné." Published by permission of the author.

Angelina Muñiz-Huberman. "Death, Exile, Inheritance." From *Cuerpo entero*. México: Corunda, 1991. Published by permission of the author.

Moacyr Scliar. "A Centaur in the Garden." Published by permission of the author.

Ilan Stavans. "Lost in Translation." From *The One-Handed Pianist and Other Stories*. Albuquerque: University of New Mexico Press, 1996. Published by permission of the author and the University of New Mexico Press.

Mario Szichman. "Distorted Words, Distorted Images, Broken Languages." Published by permission of the author.

For Jim Kates

It is said that King David had an extraordinary harp. Before he went to bed, he hung this precious instrument by a window near his head. During the night, the north wind blew on the strings and created wondrous music. That harp music would cause King David to arise and begin to compose. According to legend, he wrote the Psalms while in a trance-like state. The poetry flowed freely from him. It is also said that King David had the ability to see into the past and the future. If that is so, King David's Psalm 137, "By the Rivers of Babylon," is the first literary work of the exile to respond to life in the Diaspora.

JEWISH LATIN AMERICAN WRITERS, INSPIRED INTERPRETERS OF THE DIASPORA, HAVE HEARD KING DAVID'S HARP.

CONTENTS

Acknowledgments

King David's Harp was remarkably easy to edit. The contributors were active participants in the task. From the project's inception, they were enthusiastic about collecting Jewish Latin American autobiography. "What a wonderful idea!" Moacyr Scliar wrote. "I will write something special," Marjorie Agosín promised.

This project brings together essays from people who are or could have been old friends. The writers come from many places: Marcos Aguinis and Ricardo Feierstein from Buenos Aires, Angelina Muñiz-Huberman and Margo Glantz from Mexico City, Moacyr Scliar from Porto Alegre, Brazil, José Kozer from Spain, Alcina Lubitch Domecq from Israel, Isaac Goldemberg and Mario Szichman from New York, Marjorie Agosín from Wellesley, Ilan Stavans from Amherst, Ariel Dorfman from Durham, and Ruth Behar from Ann Arbor.

Ilan Stavans, series editor of "Jewish Latin America" and a contributor to this anthology, provided welcome insights and a wealth of experience from which I could draw. His suggestions were sagacious and immediately applicable. He is both an experienced critic and a supportive friend.

I wish to thank especially Celeste Kostopulos-Cooperman, Joan

E. Friedman, David Unger, Susan Bassnett, and Ilan Stavans, the extraordinarily talented translators who made this collection possible. I greatly appreciate the patience and precision of Cola Franzen, Jim Kates, Mark Shaffer, Trisha Vita, and the members of the New England Literary Translators Group whose high standards led me to improve my own translations from Spanish. I thank Francisco Mondavi for his helpful comments on my translation of Moacyr Scliar's Portuguese text.

I am especially grateful to Annie Clark, who did bibliographical research and so many other tasks and in doing so left a bit of herself in this book.

At Northeastern University, Harlow Robinson, Chairman of the Department of Modern Languages, was unwavering in his support of this project. Jim Ross, Chairman of the Jewish Studies Program and a specialist in the Jewish Diaspora, urged me on from the start. Sermin Muctehitzade, herself a member of the Turkish Diaspora, helped me to clarify social issues. I would also like to thank the staff of Northeastern University Library's Inter-Library Loan Services, whose skills I often put to the test.

Dana Asbury, Acquisitions Editor at the University of New Mexico Press, with good spirits and good sense, made the entire process smooth and pleasurable. Elizabeth Varnedoe, Manuscripts Editor, oversaw every detail with care and attention.

I thank my wife, Norma, and my daughter, Beth, for their patience and love.

INTRODUCTION

In *King David's Harp,* Jewish Latin American writers speak for themselves about their lives, their work, their Jewish identity, and much more. The anthology includes fifteen autobiographical selections in which noted Jewish Latin American writers discuss their Judaism, their writing, their crucial formative experiences, and the Jewish community in Latin America and in the United States. These writers come from Argentina, Brazil, Chile, Cuba, Guatemala, Mexico, Peru, and Venezuela. About half live outside of their country of origin. Except for Alberto Gerchunoff, who died in 1950, all of these writers are actively involved in creating new literary works.

Many of the authors included in this volume write as members of a minority in xenophobic cultures. While some of them and their coreligionists have prospered or reached important positions, won prizes, worked as graphic artists or editors or professors or even cabinet ministers, most have never felt accepted by Latin American readers. To give one example, Samuel Rawinski, Costa Rica's leading writer, who has an extraordinary command of Spanish style, is begrudgingly and only at times accepted as a member of the country's literary community. Isaac Goldemberg was a world-class writer, whose work was being discussed at literary conferences, before he was accepted as a Peruvian writer by the Peruvian literary critics.

There is thematic unity in *King David's Harp*. While there are differences of opinion, sometimes sharp, certain basic concepts recur. Obviously, in writing that is both Jewish and autobiographical, memory is of the utmost importance. Memory of the old country, parents and grandparents, arrival and culture shock, growing up, places lived in, "making it in America," artistic, business, or political achievement, anti-Semitism and the Nazis. There is ambivalence about personal and collective memory, a constant evaluation of Jewish identity as a personal issue and in a Latin American context, a mixture of negativism and unexpected expressions of optimism, a mourning of the Holocaust and fervent Zionism. The major Jewish issues of the twentieth century come together in these essays: secularism and the mysticism of the Cabala, traditional faith and apostasy, exile, refugee, or immigrant status, the viability of Yiddish, making *aliyah* (immigrating to Israel), and struggling for success in the Diaspora. Jewish issues local to Latin America are also important: Jewish labor organizations, socialist Zionist groups such as HaShomer HaTzair, the viability of social clubs and synagogues, and terrorist bombings directed at Jewish organizations. Also central are the pervasive issues of assimilation, conversions, mixed marriages, and divided families.

Along with their Jewishness, all of these writers identify themselves as Latin Americans no matter where they may currently live. Just a few examples follow. Marjorie Agosín makes regular trips to Chile, where she has long been involved in the movement for human rights. Ruth Behar has focused her anthropological studies on the Hispanic world and has returned several times to her birthplace, Cuba. Ilan Stavans co-edited *Growing Up Latino*, wrote a perceptive study called *The Hispanic Condition*, and edits *Hopscotch*, a journal for Latino readers. Isaac Goldemberg is the director of the Latin American Writers Institute in New York, a body dedicated to the support of Latino culture in the United States; he also edits the bilingual literary journal *Brújula/Compass*. Marcos Aguinis has been continually involved in Argentine politics, rising to the positions of minister of culture and minister of state. Ricardo Feierstein refers to himself as a cultural mestizo, the combination of his Jewish and Latin American heritages.

A collective interest in Latin American literature and politics runs through the essays: César Vallejo's broken lines, Jorge Luis Borges's labyrinths and Julio Cortázar's multiple realities, Pablo Neruda's wide vistas, and Octavio Paz's sagacity. The presence of Fidel Castro, Juan Domingo and Eva Perón, and Salvador Allende hovers over certain of the pieces; in profound ways, these figures directly influenced the lives of some of the essayists. The essays are filled with movement, both physical and intellectual. These writers give the impression of being in constant motion (Kozer, Stavans). They, and their parents and siblings, change countries, languages, political systems, continually adapting to what they find (Dorfman, Lubitch Domecq). Often with little notice, but at times in a highly premeditated fashion, they have changed neighborhoods and continents (Muñiz-Huberman). Others are extraordinarily productive while remaining in their country of birth (Aguinis, Feierstein, Freilich de Segal, Glantz). They leave languages behind or else insist on writing in them in places where the majority speaks another tongue (Agosín, Goldemberg, Szichman). Most are multilingual; some, born in Latin America, spoke Yiddish as their first language (Gerchunoff, Stavans), only to become deeply attached to Spanish or Portuguese later on. Some moved on to English when it seemed natural to do so (Behar, Stavans).

Judaism itself has a different meaning for each of these writers. While most of them do not subscribe to the beliefs and practices of Orthodox Judaism, all are quite familiar with them from childhood experience. For most the Sabbath and the holidays that mark the Jewish calendar have significance. Many remember the supportive but stifling Jewish extended family imported from Europe along with Yiddish or Ladino and a few ritual objects. On one end of the spectrum, Angelina Muñiz-Huberman and Alcina Lubitch Domecq are guided by the esoteric wisdom of the Cabala. Lubitch Domecq emigrated to Israel, where she has joined study groups of Orthodox women. In the middle, Isaac Goldemberg and José Kozer infuse their poetry with biblical and other Jewish imagery. Ilan Stavans and his family attend a synagogue in Amherst, Massachusetts. At the other extreme, Ricardo Feierstein, Moacyr Scliar, and Marjorie Agosín proclaim themselves to be secular Jews, tied to the Jewish community but not to Jewish religious belief. Feierstein has been a Jewish community professional and the editor-in-chief of a Jewish publishing house, while Freilich de Segal concentrates on Zionist activities in Caracas.

HISTORICAL ANTECEDENTS

Jews started fleeing to Latin America during the earliest days of the Conquest. The first to arrive were *conversos*, Jews who had converted to Catholicism but whose conversion had not been enough to stave off the menace of the Inquisition, and *marranos*, Jews who pretended to be Catholic but who practiced Judaism in secret. These escapees were few in number and, without an available community, were quickly assimilated into the general population and the vastness of the landscape. In the mid-1600s, a small group of Dutch Jews established a community in the Dutch enclave of Recife in Brazil. When the Portuguese recaptured the territory, these twenty-three Jews, fearing the return of the Inquisition, made their way to Manhattan Island. Over the anti-Semitic protests of the governor, Peter Stuyvesant, the directors of the Dutch East India (a number of whom were Jewish) allowed them to stay. A few years later, the British defeated the Dutch, and these new residents became the first "New York Jews." Small Jewish communities were also established in the Caribbean, particularly on the islands of Caraçao and Aruba.

From the early eighteenth to the late nineteenth century, Jewish immigration from Europe was directed to the United States and, to a much lesser extent, Canada. Waves of Jewish immigration from Germany and other German-speaking areas of Europe chose to bring their "modern" Reform Judaism to the Midwest of the United States where they could live in Milwaukee, Cincinnati, and Saint Louis, among German Protestant neighbors. During these years, very few Jews decided to settle in Latin America.

This changed in the 1880s when there was a pronounced increase in anti-Jewish violence in Russia and Eastern Europe. Economic convulsion hurt Jewish tradesman and traders as well as the neighboring peasants, who blamed the Jews for what was happening. By the end of the century, the situation had worsened to the point that virtually all Jews lived in fear for their lives. Millions left for the United States, the Goldene Medine, or Golden Land.

At the same time, Sephardic Jews from Morocco settled in Argentina and Brazil, often in the interior. These were followed by emigrants from Lebanon, Syria, Turkey, and, later, the Balkans, to Panama, Uruguay, and other countries. In general, they were poor, some speaking Arabic or Judeo-Arabic. However, the majority of these Sephardic Jews spoke Ladino and adjusted to their new countries considerably more easily than did the Eastern European Jews. For many, the entry to middle-class life was rapid.

Hearing of the economic difficulties facing immigrants to North America, Jews searched for other safe harbors. Coincidentally, certain Latin American governments, Argentina in particular, were in the midst of an economic boom and were seeking skilled, white Europeans to populate the vast territories within their boundaries. Although Jews were not their first choice, they fit the definition more or less, and their immigration was allowed, even solicited. The Jewish establishment in Western Europe was quick to respond. In particular, Baron Maurice de Hirsch, an Austrian-born, enormously wealthy British peer, donated vast sums of his own money to establish the Jewish Colonization Agency (JCA). Hirsch sent his agents to Argentina, Brazil, and the United States to purchase huge tracts of arable land. Land, though often of dubious potential for cultivation, was acquired or leased in several Argentine provinces, especially Entre Ríos, in the Rio Grande du Sul in Brazil, and in a number of American states, most notably New Jersey and South Dakota. Meanwhile, other JCA agents recruited Eastern European Jews to settle in cooperative communities on the land. The Argentine experiment was by far the most successful; there were numerous settlements, with, at one point, one million acres being farmed.

In 1924, the Immigration and Naturalization Act ended large-scale immigration to the United States. Because of a formula that was calculated to be prejudicial to Jews, Jewish immigration dropped drastically in 1925 and did not rebound until the *refusniks* were allowed to leave the Soviet Union late in the century. Some immigrants were diverted en route, and many families were separated, some permanently. From 1924 on, Jewish immigrants arrived in Latin America in significant numbers, principally in Mexico, Cuba, Chile, and Argentina but also in the Dominican Republic, where a Jewish settlement was established in the provincial town of Sosua, and in Colombia, Venezuela, Panama, and Bolivia. Before and after the Second World War, Jews made their way by circuitous routes, and often with the aid of existing Jewish organizations, to the centers of Jewish life in Argentina and Brazil. Holocaust survivors found themselves living next door to Nazis, who virtually controlled sections of southern Chile, or stranded in Central American capitals. Others journeyed to Cuba and Mexico in the hope, most often unfulfilled, of gaining admission to the United States.

Those Jews who arrived in the late nineteenth century often found work in agriculture in the farming colonies or as pack peddlers who carried enormous loads of household and agricultural items to rural villages where outsiders were rarely seen. As the urban economies improved, workers, including many Jews, were drawn from the countryside to work in the new factories. Later immigrants skipped the rural phase entirely and stayed in the cities. In the 1920s, these immigrants would brag, "You land on Monday, you find a place to live on Tuesday, you start work on Wednesday." Compared to the reports of misery from relatives in New York, theirs seemed the better deal. Others found work as shopkeepers, tradesmen, and furriers and in the burgeoning needle trades. Still others, nicknamed *cuenteniks,* sold household goods and personal items on time. Gradually, Jews developed larger businesses and, where possible, their own banking systems. The Jewish press in Yiddish, Spanish, and Portuguese grew quickly, with reporting coming directly from Europe and the United States. The Yiddish theater flourished in the larger cities; visiting troupes came from New York.

Eventually, a few Jewish entrepreneurs became millionaires with considerable personal influence. A few succeeded in politics, though not in Paraguay, where Jews, who could practice as engineers and physicians, were forbidden to study law, the key to political success. Others became entertainers, musicians, and even chess champions.

Jewish immigration to Latin America started in earnest almost fifty years after the substantial German-Jewish immigration to the United States. This difference has had several effects. For one, it is not unusual to find American Jews who are fourth or even fifth generation in the country; most are at least second generation and relatively few are immigrants. In Latin America, the majority of Jews are immigrants or of the first or second generation; the third generation is only now being born. While diminishing somewhat in recent years, the use of Yiddish, both as a vernacular and as a medium for literary expression, retained its vitality well into the 1980s. For those who left the "Old Country," the memories are not so far away. The Holocaust touched most directly and personally those who had immigrated during the

1920s or after, as many had remained in close contact with relatives in Europe. In some cases, these very relatives came to Latin America after the liberation of the concentration camps.

From the 1970s on, the Jews of Latin America suffered a series of shocks from which they will probably never entirely recover. At the same time that many were beginning to prosper financially, political changes made their lives increasingly insecure at best and in mortal danger at worst. After the Cuban revolution in 1959, most Jews, who had, in any case, been there less than one generation, boarded the airlift to Miami. Although most of the thousand or so who remained are involved in Communist party activities and have disavowed their Judaism, there has been, in recent years, a limited revival of Jewish life on the island. As Marjorie Agosín points out in this volume, Chilean Jews with ties to the United States were subject to death threats during the Socialist regime of Salvador Allende; many left the country. Shortly thereafter, when, following the coup led by General Augusto Pinochet, the new right-wing government started imprisoning and murdering its leftist opponents and even those merely perceived as enemies, other Jews fled.

From 1976 to 1983, the situation in Argentina was terrifying. The military junta was particularly harsh on its perceived Jewish opponents. Some had undertaken antigovernment activities, but many had not. Jews were arrested in numbers that far exceeded their tiny percentage of the population. When abducted, they were treated more harshly than non-Jews. The American rabbi Marshall Meyer acted as negotiator with the torturers, saving a number of lives, including that of the newspaper editor Jacobo Timerman. Timerman's book *Cell without Number, Prisoner without Name* brought international attention to the kidnapping, murders, and "disappearings" of Argentina's Dirty War. Those writers who could, fled the country. The novelists Mario Szichman, Gerardo Mario Goloboff, David Viñas, and many others left permanently.

With the return to democracy, the situation of Argentina's Jews seemed to improve markedly. However, in 1992, the Israeli embassy in Buenos Aires was destroyed by a car bomb. None of the criminals responsible have been apprehended. In 1994, another car bomb destroyed the offices of the Asociación Mutual Israelita Argentina (Argentine Jewish Mutual Association, or AMIA), a center of Jewish communal life. Eighty-six were killed and more than one hundred wounded. The psychological effect on the Jewish community continues to be devastating. Communal structures and services, developed over decades, have only partially been restored. The perpetrators have not been caught, and a pall hangs over Jewish life.

The existence of the half million Spanish- and Portuguese-speaking Jews of Latin America is scarcely acknowledged outside the region. Even with the trailblazing work of Robert Weisbrot, Judith Laikin Elkin, Jeffrey Lesser, Naomi Lindstrom, Saúl Sosnowski, and a number of other scholars affiliated with the Latin American Jewish Studies Association, the American public, including most Jews, is largely unaware of Jewish populations in Brazil and in virtually every Spanish-speaking country of Latin America. Latin American Jews are invisible to all but their relatives in other countries, a few international Jewish organizations, and Israel, which sees them as a source of educated immigrants.

JEWISH LITERATURE IN LATIN AMERICA

The literary and intellectual production of Jewish Latin American writers (with a few notable exceptions) is only recently becoming known outside of Latin America. Ariel Dorfman, Marjorie Agosín, and Ilan Stavans have achieved international status, and their works are widely available, some in a variety of languages. Stavans edited *Tropical Synagogues: Short Stories by Jewish Latin-American Authors.*

Rita Gardiol has compiled *Silver Candalabra: Jewish Argentine Short Stories*. Literary criticism has been helped enormously by Darrell H. Lockhart, whose monumental *Jewish Writers in Latin America: A Dictionary* provides biographies and literary histories of writers from virtually every Latin American country. Lois Baer Barr's *Isaac Unbound: Patriarchal Traditions in Latin American Jewish Literature* provides an in-depth critical study of six important writers.

For almost a century, however, Jewish Latin American writers have been interpreting and cataloging the Jewish experience, helping their readers to deal with an often hostile environment, and creating exquisite love poetry and polemical political tracts. The Jewish Latin American literary tradition began with Alberto Gerchunoff's *Los gauchos judíos* (The Jewish Gauchos of the Pampas; 1910), which rhapsodized life in the Jewish agricultural colonies in northeastern Argentina. The Ukrainian-born Argentine writer César Tiempo produced poetry and drama that explored the immigrant experience in an urban setting. After the Second World War, Jewish writing appeared in many Latin American countries and took many forms: the Dominican Republic's Edgar Paiwanski-Conde's three-dimensional poetry; the Cuban poet José Kozer's harsh, jagged imagery; Uruguay's Teresa Porzecanski's search for connections to her ancestors' opulent past in Aleppo, Syria; Mexico's Esther Seligson's extraordinary fantastic voyages; Guatemala's Víctor Perera's ongoing nostalgia; Brazil's Clarice Lispector's revisions of biblical narrative and Moacyr Scliar's comic parodies of Jewish urban life; and in Argentina, Mario Szichman's biting satire, Isabel Balla's memories of the Holocaust, Alicia Borinsky's stylistic experimentation, Silvia Plager's exploration of male-female relationships, Tamara Kamenszain's ability to portray the flow of time, and Alejandra Pizarnik's crushing self-destructive despair. The dramatists Samuel Eichelbaum, Osvaldo Dragún, Ricardo Halac, Aída Bortnik, Sabina Berman, and Ariel Dorfman have written and produced theater for both Jewish and non-Jewish audiences. Educated and formed to a greater or lesser extent in the Jewish tradition, these writers have had to confront persistent prejudice in Latin America or, having decided to leave, to experience the shock of adjusting linguistically and culturally to the United States, Israel, or elsewhere.

THE ROLE OF THE WRITER

On the one hand, the Jewish Latin American writer who has chosen to explore Jewish themes takes on the role and responsibilities of scribe of the community. At their best, they serve as the mouthpiece for their respective Jewish communities. Local issues, characters that the reader can identify with, communal history become the clay with which this writer forms poetry and prose. Growing up as a Jew and the search for a personal identity that includes being both Jewish and Latin American, encounters with the world at large, the response to anti-Semitism, be it overt or subtle, are the themes that repeat throughout this literature. Since Gerchunoff's The Jewish Gauchos of the Pampas, Jewish Latin American writers have produced a steady stream of works that explore these questions: Bernardo Verbitsky, Es difícil empezar a vivir (It's Hard to Begin Living; Argentina, 1948); Angelina Muñiz-Huberman, Tierra adentro (Inland; Mexico, 1979); Isaac Goldemberg, La vida a plazos de don Jacobo Lerner (The Fragmented Life of Don Jacobo Lerner; Peru, 1979); and Ricardo Feierstein, Mestizo (Argentina, 1994). Rosa Nissán's Novia que te vea (That I See You as a Bride; Mexico, 1992) and Hisho que te nazca (May a Son Be Born; Mexico, 1996) provide a vision of the Sephardic immigrant and postimmigrant experience in Mexico.

On the other hand, Jewish Latin American writers work within a constrained environment. Extremely few, whether they have chosen to remain in their native countries or have emigrated to the United States or elsewhere, have been able to support themselves with their literary writing. Many are professors of literature, journalists, or editors and thus can devote little time to their writing. What is worse, most write for small audiences. Jewish publishing houses such as Acervo Cultural and Editorial Milá in Buenos Aires, though of excellent quality, are small and understaffed. Though the Jewish population of Argentina hovers at around two hundred thousand, sales of five thousand copies of a work of Jewish interest are considered impressive. Throughout Latin America, the great majority of these sales comes from within the Jewish community. Moreover, it is cumbersome, if not impossible, for small publishers in one country to sell their books in other countries. (Only Marcos Aguinis, who has an international following, is able to sell fifty thousand copies of a novel, still a small number by American standards; the Chilean Ariel Dorfman, a professor at Duke University who publishes in English as well as Spanish, has considerably higher sales.) Many writers, like the Argentines Bernardo Kordon and Isidoro Blaisten, while not denying their Judaism, have opted to write for the trade market and avoid Jewish themes altogether.

The Jewish Latin American writer's life can be quite difficult and even dangerous. Though a community figure of some importance and reknown, the writer is subject to criticism from Jewish readers who may even be childhood acquaintances. At various points in Latin American history, Jewish novelists, poets, and essayists have had to dodge governmental critics and censors. In his contribution to this volume, Aguinis describes how he has spent much of his career writing in ways that would fool antagonistic censors. For those who have chosen to live outside of Latin America, the situation is only slightly better. Although there is no censorship in the United States, Canada, France, or Israel, the questions of language and readership are serious ones. Jewish Latin American writers who were immigrants from Europe had to decide whether to continue within the traditions of Yiddish literature or change to Spanish or Portuguese. First-generation writers have tended to write in the language of the country in which they were born, but for those like the Argentine short story writer Samuel Pecar who emigrated to Israel, the decision has been a difficult one. Others like the Chilean Marjorie Agosín or the Argentine Alicia Borinsky who have lived in the United States for many years continue to write their works in Spanish and publish them in their native countries; but they also work closely with Irene Kostopulus-Cooperman and Cola Franzen, respectively, superb translators who render the works into English. Writers who publish in Spanish in the United States are generally limited to Latino literary magazines and editions published by small presses. Cuban-born Ruth Behar writes poetry in English, while Mexican-born critic and novelist Ilan Stavans, now living in Massachusetts, switches from Spanish to English and back, depending on the project. The Argentine-born novelist Mario Szichman, who lives in New York, writes mainly in Spanish and publishes his works outside of the United States. Only Goldemberg, Stavans, the Brazilian short story writer and essayist Moacyr Scliar, the Argentine Gerardo Mario Goloboff (who resides in France), and, most definitively, Dorfman (who only occasionally writes about Jewish themes) have been able to garner an international readership.

Jewish Latin American writers find themselves within three literary traditions: Jewish (biblical, Talmudic, Yiddish—Sholem Aleichem, I. L. Peretz, Mendel Mocher Sforim, Isaac Beshevis Singer; Hebrew—Chaim Nachman Bialik, A. J. Yehoshua; German—Franz Kafka; Russian—Isaac Babel; American—Bernard Malamud, Woody Allen); Latin American (the writers of the "boom" period of the 1970s and 1980s—Jorge Luis Borges, Julio Cortázar, Alejo Carpentier, Mario Vargas Llosa, Carlos Fuentes); and Jewish Latin American (the Argentines Alberto Gerchunoff, Samuel Eichelbaum, César Tiempo, Bernardo Verbitsky, and Humberto Costantini as well as the Venezuelan Isaac Chacrón). The Jewish Latin American writer has an extraordinarily rich but often contradictory legacy from which to draw.

As minority writers, they are simultaneously Latin American writers and Jewish writers.

Yet, in spite of all these difficulties, poetry, fiction, nonfiction, and theater have been and continue to be written and published and reviewed (in the Jewish press and occasionally in mainstream magazines and newspapers). "La presentación del libro" (the Book Presentation), a roundtable discussion through which a new book is publicized, is popular entertainment in the Jewish community. Jewish newspapers often include new poetry on Jewish themes and extracts from novels and nonfiction works. Bookstores dealing in Jewish literature and carrying dozens of titles in a variety of languages do business in major Latin American cities.

THE AUTOBIOGRAPHICAL ESSAYS IN THIS VOLUME

The writers included in this volume have much in common beyond their Judaism. First and foremost, they are writers—poets, novelists, journalists—people with a professional and personal commitment to getting a precise effect from the words they choose. Unfortunately, this makes their autobiographies somewhat suspect as testimony. On the one hand, many of these authors are blessed with extraordinary memories. On the other hand, they are creative individuals, used to making things up from whole cloth, or at least presenting a version of events. Obviously, this volume placed certain constraints on them. First, it overemphasizes the Jewish aspects of a life. Second, there are the restrictions of space. To provide a panoramic view of the Jewish Latin American writers' experience, each contribution had to be limited in length. In some cases, only a phase of a writer's life is discussed, perhaps skewing the greater picture. However, that these writers are experienced in rearranging or retelling tales does not lessen the veracity or importance of what they are saying. They take seriously their responsibility to tell a tale, that is, to make known the Jewish experience in Latin America, even if their techniques are not those of a historian. They are, in many instances, writing about how writing itself determines the course of their lives. While it may not be that "all autobiography is fiction," these essays are not always unbiased or unprejudiced.

Nevertheless, these slices of autobiography are riveting. They portray complex individuals in circumstances that are often perceived as restrictive, frustrating, and unforgiving. Jewish childhood in Latin America, even if only vaguely remembered, is a repeating theme; grandparents with their ties to the old country play an important role. Tales of displacement, loss, repeated emigrations, and encounters with Nazis outweigh reports of adjustment and production, though these are not absent. These autobiographers not only report on what happened (or may have happened) in their lives. Some envision themselves as role models or teachers, either positive or negative, for their readers. In all cases, these are lives that have been lived to the fullest.

Some of these essays were previously published or appeared as parts of larger works. Most were commissioned for this volume. They have been arranged chronologically by birthdate, so that the reader can witness the unfolding of Jewish life in Latin America in the twentieth century. Alberto Gerchunoff's essay appears first. His influence can be seen in the works of many of those who follow. Since its inception, Jewish Latin American literature has developed into a coherent *movement* with shared themes, experiences, and even friendships. It begins with a Jewish gaucho on horseback and persists in the writings of many wandering Jews, fleeing the Holocaust and looking for Zion in Latin America and later in the United States and Israel. Many Jewish Latin American writers have had to move on more than once, looking for an elusive "normal life." Despite it all, they have created a collective vision that is Jewish and Latin American.

Each of the writers in *King David's Harp* has had to cope with an environment, or series of environments, that is profoundly different from that known by the parents' generation. Some have become immigrants themselves; they have left Latin America for the United States or Europe. Possessing stubbornness and determination, they share a fierce will to be successful. And they have been.

Alberto Gerchunoff
Argentina

Novelist, short story writer, cowboy, metalworker, peddler, journalist, newspaper editor. Alberto Gerchunoff (1884–1950) lived to tell the tale of early Jewish life in Argentina. His first novel, *Los gauchos judíos*, remains his best-known work and his most controversial. Born in the European shtetl, he arrived in the Argentine pampas when only six, his parents seeking a better future in the agricultural colonies supported by the Baron de Hirsch and the Jewish Colonization Association. As a boy, Gerchunoff quickly assimilated local ways: he spoke Spanish, became a skilled horseman, and grew to love the land.

Gerchunoff's life thereafter was a balancing act of opposing experiences. He started as a country boy yet spent most of his life in the big city. He was a farmer and a factory worker, a country journalist and later an editor for *La nación*, the country's most influential newspaper. A native speaker of Yiddish, he came to dominate literary and journalistic Spanish. He loved school but was mainly self-educated. He favored assimilation into Argentine society but had great pride in his Jewish heritage. Intensely patriotic, he tended to understate anti-Semitism in Argentina. Though concerned about the fate of the Jewish people, he was slow to support the state of Israel. Though foreign-born, he became a dominating figure in Argentine intellectual life. Prolific throughout his life, he wrote social satire, numerous short stories, and studies of Cervantes and Heine.

The autobiography included here (the date of which is unknown) was probably written before Gerchunoff had reached middle age, certainly before the anti-Jewish violence that broke out during *La semana trágica* (Tragic Week) in Buenos Aires in 1919. An extended essay, this autobiography has been edited and its archaic language modernized.

A JEWISH GAUCHO
Alberto Gerchunoff

Moisés Ville was visibly progressing. Behind the tents, the lush horse pastures were giving way bit by bit to cultivation, and the furrows were becoming damp and dark. Squeaking carts, drawn by pairs of oxen, brought wire and posts, and the plow creaked while turning over thick clay. The tame cows and the docile horses decorated our tranquil way of life, their presence evocative of olden days of peace, the ancient days of the Bible. During the warm mornings the Jews greeted each other as they drew water from the wells; their robust voices covered over by the harsh sound of the pulleys. The greetings had something ritualistic and mystical about them in that peaceable and primitive setting.

I had a white mare, agile and fleet, which would arch its neck and gallop backward, under the pull of the bridle, whenever we passed a girl from the colony. An audacious rider already at a tender age, I would lose my way on the outskirts of Moisés Ville, looking for a lost lamb or for some unexpected rhea tracks.

After midday I would go to the tent of a hunchbacked and lame Jew who taught me Hebrew and then to the synagogue with my father, since I liked to hear the old men's opinions and their interpretations of obscure passages from the texts. A tavern, owned by a Spaniard, had been opened close by us. All the farm workers would meet there, and it quickly became the focal point for the area. Gauchos from nearby ranches, wagon drivers, as well as passersby would stop off at the rancho, tying their horses to the posts in the *criollo* style, and enter the tavern. More than a few times, bitter arguments broke out. From behind the counter, the Spaniard, raising a club above his head to defend himself against possible attack, would shout them down.

The colonists saw this tavern as something evil, and they would not stop telling the town administration's local representative that it should be shut down. After all, something serious had taken place there. A suspicious-looking Jewish fellow, covered with scars, very dark, with shifty eyes and a large curved knife, had stolen a horse from Moisés Ville; the owner complained to the authorities. The police had quickly found the thief and forced him to return the animal. The Jewish fellow, it turned out, was from the outskirts, a slacker, a brawler and a drunk. After returning the horse, he spent even more time in the tavern, particularly during the afternoons, and never stopped arguing with the other gauchos.

One day, as the colonists were preparing to celebrate Passover, the slacker sat in the tavern from morning to evening, completely drunk. It was getting dark. On the road a few colonists passed by. We were in front of the tent, drinking maté. We were talking about this and that and observing, among other things, that it was foolhardy to live in Moisés Ville without a gun. But no colonist had so much as a shotgun for shooting partridges. Suddenly, a gaucho appeared, brandishing an unsheathed knife. It was an instant at once horrible and terrifying. Shouts of panic heated the air. A minute of terrible confusion passed. Soon I grasped the enormity of our misfortune. I don't know exactly how, but we found ourselves before the town administration.

Laid out on the ground was my father, drenched in blood. Clearly, the horse's owner had mistaken him for the thief. In a room inside, women were attending to my suffering mother and my older sister, also in agony, on a pair of cots. The entire distraught colony of Moisés Ville was in the patio. People had beaten the killer to death; his head lay mutilated and his body torn apart.

My father was buried in the little cemetery of Moisés Ville. On his tombstone, the Jews inscribed an epitaph that they composed in the synagogue, in classical Hebrew: "Here lies Reb Gershun Gerchunoff, beloved for his wisdom and venerated for his extreme prudence, a chosen and a just man."

We didn't leave the house for many weeks. In the evening, the neighbors came over to entertain us, and Pinhas Glusberg, former leader of the synagogue, would invariably relate an incomprehensible story about the mythical Russian general Kokoroff, with whom he had had the honor to speak. On the slightest pretext, he would intervene with the name of the famous officer I still can't quite believe existed. Pinhas Glusberg was a little old man, a talker and a dreamer with a poet's imagination. "Don't you see him on autumn afternoons, rising on a distant horizon, a ghost with white wings? Believe me . . ."

Exhausted by the memory of the tragedy, our family abandoned Moisés Ville. We moved to Entre Ríos and settled in the Rajil colony, where we became farmers in the fullest sense. I spent several years there, tilling the land with my brother, guiding the harvester, and caring for the stock. The ox driver, a former soldier with General [Justo José] Urquiza, helped me perfect the art of horseback riding. He also initiated me in the use of the bola. Like all Jewish boys in the colony, I looked like a gaucho. I wore widely cut trousers, a large homburg, and boots with ringing spurs; from the horn of the saddle hung a lasso of shining iron rings; and tied to my belt, next to my knife, were bolas used for hunting.

No Jew of my age could claim to bring a wild yearling down with a jolt better than I. Nor could anyone else stop an unbroken colt in full flight dead in its tracks with a lasso. But my favorite task was to take care of the livestock near a stream bordering our land. All the boys in the colony would meet there, presided over by the native ox driver, who, incessantly chewing on his black tobacco cigarette, would invite us to drink maté with him.

The ox driver had a special fondness for me. I would praise the songs that he sang to the monotonous chords of his broken-down guitar, and at my pleading, he would relate his adventures as a heroic soldier. He divided the tasks among the boys. He worked the land, while we planted the seed for the next season's harvest.

In Rajil my youthful spirit was filled with legends of the Comarcas Indians. Through picturesque, rustic gaucho tales, through simple rhapsodies to Argentina's past, I assimilated the traditions of the place, its collective memories, the imaginary adventures of local warriors. For the first time, my heart opened up to the poetry of the countryside, making me aware of the native beauty of Entre Ríos and igniting in me a steady pride in liberty and a love of *criollo* manners. The vast calmness of the Entre Ríos, bounded by rivers under a matchless sky, so excited me that it erased my origins and made me an Argentine.

The crops failed the day we saw the approach of a cloud so thick that it blocked out the sun. It was locusts, of course, and hours later, the orchard and the seeded fields were covered with their plague. Men, women, and children we went out with sacks and sugar pans to chase the plague away. The wheat was high, and the orchard was flourishing.

We fought courageously; roaring and shouting. But exhaustion and the locust cloud defeated us, and by the time the sweet, magnificent moon illuminated the colony, only farmers' sighs and the women's bitter laments could be heard in the saddened huts.

The curse came three years in a row.

But Rajil, like the other Jewish colonies, made progress in spite of these disasters. Social life slowly began to stir, and families from different regions quickly formed close ties, overcoming the considerable distances separating them.

The construction of a synagogue and a school was proposed. Jews convened to deliberate. Since the younger Jews predominated in the assembly, they endorsed the school first. Soon it was established in a large zinc shed, and from all over, children were brought in daily, with their lunch boxes hanging down. This was to be the very first school in the area.

I was a good student. I learned the stanzas of the "Himno argentino," the Argentine national anthem, very quickly. During recess, my friends would surround me, as I repeated the gaucho tales I had learned from the ox driver in Rajil.

My studies there didn't last long, though. My mother, obsessed with the fatal evening in Moisés Ville, yearned to leave the region altogether, and her pleading was so compelling that the whole family decided to go to Buenos Aires.

It was in 1895, and my uncertain and wandering life had begun. My mother insisted that I study, but it wasn't possible at first since someone needed to support the family. But how? None of us knew any trade at all, of course. Eventually, I found work in a Jew's business, kneading dough for Passover's unleavened bread. The bakery was far from where we lived, so that I had to get up at dawn. At night, a Spanish cart driver started me on the Spanish alphabet.

When the season of the unleavened bread ended, I once again found myself with no means of support. I had to think about a trade.

Soon I entered a mechanic's workshop as an apprentice. I was assigned to the nickel-plating section among a swarm of young shouting boys who all but drowned out the boss's hoarse voice. I spent the day bent over near a sink filled with chalk, brushing bronzes that I would put in the can of boiling lye later.

My fingers swelled and split open. The days were not as bad as the nights, when I really suffered. Yet in spite of it all, I liked the mechanic's trade, and when I didn't have work to do in the nickel-plating section, I would go down the founders' workshop or the metalworkers' to learn something. After a month, I was able to polish pretty well, and I knew how to handle more than a few machines. I would have stayed with the trade, if a shocking event had not convinced my family to pull me out. I am referring to the death of a metalworker, an Italian with enormous, wide shoulders, a rough and good fellow. One morning, on starting the motor, he got his shirt caught in a pulley. I was preparing the lye when I heard a horrifying crash.

On the floor I saw his decapitated and mutilated body; an enormous bloodstain covered the ceiling.

With affectionate insistence, my mother persuaded me to leave the mechanic's workshop. I then joined a cigarette maker from whom I earned fifteen pesos a month and lunch. My boss would pay his workers only after they had fulfilled a certain hourly quota. I learned fast. In three months, I was producing a thousand cigarettes a day. The owner didn't keep his word, though, and failed to pay me as promised. So I changed trades once again and became a ribbon and embroidery maker—a beautiful trade, which I quickly grew to like. I progressed slowly. I spun, learned how to dye silks, knitted random stripes, and became skilled in framing. I was capable of producing a decorated ribbon less than a centimeter wide.

Soon I was a first-class worker. The factory owner, a jaundiced Jew, nearsighted and quarrelsome, once told me, in the presence of the operators, that I was the most skilled tradesman he had ever known. Meanwhile, I kept studying at night. A buddy taught me Spanish grammar, history, sciences. A factory friend, a lean and witty Asturian, introduced me to *Don Quixote*, a book for which I have a singular and profound love.

My aspirations were no longer those of a simple worker. I dreamed of structuring my studies, of taking examinations at the Colegio Nacional; I longed for the glory of a doctorate. No sooner did my day at the factory end than I went to my books, mixing my reading of the dry everyday texts with those I sought after: my *Quixote*, the *Thousand and One Nights*, and Victor Hugo's novels.

Over these first serious books, I usually would fall asleep, exhausted, and when I opened my eyes, my mother's angular and wrinkled silhouette would be in front of me. She wouldn't go to bed until she had covered me up, protecting me during those winter nights from the cold wind. A medical student also gave me lessons. But it wasn't easy to study and work at the same time. I couldn't leave the shop, since I needed to earn a living.

I spent a total of three years in the factory as an ordinary worker. At the end of that period, I arranged to work half a day for a third of my salary. This way I could prepare for my exams, which, when the time came, I passed easily.

Now the problem was, where would I find the money for tuition and books?

A neighbor, the owner of a small store, offered me popular merchandise to sell in the street. This was during the crash of 1899. I would take a bulky sack and go around hawking from sunrise to sunset. I mainly sold the merchandise in the endless port area, but I also spent time in the city's outskirts. And so I walked for long weeks until I collected a paltry sum, sufficient for my immediate needs. It was this job that brought me the greatest suffering and humiliation.

I entered the school. I applied myself above all to grammar and history. Restlessly, with exaggerated curiosity, I read enormously, chaotically. I also became interested in public affairs and argued with my classmates about the questions of the day.

That was the time I obtained my Argentine citizenship card. Until then, I had not been equal to the others, that is, not an Argentine. Once when I told my grammar teacher about this problem, he first laughed heartily and then hugged me affectionately. I was sixteen years old then, two years too young to become a naturalized citizen. The next day, I was called to the school director's little office, where I found my teacher. He put me in a car.

"Where are we going?" I asked timidly.

"Well, my good man!" the director exclaimed. "To make you an Argentine . . . Aren't you really one already?"

Once again I passed my exams with high marks. But the question of making a living was still unresolved. I began to give lessons to Jewish workers. But those unpredictable little earnings were clearly insufficient even for the most rudimentary necessities.

The following year, I was no longer able to study as a regular student. In vain the school director and the teachers sought work for me. But I could find nothing. Free from the discipline of the program, I spent many hours in the National Library, poking around books. And so, bit by bit, my interests led me to journalism and literature.

I got to know a number of writers and journalists at public lectures. They grew accustomed to my presence and were quite interested in my views and stories on Jewish life. Soon I became part of the bohemian side of Buenos Aires. This phase lasted for a long time. Happily, neighborhood newspapers and youth magazines began to accept my hesitant essays.

One fine day in 1903, I was offered the position of editor of *El censor* in the city of Rosario.

Of course, I didn't know how to run a newspaper. It took a great deal of work to acquire the most basic techniques. *El censor* was an opposition newspaper, and my articles, violent like all beginner's, caused a small scandal in town, sufficient to make me a man of the press. The newspaper was forced to close down, and I returned to Buenos Aires, armed, fortunately, with a certain professional preparation.

It was then that I joined *El país* and became an effective journalist, able to take on any assignment and do a passable job of it. I stayed at this daily for years. I also collaborated on various periodicals.

My departure from Moisés Ville and Rajil had not led to my separation from Jewish people. In Buenos Aires the Jewish community was constantly growing, forming a visible nucleus for its intense commercial and industrial activities. Already, there were a considerable number of Jews in the high schools and the universities, all hardworking and extraordinarily energetic, stubborn and firm-willed, who didn't take long to distinguish themselves with their scholarly achievements.

Observing this, I conceived of a plan to study Jewish life in a free atmosphere, without outside persecution. Wouldn't it be interesting to show Judaism redeemed from the share of slavery, martyrdom, and stoicism that usually plunges it into abjection? I was, at the time, literary critic of *La nación*. Well placed and calmer than I had once been, I carried out part of my plan in 1910 by publishing a book in which I tried to describe the customs of Jewish immigrant farmers in Argentina.

I traveled a lot, edited newspapers in the interior, took over the associate editorship of *La mañana* and later the position of editor-in-chief of *La gaceta* in Buenos Aires. That, in short, is how I became a full-fledged journalist, wandering from place to place and from trade to trade. Life, in all its hardships, taught me to love being alive. It planted deep in my spirit the feeling of human pain, and more than books had done, shaped my personal ideas. This is why I love the Jewish people, for they know, like no one else, the supreme value of liberty. In Argentina, Jews, redeemed from injustice and religious stereotypes, will lose their generally accepted profile. On this soil, they will be gradually freed from the whip of persecution. This can be seen already. From the city and countryside, Argentine Jews are deeply and sincerely patriotic as are their elders, those born in Odessa or Warsaw and immigrants to this land. Argentina can be proud of this and show it to older civilizations. What would the Russian people say about such a transformation, for instance? As I carry out many official functions, I come across Jews who are university professors, which neither shocks nor irritates anyone. These Jews are Argentine citizens, nobody cares which temple they pray in, if they are Catholics or not.

In truth, the Jew lacks religious preoccupations. He is mystical without being dogmatic, exactly the reverse of what anti-Semites think. In an atmosphere of freedom, he assimilates to the country; he is remade in its essence. The venerable Baron de Hirsch understood this potential well when he founded the agricultural colonies in Argentina, an immense task of practical philanthropy, and, at the same time, a testimony to show the systematic enemies of this small suffering people, dispersed over the globe.

Neither moneylender nor martyr, the Jew is a free man. No matter what trade he embarks on—laborer on the land, factory worker, or financial magnate—in Argentina his status will not change; for this is Palestine for the Jew, a land of liberty, the Promised Land in the biblical sense of the word.

I don't sing of Jewish life only, though: above all, I am an Argentine, and, as such, a man of letters.

Translated by Stephen A. Sadow

Margo Glantz
Mexico
ॐ

Margo Glantz (1930–) is blessed with a quick and subtle sense of humor. Her work is often fun to read. Her powers of observation are extraordinary, and she is able to skip from topic to topic or scene to scene at lightning speed. Her writing style is fractured, sometimes surreal in its presentation.

Daughter of the Yiddish poet Yakov Glantz, an émigré to Mexico, Glantz grew up surrounded by Mexico's intelligentsia. She has not felt like an outsider in Mexico. On the contrary, she is considered a force in Mexican literature.

Margo Glantz is a professor of literature at the Universidad Autónoma de México, and has been cultural attaché at the Mexican embassy in London and a visiting professor at Yale and Princeton universities. She has made a substantial contribution as a journalist and as an essayist and literary critic. Her writing is quite varied, often veering off in unexpected directions. Her *Las genealogías* (The Family Tree) is a "fictional autobiography" or "pseudo-novel." Her novel *Síndrome de naufragios* (Syndrome of Shipwrecks) replays the story of Noah, while *El día de la boda* (Wedding Day) pretends to be a collection of love postcards.

The selection that follows, which shows Glantz's wit and attention to detail, is taken from *The Family Tree*.

FAMILY TREES

Margo Glantz

In those days the market at Tacuba was like the one in Juchitan. The comedian Cantinflas had a booth near our house and his partner Chilinsky's wife, Tamara, used to visit my mother. She was a very good-looking blond and nice. My parents never talked to Chilinsky, or to Cantinflas, but when I remember him I make connections between the skulls of the Noche Triste, the hairy priest of Popotla, the latest shoe styles, the lack of water, and the fiestas of Twelfth Night, when the local children were all given toys and we Jewish girls always wanted some too, and were always disappointed, even though we were pseudo-Christians.

My religious activities came to an end when my mother was bathing Susana one day (she must have been about four years old) and found a little medallion under her blouse. Lilly and Susana got a good hiding. My speedy trip through Christianity has left me with a decided preference for reading and a fascination with torture. Every Sunday I used to think about Baby Jesus sitting on my heart, and whenever I ate crunchy cakes I'd feel very uneasy, because I used to worry that it might disturb Him.

Probably the name that would have suited me best when I was a child was Rosita rather than Margarita; that's where my parents went wrong. Margaritas, or rather daisies, are white with yellow centers and lots of petals. I remember some photos that show me sitting beside other girls in my family (my cousins Lila and Haya, my sister, Lilly, Miriam, the new bride's niece) when my uncle Volodia married my aunt Celia. When she died in childbirth my uncle married my aunt Raya, who was very beautiful and wore a yellow dress, and had her hair in waves rippling over her forehead and my uncle looks very handsome in the photo, while I look gauche, my round cheeks like apples. My cheeks were so pink that my mother used to think I was running a fever, and sometimes she was right, so she would give me castor oil and hold my nose. Sometimes I'd be cold and there was a Hindu gentleman, a friend of my parents called Mr. Bezra who called me Rosita and brought me chocolates. There was another one too, a Mr. Baisboim, a bachelor who wrote poetry and who we all liked a lot; he used to call me *katchele,* duckling, because I've always walked rather like a duck, and then there was another poet, Meier Perkis, who was also a bachelor and called me *eretz Israel epele,* which means apple of Israel, because of my brightly colored cheeks.

Later, when I was older, I started to do my hair in the way I wanted, that is, in a Pre-Raphaelite style, though that was completely beyond the pale in my teenage years, because nostalgia was not yet fashionable. Then I had another hairstyle that might have been very radical. I had done my hair like that just before the Vietnam War as if I'd invented the rock opera *Hair* instead of some American gringo.

That's been my destiny, to always choose hairstyles that come into fashion later on, though when they did I was already completely out of date, and friends used to admire the way I looked like a Gustav Klimt picture, or an art deco model or a photo from the twenties by one of those men who made Coco Chanel famous. Now whenever I see pictures of the Tutankhamen exhibition in New York or I remember my trip to Cairo, a long time before Tutankhamen traveled round the world, I recognize what it means to look like a pharaoh, or rather like a pharaoh from the Lower Nile.

When I was a child my fortune was told by the flowers from Xochimilco, and those flowers often spelled out the name of Lupita, followed by Margarita. The whole family got together and we would eat Jewish food and the adults would drink beer. Sometimes we would go to my uncle's house (the one who was a baker) who had only one grown-up son, Oscar, and we all used to fight about him. That was on my father's side. On my mother's side there were two cousins, Elias and Micky, but we didn't see them very often. Whenever we went round to the bakery in Uruguay Street, my uncle would stroke my hair and call me Margarita, the name my family still calls me, which is in my passport and on my fortnightly paychecks.

The sound of my name appealed to the insect world, and we used to have to perform disinfecting ceremonies to kill off the bedbugs. The house would be covered in paper and we would go somewhere else and sleep on the floor, while the poisonous fumes would attack the insects in the house we'd just left. The bedbugs sometimes used to climb out and run and get into the feather mattresses on the beds. My mother and the maid would take everything outside in the sun and air, the mattresses and quilts, and pour boiling water over them to kill off the bugs. Her vampire-like behavior used to affect me and my sisters, and we can remember with distaste the strong, unpleasant smell on those days. That was the time when the Nazis were starting to use the ovens in their crematoriums.

Every interior male journey has its opposite; that is, there is also an external female journey. I've undertaken this sort of journey in recent months, and by exploring the nooks and crannies of reality and the countries I've visited, I find myself seeking out my own origins, especially when strange coincidences happen. Those sorts of coincidences are the reason why I love science fiction so much, and romantic adventure stories, even though they may be formulated in terms of invasions and end with frightening uncertainties that promise to hold you in suspense until next week's episode: more crunchy cakes, a few sweets, some popcorn and all the marvels of those adventures that are full of coincidences and never come to an end.

In three months I've met more people whose blood is linked to mine than ever came over to this virgin land throughout the ages, because all my ancestors are buried in Eastern Europe, or maybe in Germany, and sin is an amazing thing and we're all somehow related to the czar and to Lenin. My cousin Sam Glantz came two months ago. He is the youngest son of a brother from the Glantz dynasty that emigrated to Philadelphia and by a marvelous coincidence he has an eleven-year-old daughter called Margo, and I find my name repeated almost exactly in another language, though with a slight foreign accent. And there I am with a double, like those everlasting Cabalistic twins. "We are Schwester Kinder," says my cousin Polina from Odessa, in between her sobs, yes, Sam and I (and Sam and Lilly and Susana and Shulamis) are all children of the same bloodline, siblings in speech and appearance, and through our veins there run some of the characteristics of Great-grandfather Motl or Grandfather Osher or Grandmother Sheine. We spend several days peering at each other, looking closely at the shape of a nose or the color of a moustache, and our relatedness emerges in the way we smile or the sort of food our mothers and aunts used to cook. But blood gives out other signals too, as it flows sleepily along our veins until it gushes out into our hearts, which beat rather faster than usual. We are friends but we aren't brothers, because the truth is that there is a price to pay for brotherhood, and sometimes it's best to keep brothers at a distance, as the biblical story of Cain and Abel so clearly illustrates.

Still, even though I've met Miriam and Doris too, Sam's sisters, they made very little impression on me. Miriam used to have a big nose and was very slim, and though she still has the same nose it seems shorter now because the rest of her body has filled out. I remember that Miriam was always smoothing down the pleats in her skirt (pleats pressed in with a flatiron), and I remember Doris whose blond hair, straight as ears of wheat, was cut in a simple pageboy style, like any ordinary girl from Central Europe. They didn't look like the young Jewish girls who used to live there, those girls with dark skin and light green eyes (like my little niece Alla) and dark, curly hair, who used to be seen in the streets of Moscow and Leningrad and who were instantly recognizable. Sometimes they were confused with women from the Caucasus, but that's irrelevant. The real Russian and Polish women, and the Germans too, are all blond like my cousin Doris or like Susana, my sister, or like Ilana, the daughter of my other sister, Shulamis.

Blood can give out all sorts of signals, blood circulates and when its instincts are roused then most likely you're dealing with a relative. That's certainly the case without exception in soap operas, but it doesn't work with Sam; blood has changed its course, Sam is primarily a friend and the voice of the bloodline is not very effective over the phone that connects me one day with my cousin Oscar, elder brother of Miriam, Sam and Doris, now a professor of sociology in Brooklyn. Oscar didn't have time to see me in the high-pressure world of subways and skyscrapers, and all I remember of my cousin is a typical American voice, full of doubts and affirmations, scattered conveniently through our conversation, which was very short. Oscar is named after my grandfather Osher, but I'm sure that if my grandfather had ever gone to New York or Philadelphia the same thing would have happened to him as happened to that character of Bashevis Singer: a shoemaker who came to the United States when he was about eighty, after his wife died, when all his children had been in the United States for years, making designer shoes. Well, that shoemaker got off the boat and saw with amazement some ladies and gentlemen who looked like Polish nobility greeting him with exaggerated gestures of cheerfulness. That's how my foreign uncles perceived my mother when she went to Philadelphia in 1945, while Susana was in a hospital bed in Rochester after they operated on her bad leg, the left leg (which had always hurt her when she were small, and which always ached whenever we knocked her left hand or her right ear). My uncles were waiting for the train from Minnesota, expecting to see a lady dressed like a Redskin or all Aztec even though she was a Russian Jew just like the rest of them. That's what happens with relations and family histories. Blood flows and flows across continents, and the melting pot renders it down. All this is leading up to how I recently met Sam and his wife, who seem more like good friends than blood relatives. The problem might be due to the fact that we don't quite fit the requirements of the typical Jewish phrase "we're children of the same sister" (because you get your Jewishness through your mother) since Sam is the son of my father's brother, Moishe Itzhak, alias Morris Glantz, a pharmaceutical chemist in Philadelphia. The old proverb may well apply in the case of Izzy, only son of my uncle Leie (the uncle my father complained about because of his false kisses). Izzy died of leukemia in Philadelphia, and when I think about him I remember three visits (which seem to have followed on from one another, my mind, but which actually happened over a very long period) of his to Mexico. His refined face and his light eyes, his shortness and his curly hair, his pleasant personality, all combine to shape an image of him and make him an important figure in a story, even though we didn't share that story, first because he was so much older than the rest of us, and second because we lived in such distant, far-removed lands.

A little while ago I was talking about the kind of coincidences that happen in soap operas. I was talking about them because whenever you hope such coincidences are going to happen they never do, that's fate, but when they do decide to happen, nothing can get in the way.

Let's take an example: in this conscious and confused search for roots (a marvelous dream) I set off for Eastern Europe, cradle of my ancestors on both my father's side and my mother's. I went to Russia so as to be the first member of my (Mexican) family to retrace the journey my parents had undertaken back in 1925 before they set off for Mexico, when they left their motherland forever. My Mediterranean side came to the fore and my siblings all looked at me and told me how brave I was. To go on such an adventure in unknown lands is always the distinguishing mark of an explorer and, as I've said before, I am another Columbus, with my grandfather Osher and my grandfather Mikhail serving as navigators.

My first encounter with the homeland was Kiev. I arrived there from Budapest and landed on Russian soil, where a guide was waiting for me with a shiny black car made in the USSR. I was very moved by the journey across the plains near the Dnieper, my heart beat faster and my eyes gazed out in every direction over those steppes that were impressed into my father's memory, but when I got to the hotel a woman who looked just like one of those round Russian dolls told me that I hadn't seen steppes at all, that you had to go down to the southern Ukraine to see anything like that. I didn't see them, but I did meet several fellow Mexican travelers during a long day of guided visits to monasteries with golden domes shaped like onions, inside which were marvelous icons and frescoes. Afterward we went to the catacombs, called *laura* in Russian, which were also full of icons and coffins, all intricately carved and containing mummified bodies of hermits who rather coquettishly were still wearing embroidered velvet slippers which sometimes even had little bits of mirror fastened in.

When we came out of the *laura* an additional person had attached himself to the Mexican contingent: a professor from the University of Kiev who taught Spanish, and whose protégée had been the professor of our young guide Olga, a girl wearing glasses and an antique coral necklace that her grandmother had given her.

He was a man of about seventy, not very tall, fairly slim, with gray hair and melancholy eyes, who spoke perfect Mexican Spanish. That evening he came to the hotel where some of the tourists gave him Mexican books, and he had read Mariano Azuela, Revueltas, and Elena Poniatowska. We see him standing in the doorway. He asks me, "Are you a Jew?"

That word *Jew* is so strong it almost seems like a command, if you say *Jewish* it's less violent.

"Yes, I'm Jewish. Are you?"

"I am too. I lived in Mexico from the age of twelve. I went over there with my parents and my sister in 1924 and stayed there until 1932, the year we went back to the USSR, because my mother missed her native country so badly. It was a very cold, hungry year. Later on there was the Great War of Liberation. In 1924 we were on our way to the United States, but we couldn't get there because they refused us entry visas. We went to Cuba, but since everybody else was going on to Mexico we went there too."

"That's extraordinary! It's exactly what happened to my parents. Which ship did you sail on?"

"A Dutch ship, the *Spaardam*."

The soap opera has come true! It's the very same ship! The same adventures, the same medical examinations, one member of the family about to stay behind in the city of Riga because he can't see very well in one eye and has a patch on one lung, meeting the ship brotherhood, those photos with the same well-known poses!

There's one thing, though, that doesn't match: the dates. The gentleman facing me traveled in 1924 with his family, whereas my parents went over in 1925.

"Ask your father if he ever knew my family. My father was a very refined man, very well read, very gentle. He had always been fond of books. In Mexico he worked for the Soviet Embassy . . ."

Maybe he worked there in Kollontai's time, and maybe he'd used those huge abacuses, the ones with the beads that look like amber which they still use in shops and restaurants in Moscow, Leningrad, Odessa, and Kiev. At the embassy, where my mother saw the ambassadress always ready to go out riding with Diego Rivera. The *Spaardam* went backward and forward regularly, always the same ship, the only thing that ever changed was the passengers and the cargo, the ship's master was the same, striding over the deck giving orders to the passengers or dining with them and ready to hand over the same entry fee for Mexico in dollars and explain about the two hundred dollars required as the open sesame for Veracruz. Yasha Perelman loves the USSR. Once he studied at the conservatory and played the piano, but the war came, the Great War of Liberation as they all call it so proudly, and he was sent to the front, and afterward he began teaching Spanish to enable young guides to show us round the *lauras*.

"I can remember a lot about Mexico City. We used to live right in the center. I even had a girlfriend there."

I'm in Acapulco, thinking about Perelman in his native Kiev full of poplars and chestnut trees on the banks of the Dnieper. I'm sitting on some rocks on the beach at La Condesa in Acapulco, huge seaweed-covered slippery rocks. ("Be careful, it's slippery," says an American to me, and I answer "Yes" and go on staring out to sea.) Some sunburned boatmen go past, their hair bleached in the sea air, and try to persuade me to take a boat out to the island. I don't answer, a sort of sputnik goes threateningly past my head. I've just finished reading Truman Capote's *Music for Chameleons,* an investigation of cheating at cards that quotes Mark Twain on the wickedness of mankind a lot, when two blond boys go by, looking very suntanned ("Skol? Coconut oil?"). The sea is bathing me, as it is them and filling the Pepsi Colas they're drinking with foam, they laugh, they're nice looking, wearing red swimsuits, and one has real goggles, motorcycling goggles, their bodies are magnificent, they laugh again, the sea goes on bathing me, leaving a salty taste in my mouth and sand in my eyes and swimsuit, I feel part of the ocean, I'm in the beginning of all things, I sink into the sea and the waves lap at my muscles. The sea reaches the rocks and I remember Perelman remembering Mexico and Mexican songs and the old streets where his girlfriend used to live, in the streets down by Guatemala? or the Corregidora? It doesn't really matter, he went there in 1929 or 1930, he can't remember who the president was then, he's thinking about his girlfriend or about Agustín Lara, the singer. He asks me if I like the song "Rosa" and I say yes. He listens to it often, he says, his apartment is a very small one, he lives with his Ukrainian wife who doesn't understand any Spanish, he's very fond of her, and he loves his son too and his one grandchild, but he still likes to decorate the walls with reminders of Mexico, with things like a huge Mexican hat, and he has albums of Mexican songs, Greever, Cuty Cardenas "who died in a barroom brawl when I was in Mexico."

Yesterday I went into a jewelers in La Costera—La Costera, with its filthy sand and exposed pipes and acres of cars—just like our own town in fact. I saw something I liked, a very unusual ring with a shiny cluster of stones. I went in and asked the price.

"A hundred and fifty dollars."

"Dollars? Don't you sell things in Mexican money?"

"Even Mexicans think in dollars these days, that's why we do it."

There are two completely different Mexicos, and this is totally unlike the one Perelman means when he says:

"When the Bolshoi Ballet came to Mexico the first time they asked my advice about the sort of music they could use. I taught them 'Las mañanitas' and 'Las golondrinas,' and later they told me that people liked that a lot. I do miss Mexico, and when I feel totally homesick I put on the record player and listen to some of Agustín Lara's songs, I get my map out and I use my fingers to travel round."

In Moscow I talk to Carlos Laguna, who has been in charge of the embassy shops for the past fourteen years. I tell him my story while we eat caviar and mushrooms and drink vodka in the Arkanguelsky gardens, near the beautiful church with its violently colored twisted domes, a miniature version of St. Basil's Cathedral.

"Is it Perelman?" he asks.

"Do you know him?"

"Of course I do, he's always interested in news from Mexico."

Then we go into the church, which is full of old ladies around seventy or eighty, dressed in black with head scarves tied under their chins. There is only one man, who is also very old. They say their prayers, kneel down, kiss the ground and the icons, and there are flowers everywhere. We go out again and on to Peredielniko, where we visit Pasternak's grave. Beside him both his wives are buried. Some young people are there too, and the grave is covered with flowers. Russians love flowers, they are always carrying bunches of gladioli or carnations around, and brides lay flowers on the graves of unknown soldiers who died during the Great War of Liberation, our guide says very solemnly.

Back in Mexico I tell them what happened. My parents can't remember any Perelman family. On Saturday or Sunday we're all together at the table, and I'm telling my story again to the rest of the family when my father suddenly gets excited and stammers: "Perelman? . . . Perelman? Of course I remember! *er iz geven a guter Id* (He was a good Jew). Don't you remember, Lucia? You don't? I do, he used to have a magnificent moustache."

My sense of nostalgia grows and grows, keeping up with my new friend, in fact it isn't nostalgia, it's melancholia, sweet, sticky and rose pink, like the song that Lara sang in the 1930s, when a Russian Jew was a young man of seventeen, chasing girls in La Lagunilla, back in the days when he missed the northern snows.

Once I start talking about coincidences, there's a lot more to tell. I think about the Jews crowded into the ghettos in Odessa, and I see them as Babel saw them, all aspiring to live until they were a hundred and twenty years old, sitting along the low walls of the Jewish cemetery (which has long since vanished) and gazing out over the graves of all those people named in epitaphs. Sometimes I like to think about them, because my family doesn't have any heroic episodes in its past, it just has a few hiccups, like what happened to my brother-in-law when he was arrested as he got off an airplane in the United States, because his name was Jacob Guzik, and the people reading the blacklist thought they were dealing with the famous gangster by the name of Jake Guzik, the man who had been holding for ransom both the police and the underworld in Chicago, in much the same way as Leibl the King had held for ransom the Jews and the local police in the Moldavanka quarter of Odessa when the czar was still in power. The customs officials realized that they had had been misled and that they had got the wrong man, that my little, bearded relative was not the equally little but very dangerous Chicago gangster. They let him through, and here am I, writing about it all.

Sometimes I write down the conversations that my mother used to have with her friends, during recreation in high school, all those neighborhood girls from Moldavanka, and although they didn't talk about Leibl the King, they did talk about Mishka Yaponetz, Japanese Mishka, whose gang lived in the same area.

"Yes, Deribasovskaia was a very high class street, and so was the street I lived in, but Moldavanka was very poor, there were even beggars there, and sometimes there were 'blind' ones who weren't really blind and who used to wrap their feet in rags when they went out begging, and then they'd mug people and work as pickpockets, just like used to happen in Tempito, where you went with your father to buy shoes. I was amazed when I heard that things like that were actually going on in Odessa, which my friends all knew about, though I was actually pleased later on when they told me that those same members of Mishka Yaponetz's gang had fought against the Cossacks in 1919 or 1920 (that was the time of the pogroms in our area). Those

Cossacks were white Russians, they were killers and rapists. The gang killed them because they'd been burying people alive and beating and torturing. Hitler could have learned a few lessons from them. Mishka and his gang crushed them, they wiped them out and then went back into the ghetto and disguised themselves and put on bloodstained bandages as though they had actually been victims."

As I'm writing, Renata comes into my study in a rage and says: "Mother, the only fun in this house is the sound of that typewriter."

I tell Cristina this, and she suggests that I try to sell that statement to Olivetti, the makers, to help pay the cost of going to a psychiatrist in an effort to try and reconcile my daughter either to life or to her mother. I think it's enough for the sea to go on lapping at our feet, as is happening at this very minute. I also prefer to save my money, as I climb the steps opposite the sea that calmed Potemkin, the Chornoe More, the Black Sea, with my nephew Petia. He has green eyes and lives with his parents in a room in my hotel.

Later still I am walking down an arcade filled with baroque statues and crystal ceilings with another relative that I have only just met, and am learning more about the world. I cross the street, escorted by my two companions who are both engineers (everyone in the Soviet Union today seems to be an engineer; the same thing used to happen here in Mexico when everybody had a degree, including the tram drivers and community workers). They show me round the city and take me to the nicest places: the opera house, the Voronsov Palace, Pushkin's house, Red Army Street with all its cake shops and the parks full of old ladies selling flowers, the museum, an old merchant's house, Deribasovskaia Street, which still retains its old czarist name, like Peter Street, who was important "because the revolution thought of him as a good governor," as a guide told me yesterday. Deribasovskaia, I learn, is named after General De Rivas, a Spaniard who fought against Napoleon.

"Yes," says Mother, interrupting my account of the places I'd visited, "I went there once as far as the Nikolaievsky Boulevard, I don't know what they call it nowadays, and I was just passing Count Voronsov's Palace, the one who was jealous of Pushkin. You must know where I mean, it's near the sea, and I heard shouting so I went up the staircase and into an enormous room full of antique furniture, Louis XV style, gilded furniture, not like the imitation things they make today but genuine antique Louis XV furniture, and I saw some young boys sitting round a bonfire in the middle of the polished floor singing and passing bottles round, and I felt really upset because it didn't seem right for them to be destroying such lovely things, it was pure vandalism. Now they really look after things in the Soviet Union, they have a lot of museums, Russians were always very honorable people, but in those days things were very difficult and the government was always changing and you didn't know what was going on from one day to the next. I was very young, and my brother Salomon was a civil servant. He was in charge of removing furniture from a palace that belonged to one of the Rothschilds' friends, and he gave the furniture to people who had once been servants in the palace and let them do whatever they liked with it, because he had no idea where it was all going to end and if anything would be saved at all."

"That furniture might even have ended up in the National Museum where I went with Petia."

"Yes, that sort of thing did happen. They liked me at school, they used to hug me a lot and try to get me to join the Young Communists and break away from my bourgeois past, but when they saw that I wasn't very interested, they stopped being quite so nice to me. I remember once I was with a friend who lived in the apartment below us. A young man came up, one of our friends, wearing a uniform and carrying a pistol. He really thought he was something special, and I asked him since he had a gun if he knew how to fire it, and he took it out and actually grazed my skin with a bullet. I never did tell my mother about that."

The statue facing the steps in Odessa is a statue of the great lord
Richelieu, a relative of the famous cardinal, who lived in the city for
many years, but the street once named after him is now named after
Lenin. My father lived nearby, by the opera house, but that street is
still called Richelieuvskaia. I went there with my guides, Petia and
Zaik, reliving the image of my father as a young man, a bright-eyed
youth wearing a striped cashmere suit and a matching Spanish-style
waistcoat (just like the one my older daughter Alina wears nowadays),
a watch chain hanging from his left pocket with a Star of David, that
pocket reminds me of other pockets, also on the left, in waistcoats
draped over the end of the bed, when my parents were asleep and I
used to hunt for coins that consoled me in school time, since I used
to eat cakes during recreation periods in those miserable secondary
school years and fancy shoes, which can't be described in any other
way, because they look like the sort of thing Clyde (of Bonnie and
Clyde) or some godfather figure would have worn (two-color shoes, in
coffee and white), and that's my father, a godfather in the truest sense
of the word, a great father like the one in the photo, framed in purple
velvet and silver given as a wedding anniversary present to my sister
Susana: "There you are, Susana," says my father, "a father's present."

Translated by Susan Bassnett

Marcos Aguinis
Argentina

Marcos Aguinis (1936–) is blessed with a wide array of talents and the energy to use them. Neurosurgeon, psychoanalyst, former minister of culture and of state, journalist—his is a constant presence on the Argentine literary and political scene. He is driven to cure the world's ailments, or at least do as much as he can. His writing focuses on ethical issues—Israelis and Palestinians, the Spanish Inquisition. Aguinis abhors boredom, judging it the worst of the sins. A master of character development, he creates characters and situations that are sometimes disturbing and often provocative. Among Aguinis's best-known novels are *Refugiados: Crónica de un palestino* (Refugees: Chronicle of a Palestinian), which treats the Israeli-Palestinian crisis; and *La cruz invertida* (The Inverted Cross), a study of conflict in the modern Catholic church. *La gesta del marrano* (The Marrano's Gesture) deals with individual integrity during the Inquisition. Considered one of the most important writers in Argentina, the prestigious publisher Sudamericana recently issued a retrospective reprinting of his works. Aguinis is an active member of the Jewish community in Buenos Aires and speaks regularly at synagogue and communal functions.

In this essay, written especially for this anthology, Aguinis is wise and worldly, ready to repudiate injustice wherever it may occur. But he has not lost his sense of humor.

BOREDOM IS THE WORST OF THE SINS

Marcos Aguinis

When I am asked at what age I began to write, I say five years old, when I drew my first down strokes. When I am asked about my literary vocation, I state precisely that I began at twelve, when I wrote several short stories and filled two hundred pages of a notebook with an unpublishable novel. At thirteen, I wrote a large article about peace, influenced by the books of Stefan Zweig, that was stupendously rejected by the newspaper of my childhood town. Later on, I wrote other essays, biographies, and more stories that were read and devoured only by the moths. They constituted my place of apprenticeship.

Having to choose a university specialization, I didn't enroll in Literature or Philosophy or History, because those schools—in my native Cordoba—were controlled by backward figures, steeped with a Catholicism closer to the Inquisition than the Gospels. I decided in favor of Medicine because—I said—nothing would bring me closer to man.

I must confess that I never felt comfortable with the choice. It had positive aspects, among them the ability to get closer to the pain, anguish, desperation, and also the gratitude of human beings. I became calmer about it when I learned that many physicians were brilliant writers, from Rabelais to Anton Chekov, Arthur Conan Doyle, Pío Baroja, Somerset Maugham, Cronin, Axel Munthe, and Güimaraes Rosa. To resolve my doubts, I wrote the biography of someone who eight centuries ago was an extraordinary physician and humanist: Maimonides. I didn't resolve my doubts, but that was the first book that I was able to publish. Now I consider it a youthful sin.

Another positive result was that, thanks to my medical career, I won fellowships that brought me to Europe, among them, the Alexander von Humboldt Stiftung. I stayed for a year in France and another in Germany, with youthful trips into the neighboring countries. I dedicated six months to Freiburg im Breslau and three to Cologne. Not only did I learn medicine, but I also gained the inspiration for the novels that I wrote some years later. One is entitled *Refugiados: Crónica de un palestino;* it takes place in Freiburg at a time when dialogue between Palestinians and Israelis was impossible. Freiburg was a neutral setting, and that dialogue was linked with a notable reagent: the existence of German refugees, also victims of war, like the Israelis and Palestinians. The three sectors slowly came to recognize each other as brothers in the tragedy. Art's capacity to anticipate itself— what Sigmund Freud pointed to as a mystery—occurred in that novel. The protagonists of my novel, after difficult trials, affirm that there will be peace, understanding, and affection between Palestinians and Israelis; they said it when nobody else even dared to dream it.

The greater part of my existence was spent under the yoke of authoritarianism that scorched Argentina. The repression obligated the use of ellipsis; to say what was burning in one's guts and at the same time, not lose the book that one had written or one's life.

My second novel is entitled *La cruz invertida.* It was inspired by the German priests who prepared revolutionary documents for the Second Vatican Council. They spoke of ecumenism, freedom of conscience, and human rights, themes that were almost subversive for the episcopal establishment. I was amazed, because Catholicism in

Argentina was insensitive to social urgencies, to modernity, and to the opening of the Church. That novel too was more perceptive than the political scientists. Years later, critics called it a "prophetic novel," not only for its impertinent critique of corrupt power but also for announcing the persecutions, tortures, and delirium that were to make the decade of the seventies so filthy. It received the Premio Planeta, in Spain, which was at the time the most important in the Spanish language. The government of the dictator Francisco Franco had intended to ban it; but since its author was an Argentine, they let it go through. The Argentine military government also wanted to ban it, but, as it had been given a prize in Spain, they also abstained from censoring it. Isn't it humorous that the two tyrannies had worked together to guarantee the liberty of expression?

Up to now, I have published sixteen works, including novels, essays, stories, and biographies. I have the impression that I was fortunate—for having been able to dodge the henchmen of the dictatorships, for having been able to depend on publishers willing to publish my works, and above all, for having had the gratification of expressing my ideas to many people, because from year to year the number of my readers has grown.

It so happens that in Argentina we writers are often consulted on issues about which we are not experts. They ask us for direction, convinced that we artists possess a special organ that allows us to see in depth and in breadth the human panorama. For years, I was a severe critic. And when, in 1983, democracy was reestablished in a form that promised to be more durable, I understood—with many colleagues—that it was not enough to stay in the comfortable position of the critic: we should offer our shoulders, hands, and head. I was designated a member of the new democratic government in change of cultural matters. And then I created a program of democratization that obtained the support of UNESCO and the United Nations.

This stage completed, I returned to my private life. My story closes like a circular short story: in puberty I began as a writer and in my adulthood I ended up as writer. For a long time I was a neurosurgeon and then a psychoanalyst, minister of culture, minister of state, columnist in newspapers and magazines, lecturer, democratic leader, lover of the arts and sciences, untiring traveler. I suppose that all of it has served my literary creation, because no writer, no matter how controlling he may be, can determine what occurs in the multiple experiences that penetrate his soul, where the pots of his intimate cooking never cease boiling.

My critics and commentators through two decades have maintained that my work, like that of almost all writers, revolves around a half dozen obsessions, although the books may appear very different from each other.

I agree. My books have created distinct characters that inhabit different scenarios, except in a few short stories and novels where certain creatures reappear with certain irony or shame. I am aware of this tendency to rewrite. When I am asked about it, I say that I change characters and scenes for reasons of courtesy, so as not to bore my reader. But if I dare to confess the truth, I say that I do it so that I don't bore myself. Boredom, in my judgment, is the worst of the sins.

But this variation, including the formal, doesn't encompass small matters only. The list would include disgust with injustice, solidarity with the weak, revulsion toward the "owners of the truth," fanaticism for life and its celebration, admiration of spiritual courage, and adherence to beautiful and vigorous prose. These elements combine in a thousand ways, and they are seen through characters, conflicts, circumstances, and diverse scenes. But they reappear incessantly. In my texts, criticism, irony, humor, and atrocity abound; but also kindness and clear proofs of human limitations that we would do well to accept.

In other words, with the most fluid and formidable language of which I am capable, I denounce injustices, salvage lost causes, get furious with hypocrites, and reduce the dangerous "lords of the truth" to grotesque ridicule. I don't write poetry, but my prose suggests it, not as an adornment of false flowers, but to express the often-infernal labyrinths of the human condition. My narrations are aesthetic products, where the aesthetic doesn't hesitate to strengthen itself with thought. Thought is also conflict and, if it is properly treated, generates the maximum tensions. I don't avoid it; every character not only runs, he maneuvers, fights, and feels; he also reasons and questions.

My novel *La gesta del marrano* is based on a terrible historical event: in January 1639 a doctor was burned alive, in the city of Lima, for having confronted the Inquisition by remaining faithful to his convictions. This has a great deal of meaning in itself because it is the first case in America in which someone fought in an overt manner and died heroically without giving in, to defend his right to the freedom of conscience.

The work is a vast hymn to liberty. Within it unfolds the drama of Indians, black slaves, pious Catholics, and persecuted Jews. The reconstruction of the period as well as the natural and human landscapes provide both poetry and tension. The characters suffer and enjoy themselves as they can in the midst of an implacable Inquisition. But that Inquisition is not simply the organism that has been given the task of discovering heretics and witches in order to send them to the fire; it is also the womb of what would happen again in successive centuries, in particular, during our twentieth century. In effect, that novel was enormously successful with the critics and the public, and for two years it was on the best-seller lists. I don't attribute this to its special artistic merit; passionately telling us something from the past. In fact, I am describing the present. This awful present disturbs us. The Inquisition of those days was the model for totalitarianisms, dictatorships, and fundamentalisms that have devastated the planet and humanity, and even now intend to continue to generate grief and pain.

The Spanish and Portuguese Inquisition, with its Latin American branches, was directed by arrogant villains who considered themselves owners of the truth, who used religion (or ideology) to satiate their hunger for power, who stimulated and rewarded denunciation even among close family members and constructed a farcical legal apparatus for their exclusive benefit. There was always a legal apparatus with judges, prosecutor, and defense attorney, although the victim had already been condemned before they arrested him. The Inquisition—and its present-day representations—systematically practiced torture to obtain more names of supposed offenders, because with more victims, there could be more terror and more power. Torture was carefully registered by the notaries and carried out under the supervision of some doctor who, before the coming of death, could advise its postponement for a while with the intention of continuing the process more successfully the next day.

Nazism, Stalinism, and the Latin American dictatorships owe a great deal to the Inquisition. From it, they obtained methods and mentality. We have to continue fighting against it today, here and everywhere.

My latest essay is entitled *Elogio de la culpa* (Elegy of Guilt). Inspired by *Elegy of Madness* by Erasmus of Rotterdam, it reviews the spiny function of guilt. Guilt appears as a woman, who, in first person, describes herself and narrates her long activity in man's heart since prehistoric times, since the mythical Cain killed his brother, Abel; she insists that, thanks to her, men don't end up killing each other. She sees herself as powerful and cruel. Nevertheless, she accepts that she has bad aim; instead of hurting the villains, she more frequently wounds the good and the just. Also, she confesses that she produces severe mental pathologies. Toward the end of the book, after railing against the injustice, corruption, and violence of our times, she agrees to pass her scepter to someone better than she. It is her daughter, who is more refined and doesn't generate mental pathologies. She is named Responsibility. The conclusion is that great pain kills, but total anesthesia is equally lethal; a lot of guilt is very serious, and a lack of guilt is too. The theme remains open to debate.

Translated by Stephen A. Sadow

Angelina Muñiz-Huberman
Mexico
&♥

Angelina Muñiz-Huberman (1936–) looks inward, studying her thoughts and finding a great deal to value. Always conscious of being an exile, she never quite feels comfortable, never quite part of the land she lives in. Her writing is carefully crafted and sometimes eerie. Muñiz-Huberman became a Jewish writer, something she had not intended. She learned that she was a distant descendant of Sephardic survivors of the Inquisition. After extensive contemplation, she underwent formal conversion to Judaism. In part as an act of self-exploration, she has compiled an important collection of Sephardic literature and another about the Hispano-Hebraic Cabala.

Muñiz-Huberman is a professor of comparative literature at the Universidad Nacional Autónoma de México. In her writing she explores hidden, secret, and magical places. Her novels and short story collections such as *Morada interior* (Interior Abode), *Huerto cerrado, huerto sellado* (Enclosed Garden, Sealed Garden), and *De magias y prodigios: Transmutaciones* (Of Magic Acts and Prodigies: Transmutations) present reworked myths and magical transformation as well as spiritual and psychological crisis. Always, her use of language is precise and carefully controlled.

This essay, which shows the isolation of exile and the thrill of writing, was previously published in Muñiz-Huberman's collection, *Cuerpo entero* (Entire Body).

DEATH, EXILE, INHERITANCE

Angelina Muñiz-Huberman

DEATH

Death is the first experience from which I set forth. My companion since infancy. Death observed. Death spoken. "Our everyday thing," as I have called it in a poem. That which I felt hang over me in the manner of a quiet condemnation. Absolutely familiar. Not disturbing. Full. Fecund. With which I always had a dialogue.

Death, for me, was a benign figure. I had its picture in front of my eyes: that of my brother at eight years old, just before he died. That is, a living figure, though immobile. I was accustomed to speaking with my brother-death and his answering me. My internal splitting was not directed toward a fictitious "you" but toward the present reality of a being who was mentally alive. For that reason, I never resented solitude. I acquired the ability of being myself and my brother at the same time. On some occasions, I would act like myself, and on others, like him. My great childhood secret was to live death. In my hand. Inside, deep inside of me. That caused me to create my own games. A floor tiled in black and white made me repeat yes, no, yes, no, life, death, life, death, and the last one would seal my destiny. In the same way, to jump on one foot or on two indicated life or death. As well, paint peeling on a small protrusion of the patio wall of the school would indicate death. Also, any empty place, fault, opening. To count up to a determined number to find out if you would live longer. Waking up in the darkness and not being sure if I was in a coffin. Surprised by the dawn that had opened my eyes to the new day.

The great test was to reach my brother's age. As long as I hadn't turned eight, my life was in danger. If I were to be able to reach eight, I would be saved. If I keep in mind the fact that I was two when he died, I lived for six years waiting for a certain death.

Contributing to all this was the fact that for my parents the theme of death was never prohibited. My father, an Andalusian given to tragedy, feared it and invoked it. My mother, a Castilian, accepted it naturally. There was a certain delight in describing my brother's death to me, without omitting details. And every death from then on.

In spite of the familiarity, I rebelled: I didn't want it to occur. In my experience, everything confirmed it. The little chick that I thought was asleep in my fingers and turned out to be dead. My dog, attacked by rabies. In my readings, above all. Those children who would die in *Corazón: Diario de un niño* (Heart: Diary of a Child), by Edmundo d'Amicis. And the wars. The unbearable wars. I grew up with two wars in the background. The Spanish Civil War and the Second World War. Where the dead were millions.

This death that was loved and welcoming, this death-brother, clashed with Mexican death. A new profaned, trivial death that appeared in the headlines of the periodicals: "He Killed His Mother for No Reason with a Sharp Knife"; "He Killed Him Because of a Dirty Look"; "Life Isn't Worth Anything." It was another death; not my loving one. And that certainly shocked me.

It occurred at a certain moment that I denied it. My brother hadn't died. He grew up with me, at my side. I forced myself, because my parents wanted it that way, to be like him. My games were warlike. I had changed myself into a *guerrillera*; a wooden gun and an aviator's helmet were my favorite toys, and with my brother I left to fight against Franco.

Death, with all that it demanded of me: a mode of behavior that made me profoundly appreciate life: it led me to another idea: God didn't exist. I argued the point with my brother and I won. "No. If God would permit your death, then he doesn't exist." My conclusions were radical and took care of the question once and for all.

I sought a way to transcend the situation. The silence and the ignorance of a life, his perennial oblivion, as would occur with my brother when neither my parents nor I were alive any longer, made me yearn for an afterlife. With that rationalism that was very typical of my childhood, I thought that only by being a writer could I achieve it.

The relationship—death-memory—was revealed to me on a very special occasion.

It occurred during the first vacation that my parents and I took after arriving in Mexico. The place, chosen by chance, through a game (with eyes closed, in front of a map of the republic, where the finger touched), was Chachalacas. On the beach, a vast and empty beach, my mother spoke to me seriously, and said to me that from this moment on I ought to observe the world around me and record it in my memory, bit by bit. That I was already old enough—six years—so that I wouldn't forget anything. Then, when holding her hand I entered the sea and saw the undulation of the sand under the transparency of the water, I felt faint. I thought that was the end, and that I would die at that moment.

And so the memories of the sea, of the dunes, of the unreachable horizon, combine beauty and tranquillity with disappearance and death. But, once again, a death very much attached to life that furnished a certain sort of happiness.

Intensely linked to death, the trace of exile has always stayed with me. This going from country to country created my inner dwelling. I was versed in the traffic of spaces. I would be able to live in any part of the world; as soon as I arrive at a place, even if I'm just passing through, I adjust to the streets, the landscape, the houses, the walls at my gaze. And the means come to me. The ease with which I adapt is famous. (Even in the limited space of an airplane seat, I install myself in my own room and I read and write as if in a palace.) And of course the idea of transience is the idea of mortality. And the idea of exile includes both.

If, in truth, exile is obsessive, it has become a negative burden. It accompanies me, and it will accompany me forever. Exile is so much a part of me that, like a part of my body, it cannot fall away. But it doesn't overwhelm me or provoke me to lament or paralyze me. Better said, exile is just the contrary, it has made me take different forms, in new directions, in great open spaces, without limits or borders. In freedom and almost in anarchy. In such a way that it permits me to choose the landscape that I like best from the place and the time through which I pass. No country exists that I can call my own: I simply choose the landscape I like best. As for people, it has never occurred to me to divide them into nationalities: I group them by the amount of love we have for each other.

Advantages and disadvantages? Of course, like any human situation. A combination, then, of lucidity, but by the same token, of distancing and realistic vision that can be marked with pessimism. And, in spite of that, no. I reject pessimism. On the other hand, I stick with unadorned observation of one who doesn't fool oneself and doesn't want to fool others. The great shock is when others prefer to be fooled and to hide the truth. Then, they shut you up. But this doesn't matter to me: in the same way, I know what things are. Finally, truth comes to the surface.

If the exiled person has learned one thing, it is patience. And patience is the best laborer, slow, sure, and productive.

To be a refugee was to belong to a special group. Chosen. Different. Pointed to. The fact that, by my parents' decision, I didn't attend a Spanish school in my early years, didn't make me, for that reason in itself, forget my origins. Later, during adolescence, in an attempt at equilibrium, I convinced them to let me attend the Academia Hispanoamericana for the last two years of the *bachillerato*.

During my primary education, in the Gordon School, I played with nationalities as it suited me: I was French, Cuban, Andalusian, Castilian, refugee, or Mexican. In High School No. 18, I felt completely absurd each Monday, when, for having achieved the highest grades, I carried the Mexican flag and sang the national anthem, while inside I thought that what I should be singing was Riego's hymn.

I felt at home at the Academia Latinoamericana. I recovered the use of the "vosotros" as a mark of identity, though now I only use it in an intimate way if I am among Spaniards. On the other hand, with Mexicans, I use "ustedes" in the same intimate way. Both pronouns place me, without my thinking about it, in one situation or the other.

I know that because of exile I developed a peculiar way of speaking. A neutral speech. I avoided Spanish and Mexican idioms except for those that truly cannot be substituted. Also as a writer I aspired to a universal expression. From the time I was little, I was dependent on language, and I absorbed that of my readings. From my parents, I received a language that was carefully formed on my father's side and very expressive and enlivened by proverbs on my mother's. As I was an only child, integrated into the adult world (we were the "Trinity" as my father would say, or else "the benzine ring"), I devoured lexicons, and what I most wanted was to know the meaning of all the words. I surprised my own parents when I asked for an encyclopedia for my birthday.

This phenomenon of exile that makes you more attentive to the slightest difference or inflection of the country where you arrive led me to employ different ways of speaking, according to where I might find myself. If I wanted to be understood, I had to violate my natural expression, but within certain limits: I permitted myself changes in vocabulary or in the use of the diminutive, never in the other grammatical aspects that touch on the essence of the language. Having lost my own land, I grasped the land of the words. That became sacred.

One more negative aspect of exile was the free and open criticism—among refugees—of anything Mexican while at the same time giving to the outside world the impression of gratitude. These things caused me to keep quiet and to stop believing in the world that was in flower. I was forcibly pulling back, and my contact with the outside was closing.

I believe that because of this my first childhood friendships were with children who were also from minority groups: a Jewish girl, a Guatemalan girl, a Swiss girl. During my childhood and adolescence my friends were refugees.

As the exile's world can include other spheres and be connected to outsiders, for example, beings that society isolates puts them off-limits, I ought to mention two examples, two people who mean a lot to me. One of them was my friend C., like me a child of immigrants, with whom I spent every weekend and vacation. With whom the game of the imagination didn't have limits. With whom my world was circumscribed even more. C. didn't have brothers and sisters as I did, or friends either, not a single friend. It happened that C. was mentally retarded, and he lived in his own personal exile. How we created a paradise still moves me. (And at times I think that exile is the re-creation of a lost paradise.)

C. and I had to invent everything all over again: starting from the beginning by naming things: creating objects: changing rules: creating our own language: protecting ourselves from jokes and laughter. Our games were games that other children didn't play.

For example, I must have begun to write to him. This is an anecdote that I have told on other occasions. We were in Cuernavaca, and after we had finished our games, without knowing what else to do, it occurred to me to suggest to him that we write a story. Said and done. I don't know what he wrote, but it was something scribbled on the paper. I wrote my own four scenes, which I still have.

The story of my friend has changed into different stories during the course of my life. And this has been like taking up again our interrupted games. Our closed paradise. Since he is no longer alive.

The other case was that of María, the dwarf. She was the daughter of the first servant who worked in my parents' house. I think that she was more than twenty years old, perhaps thirty; it is difficult for a child to guess ages. What I do know is that I was taller than she and that when she sat in a chair, her tiny feet bounced up and down. She also suffered from some kind of retardation and from a speech impediment. The mother always carried her around with her because if she had left her at home, they would mistreat and abuse her. And so she also was my companion. Her specialty was cleaning lentils, beans, or green beans with the greatest patience and impeccability in the world. Her skill: making figures out of *plastelina* with which she played with me.

María presented me with the problem of religion. She took me to church for the first time. I who had never stepped inside of one, and who, guided by my linguistic inclinations, said "inglesia," thinking it was a place that had to do with the English and not the Spanish. Which reminds me that when, in school, they called me an atheist (*atea*), I responded very tranquilly that they were mistaken, that I wasn't an Athenian (*ateniense*).

If, on the one hand, my education at home was very democratic *and* I never knew of hierarchies, I was always at my parents' level; on the other, I grew up like a true savage. No one spoke to me about religion, nor did I have any fear of God at all. María was my initiator and the one who caused the fear in me.

That day, when I entered the Church of Saint Rose, was one of absolute fear. The half darkness, the statues, the pain, the blood, the fervor, they all moved me. I've mentioned this experience, too, in other of my writings. More and more, I defend the importance of the roots leading from childhood. The strongest sources for the creative effort.

So religious exile was another burden that I counted. After several negative experiences, I learned to answer ambiguously when the children asked me if I was going to mass on Sundays. Then, in High School No. 18, when there was the New Year's Mass, I pretended to be sick so I didn't have to attend.

INHERITANCE

That I chose to be a writer—when I passed the limiting age of the death of my brother—caused a division between my parents. My father said no, as he had to correct what I wrote, and my mother supported me. My father criticized the lack of clarity in my writing, and my mother adduced that it was because of his corrections that the confusion occurred and that I should be allowed to write however I pleased. After all this, I heard and took note.

Moreover, there was another circumstance, and it was more serious. My father had sworn not to return to writing after my brother's death. (He didn't keep the vow, as he began to write poetry.) And if I wrote, the curse could fall on me—that of being young—and when I published my first texts I never received one single favorable comment from him. But my mother was on my side.

My maternal inheritance was of a different sort. My first readings were directed by my mother. She liked to read to me out loud, and I remember the two of us on the bed, spending hours, she reading, I listening. She taught me poems that I memorized, and she wrote in my little notebook special facts from history or geographical information, like the countries and their capitals, the highest mountains, the longest rivers. She spoke about Spain, about her summers in the Guadarrama mountains or on the beaches of San Sebastián. During that period, I drew Republican flags on every piece of paper or on every book that came into my hands.

My mother was from Madrid, from which followed that my linguistic logic was perfect (*madre-madrileña*). Her family came from El Casar de Talamanca. Before that from Guadalajara. And earlier yet, from Zaragoza.

One afternoon, on the balcony of our first house in Mexico, at 185 Tamaulipas Street, my mother confessed to me that she was of Jewish origin. That is, my mother's family had conserved that tradition for centuries upon centuries. Her Judaism was by now quite diluted, and she mixed it with forms taken from Christianity, though also diluted. My grandmother Sebastiana knew some words in a Hispanicized Hebrew. She had passed it on to my mother, so that, in turn, she would pass on to her children, as a sign that would identify them as Jews. This sign is called *shadai* and consists in the pinky and the ring finger and the first finger and the index finger with a separation in the middle. Later, I learned that my mother's last name, Sacristan, apparently so Christian, was nothing but the translation of the Hebrew Shamash.

Starting with this discovery, strengthened by my mother's readings from the Bible, I took on the task of studying Judaism. When, many years later, in the university, I studied the work of Américo Castro, the panorama of my origins became clear to me.

THE GAME OF WRITING

My world as a writer has been a world rich in solitudes. I took myself away and I closed myself off because of something won the hard way: the right to write, a privilege that not even all the words from all languages can express. It is an office of such responsibility and of such ethical meaning that the only possible comparison that occurs to me is that of the Cabalist who rewrites the sacred texts with greater perfection, because to mistake a letter would be to destroy the universe. Therefore, my aesthetic is an ethics of language. I select the precise word, that which means exactly what is needed, and I disdain fashions and circumstantial attitudes. I head for the center and I stay away from the bark. If I use an adjective, I adjudicate the value of a nominative and bring it back for the quality of surprise. I don't like habitual and worn-out usage: I renew, undo, and reconstruct. But without ever losing the harmony: even within violence, cruelty, or sarcasm. In the same way, the musical rhythm of the prose is a requirement in my style. It is something that fell to me out of the sky: the moment that I finish writing a phrase, I know if it flows or not, and I find myself pronouncing it out loud to assess the particular rhythm. I need to watch myself about this practice, since at times the similarity of a sound makes me exchange one word for another, a letter for another, in which case, I need to decide if I leave it the way it is or change it. As my work with narrative parallels my poetry, the exercise is continuous. Punctuation is an element with which I like to play and where I have established my own rules. Rules that are in agreement with the special rhythm of the phrase. To do that, I go on breaking with classic punctuation in order to highlight that part of the sentence that requires it. I cut and I break where the meaning or the background call for it. The white spaces that I use are intended to indicate a longer pause in the reading: they are an attention getter or better yet, in the Cabalistic manner, they are populated with infinite meanings that the reader may think to add. Black fire on red fire. Ink on paper.

If writing is the union of all those so precious and so valued, the act of doing it is an inseparable unity done in a single beat: like mystical ecstasy or erotic ecstasy. Nevertheless, my writing process occurs in a setting of absolute calm: I hardly alter the texts that I am developing; and if I do, it is at the same pace. The error jumps out at the moment it is committed. Above all in my favorite hour for writing: four in the morning.

Writing is an absolute pleasure of the senses and the soul: of memory and of time. It is the most pleasurable profession there could be. But loving, it is a returning to and a spinning of internal worlds that emerge from obscurity to clarity. It is a gift and an engraving of the living word that transforms the impulse toward sin into an enlightening impulse.

If I remember correctly, beginning with my first publications, I opened a breach in Mexican literature. I set out to write about what I felt to be mine and not adapt myself to fashions and ideologies that were in vogue. I tried to deepen the themes that interested me in order to offer the reader a fresh vision of things and of the world. I went forward, or perhaps I prepared the ground for what is now in fashion. I was the first to treat the theme of women in extreme situations and not as objects of cruel humor. These first stories that had languished in various magazines of the period have just appeared together as *El libro de Miriam y Primicias* (The Book of Miriam and Primicias). I collected those from the sixties but more broadly from those of the seventies, a neomystic attitude in which the world of mysticism was an answer to the contemporary confusion. I included themes from the Cabala, from Teresian mysticism, from hermetism, alchemy in modern situations.

In my first book, *Morada interior* (Interior Abode), Saint Teresa, the central figure, became a contemporary voice: without roots, without faith, in search of identity: in exile and in separation: in the center of a silent eroticism. It interested me to develop the same theme with a duality of focus: the search for religious identity between New Christian and Old Christian, and the search for nationality, Spanish exile and Mexico. Although I began with a narrative structure that was similar to that of the novel, I created my own genre ad hoc that allowed me absolute freedom of movement in time, space, characters, forms, inventions, reflections.

In *Tierra adentro* (Inside Land), I preferred a more classic narrative form, and I chose the chronological order of a noncontemporary event. I based my work on a picaresque novel of the Spanish Golden Age to create a character whose life could seem to be like that of a *pícaro* but whose ideals were not. I intended to explore the idea of exile through the means of a Jewish character who has to abandon Spain rather than give up his religion.

In *La guerra del unicornio* (The War of the Unicorn), I used language and forms of the Castilian epic, transposing the Spanish Civil War onto the Middle Ages. Alchemy and Cabala are present in this novel. These themes were also antecedents of the interest in the esoteric and medieval that continues today. The three works can be considered as my *improvement* on the historical novel genre now being written.

Once I had experimented with the collection of symbols and the neomystical forms, I moved on to another aspect. The idea of madness in creation attracted me. *Dulcinea encantada* (Enchanted Dulcinea) is an attempt at literary schizophrenia: the same character writes two novels and lives his own life as a third novel but without ever being able to write anything. The action is reduced to the center of his mind with three voices in constant implied dialogue. I take on the theme of Spanish exile from the childhood memories of a girl who is sent to Russia by her parents to escape the dangers of the Spanish Civil War, without imagining that, instead, she would have to suffer through the Second World War.

In my books of short stories, I alternate two lines: I continue with the mystical mode as a way to reflect on the creative process. Or I take advantage of the accumulated stories—heard and re-formed—to show off unique events, between violence and humor. *Huerto cerrado, huerto sellado* groups stories from 1960 to 1984. *De magias y prodigios* takes in the period from 1985 to 1987. Both include the two types of stories. The same could be said about *Serpientes y escaleras* (Serpents and Stairways), next to appear, in which the experience of going up and down marks small events in the lives of the characters, mostly Spanish refugees. The presence of Mexico stands out in this last book, as it does in the stories I'm now writing.

Which brings me to a parallel theme: exile (temporal and atemporal) and memory. A feeling world and world of memory. History and the past surge like a modifiable present. They exist in order to be changed. I mix, combine, and oppose the memories that I save in my memory, which includes that which is specifically mine, and also the collective memory that I have been collecting throughout my entire life. Then I place the memories in a virgin flow of facts. I don't transcribe reality, or rather what is beyond it or what I can imagine to be reality. It interests me to highlight the infinite textual variety: the struggle between clarity and irrationality: the constant ambiguity of the emotions: the hidden passions: the tension between word and act: the lack of law in a world of laws.

As for the formal, I govern myself with the same freedom and independence. I remove from my path anything that could be a limit, a rule, slogan. I use the genres flexibly and according to the needs of each case. Within a conception of clarities, the strident call or the "I" written with a capital letter. I believe in work without measure: not in the counting and sounding watch.

The task that occupies me now and for the near future is a trilogy of "nemofiction" that brings together the life of the Spanish exiles in the forties, as seen by a young girl. The first part, *Castillos en la tierra*

(Castles on the Land), has been completed, and I am in the process of writing the second. These books are helping me rescue from being forgotten unique experiences, but which belong to my group. Those traits, gestures, manias about that which perishes can be caught by the written word. At the same time, I write stories that are parallel to the trilogy. At times repeating the same theme and the same anecdotes, although they are developed in a compromised manner. Other times adding new facets. This parallelism allows me to repeat with variations the theme of exile that most certainly has always obsessed me, that I wasn't able to add or I added in a very ambiguous way years ago. Undoubtedly, the distance, the temporal perspective, the dispossessing help a great deal in historical understanding. And in the liberation of the pen. The hand has let go in calligraphic marks.

In this moment of my creation, I make use of the lessons received and I decant the stories that were trusted to me. I take up the origins and my mother's enthusiasm for showing me what could become a literary object returns to me. I discover that what I had thought forgotten or that which I hadn't paid sufficient attention was kept in a well that is now overflowing, limited episodes, limited in themselves, reveal themselves to me as scenes from a movable theater, paintings at an exposition, musical compasses, during every day I still live. And later, the night is left to keep rescuing the bottomless sack of memories during the welcome periods of insomnia or in the liberating images of dreams. What I disdained rises by its own value and the small becomes large. From now on, I let the deep waters of the well return to me my earliest memories, and together with the unrestrained power of invention, I dedicate myself to the internal circle of unending writing.

Translated by Stephen A. Sadow

Moacyr Scliar
Brazil
ॐ

Moacyr Scliar (1937–) is one of Brazil's leading intellectuals. A noted physician and government adviser on public health issues, he is important in Brazilian letters as a novelist and short story writer. He is one of only a few Jewish Brazilian writers (others being Clarice Lispector, Elisa Lispector, Arnaldo Niskier, and Samuel Rawet) to gain such prominence in Brazil's vast and multicultural literary environment.

Following the example of Sholem Aleichem and perhaps William Faulkner, Scliar has written many of his numerous short stories about the fictionalized inhabitants of a small, isolated town. For Scliar, the source is Bom Fim, a working-class neighborhood in the southern Brazilian port city of Porto Alegre where many Jews, including Scliar himself, have lived. He writes with humor and pathos about the travails and successes of the Jews of Bom Fim. Interweaving a number of tales in a single story, using frequent exaggeration and the techniques of magical realism, presenting a panorama of Jewish types and "droll characters," Scliar brings the world of Brazilian Jewry to a national and even international readership. Among his best-known works are *A guerra no Bom Fim* (The War in Bom Fim), which describes the growth of the Jewish middle class in Brazil; *O centauro no jardim* (The

Centaur in the Garden), the story of a Jewish centaur; and *A estranha nação de Rafael Mendes* (The Strange Nation of Rafael Mendes), a complex novel in which a man becomes aware of the many implications of his Jewish ancestry.

This essay, a retelling of Brazilian Jewish history as well as a personal saga, was written expressly for this anthology.

A CENTAUR IN THE GARDEN

Moacyr Scliar

In 1993, I spent a semester as visiting professor at Brown University in Providence, Rhode Island. Right after my arrival, they held a traditional ceremony marking the beginning of the academic year, in which professors in academic regalia parade before the student body. I was honored by being invited to be a participant in that ceremony. I can't deny that it made me proud. For the first time in my life I dressed in a professor's gown—and in a prestigious American university. But when I received the commemorative photograph, I was surprised: the face that appeared in the gown wasn't mine, it was my father's. We were never so much alike. The one in the photo wasn't a doctor who teaches Latin American literature or a writer invited to give a course on the image of the physician in literature. Rather, it was José Scliar, the Russian Jew who immigrated to Rio Grande do Sul in the second decade of this century, and who, taking things into his own hands, worked, formed a family, educated his children. It was destiny that my father wore the robes that he deserved. And so it happened that I once again remembered my origins.

I had never rejected them. I never could have rejected them, even if I had wanted to. Judaism is undissolvable. In my case it never had anything to do with religion, because I am not religious. It doesn't have anything to do with the vague and infamous concept of race. I don't have the hooked nose that anti-Semitic propaganda attributes to Jews. Neither do I have the type of Mediterranean physique that would be expected in the descendants of the ancient inhabitants of Palestine. Frequently, and with the traditional mixture of hostility and admiration, I am taken for an American. Of course, I was circumcised, but this isn't uniquely Jewish—anyone circumcised during infancy is affected in the same way.

I do have a personal story that, during my sixty years, I have come to consider as a testament of the history of this century, and a history of a group. I am part of the long heritage of Judaism, formed in biblical times and continuing to the present. I identify with the millions of human beings with whom I share the Judaic condition. I suffered with those who were persecuted, I died with those who were exterminated, and I am proud of those who have made their contribution in the arts, the sciences, literature, politics. I don't accept that a Jew can possibly be indifferent to Judaism. Such alienation is not possible, even in a country like Brazil where identities are often hidden in what I have called "the mix." The Jewish tie may be tenuous, but it is not undone.

I remember the great writer Clarice Lispector (1925–77). An immigrant from Russia like my parents, she hardly ever spoke of her Judaism—perhaps because she was married to a diplomat in a time when "blue blood" was de rigueur in the Brazilian diplomatic service. More than that, in her most admirable literature, Judaism is evident in its absence. A Jewish component is not lacking in her works but represented primarily in a melancholy way. In her last book, A Hora da Estrela (The Hour of the Star), a principal character, named Macabea, the prototypical persecuted and humiliated woman, summed up the feminine condition and the Jewish condition. During a personal conversation, Clarice told me, melancholically, of her admiration for those writers who can assert their Judaism.

Quite different was the attitude of another writer, a contemporary of Clarice, and like her, an immigrant, though from Poland: Samuel Rawet (1929–94). Author of the first great work of fiction about Brazilian Judaism, *Contos do emigrante* (Immigrant Stories), Rawet, who was a man known for emotional instability, at times turned against Judaism, calling it a conspiratorial movement. His Jewish self-hatred expressed itself in various articles published in the Brazilian press and followed him until his tragic end, a solitary death in an apartment in the city of Brasilia. Judaism can be, for many, a heavy burden.

Heavy or not, I never doubted my Judaism. My parents were immigrants; they came from Russia, more precisely from Bessarabia, a region that made up part of the czarist empire and where the Jews lived in encompassing and anxious poverty in the small villages that Sholem Aleichem described and Chagall painted. Jews, confined to this region, were subject to persecutions. The social tensions of a society violently polarized between a small moneyed class and the immense miserable masses needed to find an escape valve; the Jews were a favorite target. From the beginning of the century, Bessarabia was the scene of many violent pogroms, in particular the Kishniev pogrom (1903) that inspired Chaim Nachman Bialik's somber *City of Death:*

> *Of steel and iron, cold and hard and dumb*
> *Now forge thyself a heart, O man! And come*
> *and walk the town of slaughter. Thou shalt see*
> > *With walking eyes, and touch with conscious hands,*
> *On fences, posts, doors,*
> *On paving in the street, on wooden floors,*
> *The black dried blood, comingled here and there*
> > *With brains and splintered bone.*[1]

This situation called out to the worldwide Jewish conscience. Jewish philanthropists from Western Europe formed a company to foment agricultural colonization, the Jewish Colonization Association, or JCA. The JCA acquired huge tracts of land in Argentina and in Rio Grande do Sul, with the object of settling there the masses of refugees who were then leaving Eastern Europe. The colonizing project was not an exception. From a Europe cut into pieces by national and social conflicts, Germans, Italians, and Slavs left by the millions, facing the turbulent waters of the Atlantic in precarious ships. Their destination was a new promised land, America. In the southern cone of Latin America, where enormous expanses of undeveloped land existed, these immigrants were welcomed; as Juan Bautista Alberdi, an Argentine politician and intellectual said, "To govern is to populate." To populate with Europeans, naturally, who brought work experience and who could "whiten" the Latin American populations.

A few hundred families came to Rio Grande do Sul at the beginning of the century. They settled in the colonies of Philipson, Quatro Irmãos, and Baronesa Clara. They would receive land, agricultural tools, seeds, and some help from the JCA. But it never was a successful enterprise. To begin with, these people had little agricultural experience. In the region where they lived, there were only two distant urban centers, and the hospitals and schools were far away as well. To make matters worse, Rio Grande do Sul, an area ruled by warlords, was going through a period of continuous and bloody conflicts. During the revolution of 1923, the colonists lived in constant agitation. Armed bands frequently stole cattle and rations. Little by little, the colonists left their lands and went to the cities. They weren't the exception. The phenomenon of rural exodus, caused by the lack of suitable conditions in the country, became a constant in Rio Grande do Sul and in Brazil as a whole.

When my parents arrived in Brazil, the agricultural colonies were an episode that was practically over. They settled in the ship's final destination, the city of Porto Alegre. My grandmother Ana Scliar, a widow, arrived with her eight children. My maternal grandparents, Abrão and Edith Slavutsky, had four children. Large families were the rule in those days, when the survival of a child was always problematic. My grandparents, my uncles and aunts, and my parents went to live in a neighborhood called Bom Fim, something like the Lower East Side of New York, or Marais in Paris, or Once in Buenos Aires, or Bom Retiro in São Paulo. A poor neighborhood, of small houses— an Eastern European village in Porto Alegre. Of course, Bom Fim wasn't a Jewish neighborhood: we had Portuguese, Italian, and German neighbors, but the atmosphere was characteristically Jewish. There was a Jewish school, the Colegio Idiche, as it was known in the neighborhood, in which my mother, Sara Scliar, was a teacher; there was the synagogue, small and noisy; there was the club, with its dances, during which the boys found marriageable girls; there was the butcher shop, the general store—the streets were crammed with people: street vendors hawking their wares, rotund ladies discussing other people's lives, girls jumping rope, boys playing soccer.

At night there was never much to do. At times the neighborhood movie theaters showed a film in Yiddish; particularly popular was the tear-jerker *Uma carta da mamãe* (A Letter from Mother) that made the audience sob. When the first showing ended, many stayed for the second, trying to squeeze a little more from one ticket. Theatrical spectacles were also unusual, produced by a troupe, that in spite of its pompous name was almost always limited to a couple (Max Perlman and Guita Galina, Herman Klatzkin and Sofia Rafalovich) or possibly a lone actor (Morris Schwartz, Benzion Witler) from Argentina or the United States. The cast was filled in by local talent, aided by a prompter who, helping them remember the lines, yelled more than the actors. The show, presented in the São Pedro Theater, didn't have a starting time, but it did have a closing time: midnight, when the last bus left for Bom Fim. So that in spite of the fact that the show wasn't over, the shout *lomir guein, se iz shoin*, hurry, let's go, it's late, caused the audience to disperse. On Saturdays there was a traditional dance, enlivened by an orchestra that was not very skilled but was highly enthusiastic. Under the vigilant eyes of their mothers, the boys asked the girls to dance, keeping in mind that that could lead to a marriage proposal—and in fact, many marriages began at the Saturday night dances.

In general, though, there weren't any dances or theater productions or films. During the hot summer nights, chairs were brought to the sidewalks and people got together there. On winter nights, these get-togethers were held in people's homes, frequently in the kitchen, the most comfortable room. In summer or winter, the favorite distraction—in a time when television did not exist and when movies were expensive and theater rare—was to tell stories. This was a Jewish tradition that had great practitioners in Bom Fim. My parents, especially, were great storytellers. I became a writer, in great part, because of my identification with them, because I wanted to participate in the pleasure they had in telling a good story.

Part of social life—for the masculine sex, at least—had the bars as its locale. Bar Bom Fim was famous, frequented by a varied clientele that ranged from liberal professionals to smugglers who began to introduce into the city electronic marvels—battery-operated radios, calculators—brought from the United States.

Life in Bom Fin was hard. It was difficult to earn a living. Many dedicated themselves to street peddling or to selling on credit: they were the *clienteltchiks*, a term that originated from *clientele*. With merchandise that was easy to carry, clothing, pieces of fabric in a package (*pekel*), or a basket full of things (*koichl*), the clienteltchik went through the poor neighborhoods to *klapen*, knock on doors. Forerunner of the modern credit system, he sold on time. These sales were not written down, there weren't any notes, receipts, payment booklets, scarcely any notations in an account book—it was all done by mutual trust. Of course this trade wasn't free of risk. There were those who didn't pay: the *tchvok* ("nail," in Yiddish). The lenders were united; they had the *clienteltchik farhein*, a special type of union, and a credit cooperative (Lairsparcasse).

There were also regular street vendors. Ties were the favorite merchandise, principally in the center of the city: there the *gravatniks* worked, sellers of ties. And there were also established businesses, in clothing or furniture stores—merchandise produced in the small factories of Bom Fim.

Clothing, furniture. Later, during a surge of building expansion that continued until the end of the Second World War, the Jewish merchants and industrialists began to invest their money in the construction of small apartment houses. Clothing, furniture, houses. There is a connection here, these things that shelter, that protect, reveal a disposition, on the part of those who make and those who sell, to not only earn or to support themselves but also offer something that brings with it emotion, human warmth. He who has had to precipitously abandon houses, furniture, clothing, knows the importance of these things.

The Jewish father was in the store, in the little factory, or in the street, selling. But at home, the Jewish mother ruled. In Bom Fim, she corresponded to the traditional image of the mother who nourishes. It wasn't unusual to see mothers running after their children in the middle of the street, with a plate of food. I can give personal testimony of this. Thin, without appetite, I ate a few spoonfuls of soup by the time they turned on the machines in my uncle's furniture factory. My little brother was even worse: he hadn't eaten anything at all. It was a mystery how he survived. My mother finally found out. In front of our house there was a construction site. My brother crossed the street and asked for food from the operators, who, feeling sorry for him, fed him. Learning this, my mother made an agreement with the workers. She cooked food for the men who brought their lunch pails. My brother ended up being fed by his own Jewish mother. These precautions were, if not justified, at least comprehensible. Tuberculosis, the white plague that had decimated the inhabitants of the shtetl, of the ghetto, also afflicted the Brazilians. To feed them well was to protect the children against a terrible illness. But it fomented an Oedipal fixation in the Jewish people, and it isn't surprising that psychoanalysis has dug such deep roots in Bom Fim.

I close my eyes, and with great effort, I remember the house in which we lived, on Fernandes Viera Street. Like other houses in the neighborhood, it was very small; like the other houses, it lacked basic comforts like hot water. To take a bath (not very often, I am ashamed, as a public health worker, to have to admit), my mother heated water in a large Sol Levante cooking oil tin. By the way, she never used a gas or electric heater. It was a large wood stove; and anyone who has had to build a fire with damp wood in the depths of winter knows how it's practically an impossible mission.

In this scenario, I began to become conscious of my Judaism. Initially, it was a form of group identification. Those adults who spoke Yiddish and told stories of Bessarabia, those boys and girls who were my companions in the Jewish school, those were my people, I never doubted that. But Bom Fim wasn't a Jewish island, isolated from the world. Bit by bit, I was also becoming conscious—painfully conscious—of a difference. I was a Jew. I wasn't a *goy*. A strange word, that in Hebrew designates a nationality. It is not a pleasant word. It begins with this G, an ugly, disagreeable letter, that is frequently found in words that designate strangers: the *gajo*, the *ciganos*, the *gaijin* for the Japanese, and even the *gancho*, which doesn't take its origin from a very flattering term, perhaps coming from the Spanish *guacho*, which means "abandoned." In Hebrew several words beginning with G designate the stranger or the unknown: *gehena*, Hell or Purgatory; *Golem*, the android created by Rabbi Judah Löew. *Galut* begins with a G and means "dispersion." The biblical chosen people had ascendance over the *goyim*; but the Jews of Bom Fim were in no way chosen people. There were limits to the neighborhood, foreign boundaries, hostile land. On Holy Saturday, Bom Fim itself wasn't safe; a day after Holy Week, which commemorated the death of Christ, avenging hordes came from far away to punish the descendants of the Christ-killers. No one went out into the street to risk getting beaten up.

One day I got a portrait of Jesus. It was a gift, I think, from a pharmacy. It was a blond Christ, with soft, blue eyes filled with pathos— a good man. So good that I decided to hang it on the picture in my parents' room. My father, impatiently, ordered me to throw it away. I asked why. I received a vague answer, which didn't convince me, but I obeyed.

Paradoxically, my parents took the initiative to enroll me in a Catholic high school. The Jewish school had only the primary grades, and when I had finished, I had to continue my studies in another educational establishment. The high school in which I studied was considered to be difficult, disciplined. In fact, I became an exemplary student. Latin, for example, had no secrets for me. And my handwriting was excellent.

But there was also daily religious education. We prayed every day and we had catechism class. And from that a conflict was born. Let me hasten to say that there was no anti-Semitic or doctrinal element, or, if there was, it wasn't important. But that didn't save me from anguish. I acquired a sudden and sharp consciousness of mortality and eternal life. Heaven, that delicious place, choir of saints and angels intoning hosannas, heaven was for me a complete impossibility. Everything indicated that I was going to Hell, and that I would have to withstand, for all eternity, unimaginable suffering. I knew what suffering was, having suffered from colic during my entire infancy. But for eternity . . . God, what was this "for eternity"? As a metaphor, the religion teacher tried to give us a pallid idea of the duration of eternity. Imagine, he said, an immense column made of the hardest iron; every thousand years, a bird comes by this column and scratches it with his beak, carrying with it an infinitesimal particle—by the time the bird had taken the entire column not even an instant of eternity would have passed.

I would pass that eternity in Hell, the existence of which I never doubted. I knew where the entrance was located: behind the altar of a church in Bom Fim. There a tunnel led to a pool filled with alcohol in flames that was burning eternally. My schoolmates could easily free themselves from this punishment. It was sufficient that they prayed a certain number of Ave Marias on the first Saturdays of nine consecutive months. No matter how many sins they committed, they would repent at the hour of their death, guaranteeing for them the salvation of their souls.

Now, I still had a chance. As a Jew, I could escape Hell and obtain an entrance to Purgatory, if I were good and just. Now, for a member of a cursed race to be good and just was almost impossible. The best way would be for me to convert.

They weren't talking about a remote hypothesis. A Protestant boy, son of a Catholic mother, was converted in a ceremony carried out in the high school patio, in front of all the students. His happiness, now assured of heaven, was a cause of envy. But Protestantism wasn't so far from Catholicism as Judaism. Beyond that, I, member of the "stiff-necked people," didn't want to let my arm be twisted. I ended up forming a new religion, a Catholic sect in which I was the only believer and also the only priest. I made up prayers, rituals, penitences— which consisted in playing outside with things that I liked, for example, a new little notebook. My hope was to establish direct communication with Jesus, the good Jesus of the colored badge. Before this happened, I left the high school, entered a lay-sponsored school, and ended my own cult by forgetting it.

But I didn't save myself from the curse. I had already introjected Jewish stereotypes. Yes, the Jews were cheap. Yes, the Jews were avaricious. My new schoolmates turned to me and made allusions—in a teasing tone, of course—about the subject. I decided to give them a lesson. I would transform myself into an anti-stereotype. Did they think that Jews were cheap? I would be generous. Avaricious? I would be careless with my money. I paid for sandwiches, soft drinks, cigarettes for everybody. The Goyim looked at me in surprise, and they distrusted me.

Little by little, I was discovering that not only the Jews carried the stereotype for being avaricious, not only they liked money. Many people were avaricious, many people liked money. The world, I realized, was filled with Jews.

In 1948 the state of Israel was created, a fact that had a profound effect on my generation. Youthful protest, indignation with social injustice (of which anti-Semitism was a facet), could now be channeled toward an objective: life in a Jewish Socialist cell, the kibbutz. A sentiment I shared with hundreds of members of youth groups. Associated with all of this was a profound disgust with the bourgeois life now within the reach of Brazilian Jews.

The youth movement of which I was a member was of Marxist-Leninist-Stalinist inspiration. As such, it followed the totalitarian model of the communist parties of the time. There was iron discipline, guaranteed by rituals such as sessions of criticism and self-criticism. But it was an intense experience. To leave the city, to camp in the middle of nowhere, to sing and dance around a campfire—moments of profound emotion. The youth movement deepened my knowledge of

Jewish culture; more than that, I learned to believe in universal values, in justice, in solidarity, in friendship. It was good to have friends in whom you could confide completely. Without mentioning the love affairs, it was a time of devastating passions.

But the truth is that the movement demanded a great deal. They all, I discovered, had a messianic vocation. The conflicts that I had to face were many and painful, as in a family, as with comrades, as with friends. To leave the youth movement was a trauma that inevitably left psychic scars. In my generation, leaving the youth movement was accompanied almost automatically by entering psychoanalysis. There was the balm for our upset psyches: a treatment created by a Jew that was expressly destined to alleviate millennial Jewish guilt. Of course, that too didn't take place without suffering, but it was suffering that had a purpose.

I had other and interesting Jewish experiences. Recently trained as a medical doctor, I assumed the post of physician of the Home for the Aged of the Jewish community of Porto Alegre. There weren't many residents—there were never more than sixty—but being in daily contact with them meant stirring up Jewish memories. Among the people I treated in that institution, I was particularly impressed with a woman who, in spite of her advanced age and dementia, showed a surprising vitality—more than that, a surprising sensuality. When it was necessary to examine her in her room, I had to bring with me a nurse's aide. Without realizing that I was a doctor, she acted as if she were receiving a romantic visit from a young suitor—and she didn't hesitate to throw herself on him. Slowly, I was retelling the story of this woman, a former prostitute, one of the "polacas" as they were known in Brazil, brought over from Eastern Europe by Tzvi Migdal, a secret organization that trafficked in the "white slave trade" in the southern cone. Attracted by the promise of marriage, those women were taken from their homes and brought first to Paris, where they were initiated into the life of the brothel and learned a few words in French—the Argentine ranchers and gauchos had a fascination for French women.

In 1970 I spent three months in Israel giving a course in public health in Be'er Sheva. I discovered, in the first place, that the country didn't correspond to my idealized image of it. It wasn't a great kibbutz, the utopian society that I imagined. But it was a country of tremendous vitality and dynamism, a country in which the people faced the problems of daily life with uncommon courage. I returned from Israel proud of my Judaism—and that is reflected in my literature. From then on, I wrote stories without a defined theme (even though many stories allude indirectly to the political climate in Brazil, then governed by a military dictatorship). In that year I decided to write a novel, and it was natural that my setting be Bom Fim and my characters, the characters of the neighborhood during the Second World War. Shortly before the book was published, my mother got sick and died. It was a trauma from which I will never recover. I remember my mother constantly, and I remember her telling stories with a grace that was unique to her. The stories that I like best to tell.

In my stories about Bom Fim, I tell of childhood fantasies and the dreams of adolescence. I tell of the communists that I knew, I tell of a Jewish prostitute, and I tell of a centaur that, because of its dual nature, seems to symbolize identity conflicts to me.

Little by little, I have been developing and accepting, in a mature form now, my situation as a Jew. I don't claim that being Jewish makes a person superior, but it makes him different, and the affirmation of the difference is crucial in a world that is so homogenized. For me, Judaism isn't a religion—the religious rituals are hardly different from those of other religions. Judaism is for me a rich culture, expressed through history, literature, art, even humor. I don't know what the future can be for this culture, given the rapid process of assimilation.

I hope that I am able to make a minuscule, extremely modest contribution so that it, in some way, survives; so that Bom Fim figures on the map of the Jewish world. And above all, so that I can perceive in the photographs that portray my face, now older, the faces of José and Sara, of my parents, and of so many other Jewish parents.

NOTES

1. Maurice Samuel, *Selected Poems of Chaim Nachman Bialik* (New York: Union of American Hebrew Congregations, 1972), 104.

Translated by Stephen A. Sadow

Alicia Freilich de Segal
Venezuela

Alicia Freilich de Segal (1939–) is an activist. She has spent much of
her life as a Zionist organizer. Daughter of a journalist and correspondent for the New York Yiddish newspaper *Forward*, she was exposed
as a child to international Jewish affairs. As a journalist, she has been
constantly in touch with those Venezuelans who are influential in
politics, business, and the arts. Always active in Jewish communal
affairs, she has served as executive director of the Venezuelan Jewish
Federation. She is currently professor of literature at the Universidad
Central de Venezuela.

Freilich de Segal uses her fiction as a means of educating as well
as entertaining her readers. Her novels *Legítima defensa* (Legitimate
Defense), *Cláper,* and *Colombina descubierta* (Columbine Discovered)
investigate Jewish identity, the weight of the past on the present, and
the meaning of the state of being in exile.

Unlike many Jewish Latin American writers, Freilich de Segal is
enthusiastic about her country, thankful for the hospitable climate
Jews have found there. In this essay, written for this anthology, Freilich
de Segal focuses on her experience of Zionism in Latin America.

'RECOLLECTIONS OF A CRIOLLA ZIONIST

Alicia Freilich de Segal

This time it seemed very different. For all the other military coups the radio had played "funeral music," as the Venezuelan public called those endless selections of classical music. The was no doubt that this was different, very special. Máximo and Rebeca, tense and tearful, ears glued to the set, counted with their fingers as a distant voice counted off: yes, no, yes, no, yes.

Suddenly a brief silence. Then enthusiastic applause. Then screams, tears, and laughter. When she embraced me, Rebeca said between sobs, something like, "The majority of the world voted for the partition of Palestine. The English are leaving. Venezuela voted yes! At last we have a piece of land!! But this happiness will cost us a lot of blood."

Spoken in November of 1947, the last sentence sounded more like sour grapes yet was so typical of our ancestral rite, according to which each joy should be tempered by mourning because of what happened two thousand years ago with the Fall of the Second Temple, during the reign of Titus the Roman. There was more to it, of course. Much more. It was what we knew, suffered, and learned, through bitter experience: for the Jews as a people, happiness is never free, continuous, or long- lasting.

And yet for that singular moment, the children of the house, Perla, two years old, Miriam, three, and I, Alicia, eight, all enjoyed the unusual festive mood. In our home, for as long as anyone could remember, even at the modest birthdays and frugal Sunday dinners with *paisanos*, always, between bites of *lekach* (sweet cake), sips of tea with lemon, and sweet Yiddish melodies coming from the RCA Victrola, the conversation since forever had always been the same: Germany, Poland, ghettos, crematoriums, in other words: HOLOCAUST.

As of May 1948, with the official declaration of Israel's independence, the lively sounds of the Hora and the waving of the little blue and white flags with their Star of David, "Hatikvah," the national anthem, was sung out loud. Not even the Arab invasion that took place only hours after the establishment of the Jewish National Homeland could erase the smiles from the faces of adults and children in their daily and communal activities, thus mitigating that heavy and sad atmosphere that pervaded the entire previous decade.

That infantile and adolescent Zionism marked forever our generation of *judíos criollos*, that is, the first born in Venezuela. We were children of immigrants of the pre- and postwar Europe of 1939. From that moment on, we understood that our small and simple life *here* gravitated around great and complex events taking place in a *there* where Israel, the United States, Russia, and other powers met, unconcerned about us.

It was no accident that my father became a self-taught journalist for the *Forward* in New York and several Israeli dailies; nor that Miriam, and I, and now my youngest son, took up that profession with the goal of fighting for human rights. From the very beginning, at the back of that very small, dark, and narrow store, to the very last day of World War II, the Freilichs devoured and saved every *Universal* as well as any foreign newspapers they could find.

The radio, always on with news accounts sandwiched in between delightful sitcoms, adventure and love stories, the parental voices commenting on Zionism and Jewish culture, and the eloquent oratory of those in charge of collecting funds for the Zionist campaigns (which to this very day so ably manages the guilt feelings of the Diaspora) were the three forging elements of that Zionism, injected into us day by day, from the War of Independence to the Sinai War. This experience was totally auditory until the fifties when television invaded our privacy and destroyed part of the fantasy.

At the Moral y Luces, Herzl Bialik, the first Jewish high school in Venezuela, we were constantly reminded of the need to reconcile our "first duties" as Venezuelan descendants of the Liberator Simón Bolívar with our ancestral and therefore automatic duties toward the father and founder of political Zionism and the major poet of the Hebrew language. The most prepared Jewish primary and secondary school educators were able to find refuge in our school because they were for the most part Democrats who had been repressed by the dictatorship of General Marcos Pérez Jiménez. This made it easy for their young liberal students to hold on to their Zionism as a Jewish national liberation movement, which they saw as going hand in hand with that of the Algerians, the Irish, and the Cubans.

From the routine of that traditional homey Judaism, without excessive or obsessive religious practices, we all became one with a democratic Israel, a nation built on a secular, tolerant, nationalistic ideology. And so it functioned from the fifties until the beginning of the eighties. It continued through the Camp David Accords, my years at the Universidad Central de Venezuela, and my career teaching Spanish and literature as well as enjoying the great honor of being the first former student of the Jewish high school to return as one of its instructors.

With other Jewish graduates of the Venezuelan Republic, democratic as of 1958, I witnessed the victorious Six-Day War (which seemed, in appearance at least, to give Israel secure borders) and the surprise of the Yom Kippur War (which began to undermine that security). We lived through a visual, idealized, and reactive Zionism in the face of a growing virulent Latin American anti-Semitism based on Castro's revolutionary catechism.

The international left ended our honeymoon by hiding its Catholic-based anti-Jewish agenda behind what they called Marxist anti-Zionism. Of course, our answer in defense was equally violent.

I formed part of a small group, improvised for the emergency, to publicly answer the challenge. Ours was a unilateral point of view, the same point of view that in another place and time made Golda Meir answer: "Who are the Palestinians? I am a Palestinian." Ours was justified paranoia for being *accused* of Zionism at that point carried the same pejorative weight as that *"dirty Jew"* of forever. In addition, we suffered from a crass emotional ignorance that blocked our vision of reality. It is always so hard, if not impossible, to accept (the singularity of) someone else's nationalism. It is the cause of all conflict, all battles. We were brought up in the belief that Israel was built on an empty territory where a few natives with turbans rode peacefully on their camels. Suddenly it became clear that the presence of the Jewish state had reactivated an incipient Palestinian identity to the point of becoming a manipulable nationalism, repressed and ready to explode, unable to admit the possibility of either coexisting with or being neighbors of the Israelis.

It was as if our silk paper Zionism had lost its innocence, understood its original sin and in the face of ever-growing Arab intransigency of *no recognition, no dialogue, no peace,* found itself enmeshed in a change too difficult to assimilate. Thus our diminutive and admired David reverted into a gigantic and repulsive Goliath who heartlessly smashes its fragile adversary. This stereotype persists and weakens the soil of Zion since the Sabra and Chatila episodes of 1982.

Twenty years earlier, I had understood my need to *feel* Israel with my own hands, before starting out my married life with Jaime Segal Kuperstein, a Romanian survivor of a Russian work camp during Hitler's war. He had arrived in 1947 with his parents, Ana and Aaron, and his sister, Silvia. He became a neurologist. We created a family of four, blessed by two children: Ernest Israel, an opthalmologist, and Ariel Yehuda, a journalist, historian, and writer.

That trip to a touristic and fashionable Israel with its epic and romantic image, all the best of the novel *Exodus*, and the image of the kibbutz as a fountain that destroyed the malarial swamp, affected me less than my other voyage. The other one had been toward freedom of spirit, away from relatives and friends of my parents, all escapees of Nazi Europe. Here in Israel, on the one hand, you had all pioneers, grateful of the miracle of survival, needy of a new planet that would sincerely learn to respect and integrate the Jew and would feel shame for its original complicitous silence; on the other hand, their children, born in Israel, strong realists, unbelieving and arrogant, ready to kill to survive, did not in the least believe in *divine miracles* or in a humanitarian conscience. In both cases and complementing each other, Zionism was idealistic and practical, supernatural and ordinary.

This human contact plus the horrifying tales that I had personally heard from the lips of Aunt Guta and Uncle Abraham Hirshbein, Auschwitz survivors, constitute the *materia prima* of my intellectual, polemical, and passionate Zionism, which I tried to share and communicate in numerous articles published in the newspapers *El nacional* and *El universal* and in the magazine *Resumen*.

The following fifteen years, no longer teaching in classrooms, alternating ideological purpose, and through many articles, I dealt with other matters of Venezuelan and world affairs. I did book reviews, news pieces. I interviewed some figures who were sacred cows, others who were newsworthy, and even some who were totally unknown. Part of that journalist work was collected in *Triálogo, Cuarta dimensión, Entrevisados en carne y hueso, La venedemocracia*, and *Legítima defensa*.

In 1974, five years after beginning this editorial journalism, the Venezuelan government granted me the Francisco de Miranda Award in recognition of my efforts. Later in my mature years, my father's mental health caused a complete turnaround. Alzheimer's disease, the illness of forgetting, devastated my father for ten years until his death in 1991. The long and intermittent psychoanalysis I underwent to deal with some of the stirred-up neuroses had many hard moments from which I emerged with the desire to rescue, through literature, parallel lives.

Thus my first novel, *Cláper*, was conceived. Published in 1987, it has had three printings. An English translation was published in 1998. In it I narrate in a bifurcated first person, biographical fragments of my progenitor and of myself, in order to expose lyrically the dramatic contrast that conflicted us as "grandchildren" of the Holocaust and complicit witnesses to Zionism. The fixed point of my existence has always been someplace in between shtetl values transported to South America and acquired ones needed to survive amid the customs and influences of the Gentile world.

The situation in the Middle East, always a part of our daily bread, became even more so after the war with Lebanon. With the trauma of the Intifada, the conflictive character has become more pronounced and a new lens shows Zionism divided between *followers* and *spectators*.

There were premonitions, of course, since 1967, even with that sensational, heroic Zionism that General Moishe Dayan commanded. A million nationalist Palestinians scattered in Gaza and the West Bank of Jordan, fed blind anti-Israeli intolerance by Arab leadership, is a lethal combination now culminating explosively in the detention camps and prisons, fertile ground for sowing more Hamas-type terrorism. And Israel, in the midst of full economic expansion, is also in the midst of agonizing debates and ideological chaos. She is half liberal and secular, a fifth Palestinian semioccupied, and the rest Jewish nationalistic. The right, of course, feeds the fires of the religious militants whose extremism, identical to that of the Muslims, led to Rabin's assassination. For the very first time and with no remorse, with sincere biblical faith, one Zionist kills another, a democratic prime minister of the state of Israel. Our God lost his *oneness* and dictates to the anointed assassin, the holy messianic annihilating his brother.

Zionism is wounded to its very core. It admits two autonomous states, one Jewish, one Palestinian. Reality proves, even to moderate Arabs, that this is the only way to begin a difficult but necessary peace.

Perhaps this hurtful perception of imminent historical suicide, two Jewish people radicalized by opposing Zionisms, as happened to the kingdoms of Israel and Judea and led to the destruction of the First Temple of Jerusalem by the Babylonians, among other more personal reasons, led me to write my second novel, *Columbina descubierta,* in 1991. I created the novel with a difficult, cryptic prose, a hermeticism that paradoxically favored the most dissimilar interpretations, all very valid. It merited in 1992 the prestigious Mexican Fernando Jeno Award. The novel is based on the theories of the Spanish thinker Salvador de Madariaga, according to whom Christopher Columbus was a *marrano,* militantly Jewish, as were all the financial supporters of his first voyage. All were persecuted by the Inquisition headed by Torquemada, himself a descendant of *conversos,* converts to Catholicism, who gladly gave himself to the task of annihilating hidden Jews. My protagonist, Binhich (which in Hebrew means "knowledge") Colón, has to become several different characters to survive in this century, and her lunatic alienation was my metaphor for asking (myself) if Zionism and the Holocaust, the two pillars that bear the biography of the contemporary Jews, were indefensible delusion.

It is only now, at a sufficient distance, that I detect the authentic unconscious motivation that led me to create the novel on such secret foundations and under such a labyrinthine poetic covering. That is how I projected and at the same time covered up my profound fear of the reactions I would elicit from the fanatics in my very own community today.

So now, in the midst of the cybernetic era, one has to ask oneself about the future of Zionism. Before our perplexity, phobic because impotent, the Israel of our deepest love, the Israel of the Constitution, not the Israel of manipulated Sacred Scriptures, or the Israel of resented ethnicities. But Israel the original, the pristine, which granted citizenship and nationality on the bases of *humane* laws, this Israel might seem on the contrary to be heading toward a theocracy with its apartheid of a powerful minority exterminating any unusual traces of its very particular biblical reading.

What then shall be the thread that binds once again our feeling of belonging? How does one say, after five thousand years of history, "Who am I?" Or worse: "What am I?"

In Sarajevo, there is a 700-year-old Spanish-made Haggadah. After enduring horrible reincarnations it arrived in Bosnia where it survived in synagogues, churches, and mosques. A short time ago it was saved from burning after heavy Serb bombing of the main library. Now, this original tome, with its magnificent illustrations recounting Jewish liberation from Pharaonic slavery, is jealously guarded in a secret place, by the Bosnian Islamic police. It is considered an emblem, a talisman of survival miraculously preserved.

Could this Song of Freedom that we chant yearly at Passover be the text and symbol of Zionism for the third millennium?

Translated by Joan E. Friedman

José Kozer
Cuba/United States/Spain
꿗

José Kozer (1940–) explores every human emotion and every specifically Jewish feeling; he hides nothing. He talks about beauty and ug-
liness in the same breath. He is immersed in the spiritual mysteries
of the Cabala and the everyday mysteries of the carnal. He never forgets that his first Jewish home in the new world was next to a bordello.
Kozer seems to create poetry, lots of it, lots of it on Jewish themes,
from his inner being. It pours out of him; his words fly like incanta-
tions of some wonder-working rabbi, one who also knows of terrible
pain. Among his collections are *Y así tomaron posesión en las ciudades*
(And They Took Possession of the Cities), *Jarrón de abreviaturas* (Pot
of Abbreviations), and *Bajo este cien* (Under This Hundred). His imagery is Jewish and Christian and Buddhist; he is disturbing and he is
calming.

For many years, José Kozer was professor of Spanish and Portuguese
at Queens College in New York City. He now resides in Spain.

This essay, in which Kozer displays his feelings, his poetic techniques, and the relationship between the two, was revised for this
anthology.

NATURAL INSTINCTS

José Kozer

I enter here (March 28, 1940), Havana, a house adjoining a bordello, a little brothel of Old Havana. Everything is ready for the spectacular jump, ladies and gentlemen. Here the new generation enters, the assimilated one. (I am Cuban. Only much later would I discover, would I accept that I am that, without ceasing to be what is other, the other: a Jew from the other side of the Jordan. Let's remember that Hebrew means "he who comes from the other side of the river.") I'm already here, I can function. My use of language. That's my show. To write poems. Simulacrum, the poet. I have facts. I have instruments: only now it is something to obsess about, to work. A clear situation: a room, a table, a chair, a window, or at least the interior image of all that. And to set yourself to reinvent "because paper can put up with everything."

Here I am, in fiction, fiction of a room (*A Room of One's Own*). I can stay here inside to resist death, madness, the cataclysm of history: Let there be the Diaspora, and it was Made. But change is not rupture because poetry connects, is. The continuing force, that which scars, that which helps to cleanse, to not die, to not go crazy (how many mentally ill are produced by every immigration?). Fine: I can resist. Resist Papa who invented me, who told me and told me how to resist. Resist Mama who imposes that language of hers, soft, refined. I write: why do I seek the notation or the notoriety? Or why can't I find myself and seek to be another, unsatisfied? I seek to be grandfather, the one from the Warsaw ghetto or the grandfather of the Cuban shul, the synagogue of Old Havana.

I am grandmother who dies in the ghetto. I am grandmother, the slippered one of kitchens smelling like charcoal. I am three sisters who arrive on San Francisco Wharf and peer at the herring, at the cases, at the deformed forms of the fruit, the tubers "were ist names, Tate's" "A Que es ñame, papa?" to which my grandfather will reply, "a Zane est in Kumba / Una cosa que se comes in Cuba": I am, two languages.

There is a table, it is lunch hour. The plates are arranged in an impeccable order imposed by Mama, from the impeccable figure of my father at the head of the table. He arrived, it was two o'clock. He would enter, deliver the black or rye bread that he carried under his arm, and he would go straight to his room. From the room to the bathroom. From the bathroom, water could be heard: he would shave, shower. That ritual would last forty-five minutes. At one, the four of us would sit down at the table. Silence! Schwaig schtill! Quiet! When you eat you don't talk! Papa came out of the bathroom, handsome, immaculate, impeccable. I would hear him inside there, running the water, singing something heroic, strange. Years later I would learn that he was singing "The International," first in Russian, then in Polish. And he finished that off with the Polish national anthem, in his own original version.

We were at the table, Estrada Palma 515 between Goicuría and Juan Delgado (it's one o'clock). The dishes, the table, the kitchen door that opens and closes so that luncheon dishes come and go, the parts of the luncheon, of the variation. Variability: there is gefilte fish with *chrein* (chopped fish with horseradish) and there is *ropavieja*.

There is *ropavieja* and the fountain of latkes flows. Each dish a (another) possibility; multiplications. Parable: from a bread, breads; from a fish, fishes (many fish). Wealth: spiritual riches; that of the accepting, redemptive country and that of the original country, millenary, wandering. Each dish, each person, each member of this family constitutes another possibility, another tone of the Havana heat, another perspective from heat to cold and from cold to heat (Diaspora, right?).

Each one of them, story, instrument, vehicle of communication (to the others, for the others), is another basting thread of resistance, of survival, of continuity. They are not going to break. They (we) are going to die, but they (we) are not going to break. They are sewn together, connected. The thread and the string, the person and the host. One, is all. Cuba veered, it is Jewish, it is Eastern Europe. Since at the same time that they, we, the Cubans divide ourselves, we spread ourselves through the world: the Wandering Cuban. That's it. . . .

It seems that yes, history turned upside down, or it was always like that? Only it's now our turn, that's all.

That's it, we internationalize ourselves; we are confused, we intermingle more and more. New History? Or would it be the same Yiddishe Geshijte as always? The same Jewish history that Bertha the "lererque" might have taught to me in the house on Estrada Palma. Bertha the teacher. Everything changed? I don't know.

(JOSÉ KOZER) BIOGRAPHY: A FILE FULL OF DATES

He leaves Cuba (1958). He returns (May 1959).

Hopeful. Anxious. He leaves Cuba behind (August 1960): he doesn't return.

He works (1960–63) for three years on Wall Street: with a tie and long hair (pre-Beatles) he calls the floors in the elevators, in the streets of Wall Street. Export director for a company that sells small planes, aviation radios, and autopilots. He earns money. He is not happy.

He gets married, she is Sheila Isaac (1962). There will be progeny, a daughter Mía (la Milonga), 1966. Great immaturity. Arguments.

Drunken bashes. Three-day poker games that went on until dawn. Hero of a cheap film. Experiences with drugs. Without money. He is not happy.

He finishes a B.A. at New York University (1965). In an elevator, the same day that he receives his degree, he bumps into a professor of Spanish who invites him to study and teach at a place called Queens College (whose name I don't wish to remember?). He begins his studies, teaches as a part-time lecturer (Swineherd: the translation is mine).

1967, they promote him to Lecturer in the Department of Romance Languages (More Important Swineherd: the translation is still mine).

1968, finally he separates from his first wife. He cares for his two-year-old daughter. The mother has to be hospitalized for a nervous breakdown (wow is she crazy).

1968–70, drunk like a CUBA, day and night.

1970, after not having finished a single poem in almost a decade, he returns to writing, and for several decades he doesn't leave anything untouched or a poem undone: from that point, if he were José Kozer, he would have by now three thousand five hundred poems in his estate.

1971, Master of Arts in Luso-Brazilian Literature from Queens College. He decides not to finish his doctorate and dedicate himself completely to poetry. He can do it. That would probably be his next drunk. He smokes. He stops drinking. He buys a house in Spain (Nerja, Málaga). He smokes. He meets her, the one who will be his second and permanent wife: he begins to be happy [sic].

1974, routine. He marries Guadelupe, maiden name Barrenechea. His wife begins to learn English and confuses "gorilla" with "guerrilla." They laugh: everything is in order.

1976, nervous depression, a month in a semicatatonic state; useful fact for the biography of a poet, right? Susana Kozer is born (Susa or La Niña) looking just like her mother with her face of a Spaniard and with "the most beautiful eyes that human islands have ever seen."

1977, he stops smoking. He publishes more and more. He has already gone back to speaking (writing) Spanish. His English deteriorates.

1978, sweet consideration in all things of daily life, nothing in excess with the exception of poetry writing which can't be in excess. He is able to write three hundred fifty poems in a year. He hardly drinks. He returns to smoking but with admirable consideration.

1978–83, he continues to weigh the 155 pounds that he weighed when he left Cuba. He becomes an assistant professor in Queens College (Chief Swineherd, as I translate). I read. There are two constants: a happy marriage and his creation (without adjectives). Let's say that his life is the Liebe und Arbeit, as Mr. Freud might have said.

1983–84, new university promotion in Queens College (associate professor, or Boss of the Swineherds). Before that abstention, he sees his life begin to descend. He begins to write fewer poems per year.

1984, writing, his diaries, some creative prose and, as always, poetry, poetry.

His life will be that: to write poetry and "the rest is silence." His, then, is just another biography, one more biography.

1985 to the present, final promotion in Queens College, he is now Full Professor (Grand Captain of Swineherds): Mama, proud.

So:

First name: José (which in Hebrew means "that which is left over," or added or extra).

Last name: Kozer (whose meaning is not that of "kosher" but rather, as is known, could refer to the Caspian Sea or Cossack or, frankly, nothing).

He who is here autobiographed is the author of numerous books of poems and chapbooks published in the United States, Mexico, Argentina, the Dominican Republic, Spain. His work has been translated, I repeat, partially, into English, Portuguese, Italian, French, Hebrew; work that has been published in more than two hundred fifty literary magazines, newspapers, and literary supplements from (generally) Spanish-speaking countries. Verdehalago, the Mexican publishing house, plans to publish, in the year two thousand and something, volumes containing all his work (we'll see).

And so, it's a trivial life that of José Kozer. The anonymous as center of his creation. To awaken the poetic animal paying it the least possible attention, faking. Nothing happens, nothing gets in the way: that dissimulation centers his poetic activity. So, he gets up every day just when it begins to get light: ablations, breakfast, he sits down to work. He translates, writes in his personal diaries, reads: and from there (no always, not always) arises his new poem.

He goes to the university, gives his classes, returns home or rather he sneaks away from the university, has lunch. As a general rule, during lunch hour, intense conversations with Guadelupe: sweetness from those conversations. They share Guadelupe's excellent cooking, the fine wines of France, the words obsessive. It's well that they understand each other, well that they know how to give each other space, not interfere with each other (one against the other): a good couple.

They love each other.

The poet and the beloved: the corrosive poet and the innocent beloved. The innocent beloved purifies the corrosive poet, purifies him of the three ASAVAS: that of sensual desire, that of the desire to exist, and that of ignorance. The Beloved is a good thing.

In the afternoon, the poet reads in his upstairs room, lying in bed for hours (as Valle-Inclán and Marcel Proust might read and work). To read, throwing away, to read for death, in the way in which you might read Bernard Berenson, so admired, and D'Annunzio, so little admired.

He reads. At nine o'clock at night, he turns out the light.

ARTE POETICO

If it's true that Paul Celan said "Poetry doesn't impose, it exposes," then he spoke well. And paraphrasing Celan, I can say that with me "poetry imposes itself on me and I expose it."

I don't know where it comes from, in any particular case, I would be able to say that it comes from everywhere. And how it imposes itself, is abrupt, unexpected. It's always awaited and comes unexpectedly. How? Through a burst. A trivial image. Some words that come together from strangeness and which seem to be arbitrarily dictated. The head and the voice collect them.

Really, we are always immersed in poetry: day and night (perhaps, above all, at night). But with poetry occurs the same thing as with the music of the spheres: it sounds, harmonious, at all times, and for that reason, it is not heard. Poetry sounds at all times, and to hear it, we have to stop hearing it. The result? One (more) poem whose gestation we hardly notice: (another) poem tossed imperfectly from the perfection of poetry (Poetry?) that accompanies us day and night.

The imperfect poem (and its sensation of unreality, of indetermination), sources of insatiability, incentives of creation.

During the gestation, everything is marvelous: nevertheless, the completed poem has the effect of making us feel that there is something there, imponderable, that doesn't work, doesn't move; something cannot be (once more) adjusted. It's not possible to put your finger in the ulcer, to know with precision what is lacking: but the result is opaque while the aspiration is transparent, global. The result? That beehive of dissatisfaction, perhaps immature, always present and that, the poem completed, assaults and deflates us and again, constant pruritus that triggers the need to get involved in another poem.

That is, the necessity to again wait for the unexpected: poetry, the poems.

It returns. And in the instant that it returns, tranquility (that which strikes violently) and attacks of nerves, horror and enormous joy diluted in a silent invisible smile. It returns. And from its abundance we know that the language with which we write (we make) a poem is insufficient: dictionaries are insufficient, the nomenclatures, the tropes and figures, the damnable reverent grammar and logic which negate the disordered order that demands the poetic.

A poem, then, is always a residual incorporation, an incorporation of fecal material to a sacred center.

Oh, beautiful fecal material! as Rabelais might say.

JOSÉ KOZER: ONE TIME, NEVER MORE

On the eighteenth of August 1960 I left Cuba, and I stayed away. I stayed away from the language and from the way of speaking, away from one place though not a unique one, from the place to which, as a rule, one returns. I never returned.

I am first- and last-generation Cuban. My parents, Jews from Eastern Europe, immigrated to Cuba and were nationalized citizens (legally and spiritually). They loved Cuba. I was born there, Havana, 1940, and from there, one day, I left, Cubana de Aviación a Miami, Miami a Nueva York in a Greyhound bus, one of those in which blacks still had to sit in the back, and as I think that my daughters, born and raised in the United States are Americans (legally, spiritually), and with my death my Cuban generation will come to an end. A short lineage.

This doesn't have to be taken as a disaster, this is not tragic, it's not melodrama or mess-up: this, on the contrary, is the norm in the world in which we live. We are all of the first and last generation of something in a changing and accelerating world that evaporates us, as in an immediate and palpable sense that for me Cuba evaporated in 1960.

And so, perhaps, for several decades, to be Cuban and more concretely to be a Cuban poet implies to be or to exist in the past: let's say that at the head of the ass, the paradox may be valid; always waiting on line, pretty far from the entrance.

This posterity implies a Diaspora that I know well in an archetypical and ancestral way. Diaspora is *atopos* (the *no* place): no place and all places; not the nationality but the Orbicular Nation: in her one is taken in as to a free and open center that if one listens well, fills our pocket with poems. Diaspora, then, a center of fluidity, and at the same time, a fluidity without a center.

Posterity, the last baggage car: that is to be a Cuban and to be a Cuban poet. We are everyone. We are Polish (the name that they gave Jews in Cuba), we are all Polish; we are any old being who like Ulysses responds to Polyphemus that Polyphemus with his one, brutal eye, his huge body and his terrifying beard, telling him: I AM NOBODY. The "I" is another of Rimbaud's.

Our mother tongue, itself, it an atopic space, where the natural language (womb) is marginal, strange material that ceases to be univocal and becomes polyvocal (polyglot). Multicellular letter. Today the Cubans speak and write with Cuban national continuity and multinational contagion: our writing is filled with Peruvianisms, Colombianisms, Anglicisms, and Spanglishisms, echoes of the Slavic logos and the purifying spin, Spanish turn. And we are, then, Poles, we are adapters (in the good sense of the word) and we are, then, merchants (in the good sense of this noble trade that can be noble and can even be the salvation, against all the rhetoric and ideology, of the world, because in dealing one understands people).

And we live outside, speaking, and thinking and writing in this marginal language, made of remnants and of grease spots, surrounded by strange enclaves of foreign languages: that we, the Cubans incorporate, without pain anymore, and, what is more, without personal pain, energetically.

This posterity that, let's give an example, for a romantic poet of the first half of the nineteenth century would have been a sign of marginality, is for us Cubans welcomed norm and normality: it permits us to be NOBODY, it permits us to be of the day, but filled with shadows; and to be nocturnal at the crow of the rooster at the first light of morning. This is the fact, disadjectivized, that rules and orients us, that seduces us: we are a rice with mango, a porous receptacle:

as if we lived in a CUBA (Cuba/Kuba) of grand wines and snowfalls, stammering Spanglishs and collecting palm nuts at twenty degrees below zero: a new manna for a new poetry.

Today's Cuban poet, later, is an Alpine pilgrim, and wanders through Machu Picchu, enters in the Promised Land (any land) that is the Urals, Pico Turquino, speaks of Tibet and the High Pyrenees, since we are the entire dictionary: we accept it, negotiate it, reabsorb it and regurgitate in the (new) splendor of poems.

Poems to the promised place, posterior and perpetual, the non-place of all times: with that poetry finally we are Africans, we are children of the old Kaftan and the Kipah, we smell of ammonia, of tabernacles and synagogues, smell of strong salts and of fermented sugarcane juice with three shots of lemon juice. For thirty-eight years we spoke our poems in that language; speaking and speaking, that means writing, we live all the centers from the center, dispersed, mestizos, little by little disenchanted by false limits and by false categories of identity, nation, profession. We flee from some to others and from others to some, the form of the Caimán Type One, though not unique, that moves toward its ultimate and posterity form, rear form of an island without representation.

CATECHISM: QUESTIONS AND ANSWERS TO TRY TO EXPLAIN AN INVENTION: THOSE POEMS BY JOSÉ KOZER

The week has seven days, seven days to make poems. Seven days to ask questions, to attempt answers. Here is a questionnaire about the question of my poetry: some questions have been invented so that I can try to explain an inventor, an invention. There are eight of my change questions (inventions) and there are eight responses (reversions).

1. If it is true that in your early books it is possible to perceive the final issues, it seems clear that earlier there existed a distinct emphasis. At what point did this change take place? How do you move from the epigram and the antipoem to the story and the metonymy?

When I write, I don't pay attention to what I write. During my first stage, the consciousness of wanting to write weighed on me, the consciousness of the writing, I possessed an overflow of consciousness and, to make matters worse, I considered that to make poetry was important. For some twenty years, I write and I write, trance, transit, and moment: the poem occurs and recurs, it's an occurrence, it explodes and I forget. I know that I make poems, and I know that they are no longer epigraphic or antipoems but relators and metronymic: I know it, but I don't pay attention. It's all imprecise, unreal, indeterminate. A piece of music; I curdle a mess of stirred-up words: and so, I don't know with precision at which moment the poems get away from me and shake, go backwards on me, testify for me and veer, bifurcating themselves, trifurcating themselves, filling the page with affluents. The movement of my work, from stage to stage, is organic; it happens like breathing, waking, bumping happens. Natural developments, only pushed by a fever that needs itself, fever for making poems: and the more, the better.

2. In your book *Et mutabile* (And Change), a return to the poetry of memory, to evocations that are genealogical conjecture, can be seen. As well, your assumption of the body and of the language as a place for the meeting of traditions, stories, diverse memories becomes quite evident. It's not random that the poet several time affirms, "I am my father."

My body doesn't matter: or, better said, it can only matter to me. That is, that ego that suffers because it dies (anticipation) knows that it is surrounded by ephemeral flesh that cannot interest anyone. Therefore, this deficiency, that displeasure of the defrauded body, the body that knows it is useless to hold tight to itself, figures out that it should move to a greater body, less ephemeral (if such a thing exists). That greater body is in the chronology of the family. A clinical page of every individual that comes from others, and then is in the notion of language that links individual and family with a tradition, a community. That community, with its history, its memory, its archetypal quality, and respiratory movement, sometimes finds a meeting point, a convergence, in creation. A poem can be (it has often been for me) plaza, meeting, convocation, or summoning accepted site. In the poem, chronologies, received stories, fictions, and adaptations come together with things seen and lived, with readings, with fantasies; that "collection," that momentary globalization in the text, causes a body greater than my body, than any family, happens in language, logos projected, panting: panting that procures, that feels itself and achieves a: poem. The son is father: the collector of others' scraps creates a "new" scrap for the others. And it evades, it becomes foam: it forgets. The poem (the result) perhaps brushes against something even much greater, beyond the decade, of the grief of death and of the closed planet. Does it brush against God? Does it brush against a perpetuity? I don't know. I write poems not to know but from an obscure belief in language that wants to live, to express itself and to live: there, above, above all language.

3. In *Et Mutabile*, the love theme reappears although tightly tied to a certain impudence not bereft of tenderness. For example, when you say: "Pudgy, I love you. Clean the spit off me here: that which before they called soul. A question of words."

It's known that it is scarcely possible to write love poems "seriously." This, in the twentieth century. Garcilaso had the good luck to find a territory of Eros still virgin for poetry, territory that he could contemplate from a rhetorical language that was not yet misrepresenting a position that was quite new and recent, it was still fresh: paradoxically, it was a natural language and at the same time rhetorical. And it allowed him to write love poems without undoing them with the Provençal and Petrarchan glow, without misleading because of a fault of the rhetoric of the felt intensity of love, transmitted (transmuted), and at the same time, without falling into an overly facile, tired poetry. In the twentieth century, how to write of love if not through irony, including the impudence? To that fat girl that I love, I can only speak avoiding the declamatory desire; I can only sing of her without eloquence; that is, by the use of irony, adopting irony that dampens or covers over the trite rhetoric of love. Corín Tellado and the televised soaps are done seriously; poets have to "make jokes" about love, to play with it, and only in that way, feed it with true sap. You can't take your love seriously. You have to hit the bull's eye, hitting exactly the serious erotic language. Making it vulnerable through the sweet-talking and fucking course of laughter and the sarcasm. Serious sarcasm, serious laughter, serious love: the spittle reelects the soul. Or is it that the spittle is my glory?

4. Frequently, in your poetry, and singularly in your book *Trazas del lirondo* (Traces of Purity), you mention foul odors, pubic hairs, flatulence, in order to point out that the poet's body is not an ideal body, but on the contrary, a used up, deplorable body,

A poem is not my best biographic moment; a poem isn't, after a shower and shave: in a poem, I'm not necessarily clean, young, new, renewed. More likely a poem catches me bald, allopathic, pestilent: a poem contains the devalued verb, the contaminated ecology of the body as in the sense that it is a dumping ground of refuse. Body and text unite: and the reunion contains virtue and vice, sin and salvation, degradation and height (that "height and 'suns'" as Vallejo would say). Lethal body, text that sounds ideal. And vice versa. How not to hear the farts, how not to cause the presence of that participating, primordial slime? The artist starts with dung, a little bit of shit has to stay under his fingernails. Bakhtin already was insubordinate against that idiotic division of categories of the higher part (aristocratic, spiritual) of the body, the best and sanctified part in contrast to the lower part (plebeian, material) of the body, carnavalesque cunt, vertical toward the putrefact subterranean. We are living matter, text in a state of putrefaction and at the same time of beatific iridescence; we are violence and tameness, vitriol and virtue intermixed, without a categorical above and below, mestizo beings, all curled up. We are the paralogic language that procures a "miscegenation" or cross: varied languages, varied literatures, continuous alternations. There exists the poet who must carry all poets (that is, in all languages: Villon's, Juan Ramón's): he has to carry all the traditions on his body, all that is done. And to know it. His is an enormous, complex, multiple labor. Everything encompasses him and everything encircles him. His throat is obstructed and his voice comes out hoarse, tattered, like a hiccup. The expectorant poet; he doesn't only sing with a crystalline voice. Some time ago, with puerile pain, with puerile preoccupation, I wrote:

> I am not Federico García Lorca.
> I am not Nicanor Parra.
> I am not César Vallejo.

Today I would write that I am all of them because I am none of them, because I am Ulysses and I am No one: JK is John Keats; Joseph K. found his Kafka. He found him? In a manner of speaking.

5. I've noticed that you don't disdain the taste of things, seeing it as a kind of wisdom. So, in the same way that there is frequent mention of music and the plastic arts, there is also mention of food (wine and bread included). That love for the artisanship, for the arrangement of the table, for the creative function, is linked with the medieval halitus that is perceptible in your poetry.

There is certainly no wisdom here, only taste, only taste (a taste that is not to know, only reception, reception of superficialities). Cioran writes that the wise man produces nothing; he writes it, which is his way to say that he is not wise. Who is wise? Saying contradicts wisdom; not saying, forgetting that we live by saying and writing, annuls the register, the mark of wisdom. The creator, then, can never be the Wise Man (Socrates, Buddha, Jesus didn't write). For that reason, I don't have knowing, I'm left with taste. The taste of you in a Cuban bolero, or of a shared family table, the pop of the wine, the smile of bread, untouchable, with the mouth full, the glory of the sun: bread is midday, wine is summer, table is *agape*, friendship. Quickly, we are not alone but intertextually; affinity, in the finite, between body and moment, poem and company. Solitude shared with solidarity; the good fortune of the company, the nutritive laughter of the friends in summer, a saying from the text: a movable feast. I write, I party. A poem comes out, we were many. The table is set, I order it: there is no other fact, there is no other text, there is no other necessity: we laugh; and time doesn't exist. We chew and nothing dies, I open my mouth and the fish enriches me: I spit out words and the text laughs. The verse grows, it gets longer because I chew, swallow, drink, ingest (engorge, as Lezama says). Colored words, millet-colored words, and your own cornbreaded word that fills your mouth while you let it fall, wonders of roundness, in the poem.

6. I see your poetry as an attempt to convert reality to the ecstatic. Instead of moving cinematographically, you seem to isolate moments, obligating your reader to stop and see life not as a story but as a stopped, separated sum of instants and of presents.

The ultimate truth, to exist, is ecstatic. Poetry seeks truth in beauty and in the good, although that good may be "the flowers of evil," truth, beauty, good, sound of the "b," that "b" of "bonded," "goodness," that "b" of "bienaventuraza," "blessedness." It deals with a rise toward the ecstatic that moves me and touches me: to retain (I am anal), to stop, to contemplate. To be in the moment more than permanently, perhaps preceding a union of the temporary and the permanent; a becoming toward the temporary, the existence, "the place to be" of daily life, front room of the rear and at the same time usefulness; the ecstatic place of being, first place, immutable: established and happy place for the invariable and united. But moreover, I make my poems ecstatic because frankly that is the only technique of which I am capable: I don't have the fluidity of the novelist, but rather the ecstatic ductility of the poet who hurries and stays in the air rather than see the language become unreasonable before my language gets out of hand, the poem is made: piece, tied up, yoked together, linked. I see it through a fissure, capture it rapidly and I forget. The rapidity of Sterne, Stendahl, Diderot: and I make the spark ecstatic, or better said, that spark imposes ecstasy on me, swiftly. Something like what Sterne did in his *Tristram Shandy* when he says:

"Who are you, sir?"
"You puzzle me."

This is a jump, an unexpected, very rapid displacement; a captured spark. And a vision is fixed, perhaps nearer to the truth, to the beautiful and good ecstatic truth of the blessedness.

7. In your poetry, *mestizaje* becomes apparent, the desire to not have limits. To the temporal variations in your poetry, one would have to add the conjugal bond between colloquial language and lyrical tradition, between painting and narrative, all of it openly spattered by an ecumenical Spanish, nothing stained with Cubanisms, Mexicanisms, Peruvianisms.

I live today, I am an echo of that today; the resonance in the cavern of the day-to-day, loose constructed concentric echoes, composition of Babels, techniques, modes, instrumentations, races, diversity: an iron spring gives off materials and the poet accepts them and collects, incorporates, then, imploring from his blindness of execution and of language, a substance: the substance isn't given to him, but if that poet is Cuban, his mouth fills with roasted cornmeal cakes, then ancestral, Judaic, at the same time now and Peruvian, now and Mexican. Mexico with "x" and with "j" is the emblem of the double, of an American Europe, smashing of one, disunion and amplification, "m," modernity and desperate tradition. We are embarrassed, in desperate and dead tradition, desiring to recover a new serene tradition that unites with a happy, diverse, laughing, and smashing modernity.

In our time, there are scarcely *isms*, there aren't *isms* anymore: it seems as if we were awaiting the good news of the return of a stable and living traditionalism, dialectic, that doesn't need categories, that doesn't call itself anything, that doesn't have to be a strident *ism*, generation of '98 or of '27, dadaism, expressionism, or surrealism, since one aspires to a modernity that is a tranquil, fluid, crucible of the night air. Humble things, within limits: I know that I utopize; and what's more, I falsify. Everything goes badly (we are beings at the end of the second millennium, open beings as never at the apocalypses); and we are quite far from serenity. But modern poetry doesn't stop presenting itself and fighting for a serene, ecumenical distributive, plural modernity: I beg in some way from each poem that I write that our many excesses of disorganized plurality don't lead to a chaos of new and more terrible ideologies but rather to the embrace of all people, of all the words.

8. In what way does your interest in Oriental poetry and in Zen reverberate in your own poetry? That mysticism doesn't conflict with your Jewish background. It's visible in your last two books, *De donde oscilan los seres en sus proporciones* (Where Beings Change Their Sizes) and *El carillón de los muertos* (The Carillon of the Dead), and above all in *Carece de causa* (Lacking Cause). They contain a strong religious and melancholy charge, the same as blessedness; a type of agreement of man with the hostile world in which he lives: a "sacred" pact.

Take the Old Testament, how terrible is the God of Israel (the Father). And what happens with the soft and intervening Mother? For me, that is Cuba, New Testament, Mary; a fire that is lit (the Cuban writer Lydia Cabrera says that the "candle is sacred"), and by lighting it, you become tranquil, you become embers, hot ashes, warmth of the tropical evening. But Cuba left me: at twenty years old it expelled me. The expelled one begins to search for it and recover from all the possible forms, looking for the soft mother that Cuba represented to him: palliatives from the Hard God, Jehovah the Just, the

Implacable; the unplaceable. A Cuba that then enters me and diffuses with Zen in poems: Orientalis of soft severity, unadorned and sartorial: the religious Orientalis that has helped me balance my Jewish origin, the rending of exile, as if the burning bush returns in the form of the Caimán and the Caimán then adopts the lotus position: there inside is the ruby, jewel of tranquility, posture and center in the fragility of the flower. There are four Vedas: and the fourth the Atarva-Veda is signified by fire (Atarva, priest of fire); a fire that is Jehovah, that is Cuba the exiler, more a fire than the repetition of the sacred syllable OM and mantra soothing, seduces and reduces, controls: the fire is burned down, crackling embers, home. From home come the bread and the poems. By the light of a lamp that illuminates a table, ancestral and Cuban table, traditional and modern, were for me, once; sixteen companions.

Translated by Stephen A. Sadow

Ricardo Feierstein
Argentina
ॐ

Ricardo Feierstein (1942–) has had a lifelong involvement in Jewish communal affairs in Argentina. He was an activist for HaShomer HaTzair, the Socialist Zionist movement. During the Dirty War of 1975–83, he wrote frequently about human rights for the Jewish-sponsored newspaper *Nueva presencia*. For many years, Feierstein worked for the Jewish Mutual Association of Argentina (the AMIA-Buenos Aires), directing the Pardés and Milá publishing houses, where he was the first to publish many contemporary Jewish Latin American authors, Holocaust testimonies, and an exhaustive collection, in Spanish, of Jewish literary and philosophical classics. He served as the editor of the internationally respected cultural review, *Raíces: Judaísmo contemporáneo* (Roots: Contemporary Judaism).

Feierstein's writing is extremely varied in form: it ranges from short stories that portray Jewish life in Buenos Aires to detective stories to novels to poetry and the essay. In his long poem "Nosotros, la generación en el desierto" (We, the Generation in the Wilderness), Feierstein acts as the voice of his generation of Jewish Argentines who felt themselves to be outside of history. In the novel cycle that includes the trilogy *Sinfonía Inocente* (Innocent Symphony) and *Mestizo*, with a fifth part in progress, he employs highly innovative structural techniques to tell the saga of Jewish Argentina. In *Mestizo,* the mystery novel format becomes a platform for interpreting Jewish history before and after the immigration from Eastern Europe. In *Judaísmo 2000* (Judaism 2000) and *Contraexilio y mestizaje* (Counterexile and Mestizaje), Feierstein issues a polemical call for profound changes in current Jewish ideology.

In this selection, taken from *Contraexilio y mestizaje,* Feierstein writes of the interplay of personal experience and literary theory in his approach to the Jewish Argentine novel.

BLOWS TO THE HEART

Ricardo Feierstein

Two characteristics unify the Jewish writers born in this part of the world: cultural mestizaje and the cutting away from history. I participate in both.

I am a cultural mestizo. I am a being with two heads simultaneously turned toward the Jewish and the Argentine, the birth of the state of Israel and the American attempts at liberation, the European Holocaust and the genocide of the last military dictatorship in these latitudes.

Reviewing the proofs for my book *Contraexilio y mestizaje* (Counter-exile and Mestizaje), I said to myself, Why add pages to the many that inundate, with improbable success, the sparsely frequented bookstores? This not very original question—one every author who values himself ought to ask about each work—was answered a warm September day in 1996, through two "blows to the heart" (almost simultaneous) and a somewhat confused intuition.

The first "blow" occurred on a Friday afternoon. On the insistence of my friend Steve Sadow (who is also my English-language translator and who had just finished the English version of my novel *Mestizo*), I took him on a tour of my childhood neighborhood in Villa

Pueyrredón. A large part of the novel he had just translated takes place in those streets: Mosconi Avenue, between Nazca and Lavallol, plus a few secondary arteries on one side or the other.

The walk was very sad: the neighborhood that I remembered didn't exist anymore. Not only had most of the neighbors disappeared or moved away, it was different physically—sidewalks, buildings, street corners, and the hideouts had changed. The Villa Pueyrredón of my memory had become unrecognizable. Worse yet, Salvador, one of the few from that time, tells me—on the same sidewalk in front of his old and failing furniture store—that same Mosconi Avenue "has died." Before, there were chairs near the door, and the neighborhood conversation lasted almost until daybreak. "Now," he relates, "the stores close at 7:00 p.m., and everyone runs for the protection of his home. The street is deserted. No man's land. Even the Portuguese's bar—he died some years ago—turned off its lights and closed. It's a desert . . ."

The beginning and good-bye for nostalgia, those sidewalks and their inhabitants, with the experience of shared pluralism that crossed over those sidewalks in the forties and fifties. They are history. They only remain alive in my heart and my memory, where the protagonists still converse in Italian and Yugoslav, shouting from door to door, exchanging cultures and foods in a country of immigration. And in my writings, of course: those lines that vainly pretend to encrust a memory in the fast-moving sands.

The second "blow" occurred that same night. I had to give a lecture in the place that had sheltered my enthusiastic Socialist Zionist movement in the sixties: the place of joy and struggle, the transcendent decisions, and the experiment at life for a shared tomorrow. "To construct and to reconstruct: to unite theory and life, to be pure and rebellious at the same time."

And once again, the sensation of a search for time lost: there weren't any young people among the hundred or so that filled the room. Only companions of my age and some older yet.

Neither does that place of utopia exist any longer, except in nostalgia. And in the pages of a novel that with love gone astray, I, many years ago, dedicated to them. The new generations have stubborn fads, words, decisions, and even clothing that would put off anyone from that period. Perhaps it ought to be that way, I said to myself. The petrified memory is reactionary, useless, antinatural. The places that the velocity of history has left behind ought to be (and can be) re-created in a literary manner, bringing back to life (fixing) in what is written that emotion that now exhausts the soul.

I should publish it, I thought. Perhaps it will be of interest to someone other than myself. That did happen with my collection of essays, *Judaísmo 2000*, published in 1988. That time, too, I asked myself for what purpose, for whom, why, was this irrepressible vanity of the graphomane. Nonetheless, years later, an experience in Uruguay (where enthusiastic readers collected that text like ideological manna for their own doubts and ordered dozens and dozens of copies) made me understand that these reprinted articles about the emergency and the debates about Latin American Judaism are, also, another mode of history. A form of preserving, in outbursts and hearts and between the covers of a published book, everyday traces of a passing that is difficult to predict.

Two "blows to the heart" on the same day were difficult to take. However, the insight that finally led to the publication of *Contraexilio y mestizaje* is less simple to define. After the horrendous attack of July 1994 against the headquarters of the AMIA—preceded by the March 1992 attack against the embassy of the state of Israel in Buenos Aires—I felt that something inside me broke (and in many Argentinian Jews, I would suppose). I asked myself if the nearness and the lacerating pain of the events didn't cloud our perception of a historical process that is occurring and that we live with only with difficulty.

Said in another way, I perceive that the bomb continues to produce victims. With delayed effect, the explosion has taken the heart of the proud former Jewish community of the country. The school system is reduced in size. There is uncertainty about the future of the institutions and the organizational forms that should be adopted: a sizable number of families have emigrated to Israel and other developed countries. The suffering middle class—which includes the majority of the Jewish community—is being systematically destroyed by successive adjustment plans imposed by the savage neoliberalism of the Menem government. The political crisis is added to the economic. Avodah, the party that traditionally directed the institutions of the community, appears fragmented and wounded by the events of the last two years.

Once again, the Jewish minority constitutes an "index" of the processes that affect all of Argentinian society. Like a sensitive seismograph of general situations, its quick mimetism of the environment reproduces on a small scale the upheaval and backward movements of this time in our country.

THE CREATIVE PROCESS

Inspiration. The "lightbulb that goes on." Concentration and flight. Synthesis of the social process. Ivory tower. The attempts to explain it are varied, but the act of creation, the mechanism that allows the channeling of a series of disparate experiences, organizes them according to a rather mysterious process and forms, finally, a play or a painting or a poem, is not understood. It is likely that, in its entirety, the process will never be analyzed with scientific precision.

Freud himself, in his writings about art and literature, admits that there exists, beyond the reach of investigation, an obscure and inexplicable space that precedes the creative act.

The poet makes use of latent elements in the collective unconscious and weaves them together in a particular arrangement to produce a new work, extraordinary, and at the same time suggestive. Also, he can expand his investigation of the profundities of the human soul through routes that are inaccessible to other forms of knowledge. But the mysteries of its mechanisms persist.

I think that some of my personal experiences may be of some help in attacking these questions.

I remember that when I was a university student a teacher of advanced architecture courses never tired of repeating that we ought to limit ourselves to seeking logical and rational solutions for the posed design problems, since "the wheel has already been invented," all the original or "revolutionary" variations that we might try to create with our projects surely had already been proposed, at this level of civilization, by thousands of architects that share the current moment. In some way or other, and without referring to it, he brought to mind Ecclesiastes' refrain, "There is nothing new under the sun."

I was skeptical about this teacher. While I was willing to recognize the permanence of certain great problems through the ages—love, death, brotherhood, the cosmic dimension—that have been repeated in every historical moment and have varied only in form, in the synthesis chosen for their presentation (and not the theme itself), I couldn't forget that every one of us, each unique and irreplaceable individual, generates architectural or literary or human answers that are always different, always original.

Nevertheless, some recent experiences, of varying intensity, have led me to doubt that certainty in the individual answer.

PROSE WITH ADAGIO AND ANDANTE

Starting with my study of aesthetics, begun when I was a student of art history, everything that had to do with the *relationship between form and content* disturbed me deeply. Along with my nonfiction writing, I developed my theories in practice in a book of short stories,

Lucy en un cielo con diamantes (Lucy in the Sky with Diamonds) and in a novelistic saga, completed over the course of fourteen years, composed of four novels: *Entre la izquierda y la pared* (Between the Left and the Wall), *El caramelo descompuesto* (The Melted Candy), *Escala uno en cincuenta* (Scale of One to Fifty), and *Mestizo*.

Especially in the first cycle of three novels, collected under the title *Sinfonía Inocente*, the project—quite ambitiously—takes the musical form of a symphony. (I ought to recognize here my debt to my wife, who is a musician and who has taught me the basic elements of music that I needed in my search for a relationship between the texture and velocity of literary prose and musical pacing, a search that—I read years later—the Russian cinematographer Sergei Eisenstein developed in his theory of montage, but in his case, referring to musical bars and drawings of photographed plains.)

The saga's story—the "content," to the extent that it could be teased out—revolves around the personal experience of the protagonist, who at a crucial stage in his life (that stage of definitions and contrasts that occurs around thirty years old) painfully reaches his inevitable maturity through the search for an innocent place. This search brings him from political action to the recognition of his identity and from communal life in a kibbutz to the practice of his adult profession and to the reencounter with his human and ideological roots.

The "form" chosen for the narration of this story is rather complicated, but, to begin, it can be summarized: a change in the point of view of the narrator (first person in the first novel—*thesis;* first and third person in the second novel—*antithesis;* and third person in the third novel—*synthesis*) allows him to transcend his obscure individuality and in that way objectify—and perhaps generalize—his experience. Otherwise, the entire "Symphony" is organized in three movements, each one of which possesses an *ascending melody* (the melody), a *descending melody* (the rhythmic accompaniment), and a *contretemps*, a brief variation that is analogous to the central theme, developed in alternating chapters. These arise "from inside" the text or from the narrator's "adventure of initiation."

The literary search possesses an infinity of matrices that play with the length of the phrases: the unconventional use of punctuation and the "respiration" of each written section, with the intention of achieving variations of reading that may correspond to the musical movements.

This process, told this way, seems simple, but it took more than a decade of uninterrupted and continuous work. It was, I thought, a very original and aesthetically valuable contribution to the contemporary novel.

Nevertheless, the surprise came. Reading a book by Macedonio Fernández that had inexplicably remained hidden in my library, I found—many years after what I have just related—a note at the bottom of the page in one of his texts: *"No todo es vigilia la de los ojos abiertos,"* "It's not all wakefulness, that of the open eyes." In the course of reflecting on metaphysical problems, Macedonio notes concisely, like a marginal thought,

> Can I combine a prose that could sustain in equal order and step the sentiments that each measure stirs up in a piece of music? (Taking away, of course, all musical value of the word as sound.) Not to say that such a harmonic or melodic element signifies the presence of a forest or a river, but the precise sentiment expressed. When the amateur or professional musicologist strives for that interpretation, he distracts its force. Music and prose are two expressions, and one kind of expression cannot express another expression: forest or river can bring forth the same emotion as a certain musical passage, but one wouldn't say that the landscape expresses the forest; they are two expressions. The problem of the verbal version falls within

a generic one: the intermingling of the same themes in different art forms (a version in sculpture of a literary theme, a pictorial version of a sonata, etc.).

I am stunned. After years of intense work, I have discovered gunpowder. And, although I haven't recovered from the blow, a few months ago I came upon the essay "Technique of Narrative Fiction" by Leon Surmelian. Innocently, I began to skim its pages. I read:

> Stories and points of view can entertain in the intrigue in a contrapuntal manner and, as in polyphonic music with its melodies that are interrelated but independent, we can have a mixture of alternating, parallel and contrasting actions, with the repetition of a dominant idea, executing variations on the same theme. This is a experimental form that intends to modify the old conventional structures of the story and create a better method to reproduce an infinitely rich and varied pattern of life through abrupt transitions and an ingenious discontinuity of the thread of the story. The counterpoint can be the answer to some modern problems of the plot, although the experiment is almost completely abandoned. It is yet to be seen if a musicalization of the narrative and great progress over conventional methods is really possible.

My narcissism lies wounded. But I tell myself, the results are yet to be seen: that which is important in the end is the novel itself and its realization, before the theorizing around it.

Do I need to mention, at this point, *Roots* by Alex Haley, that profound and moving investigation of the ancestors of an American black, constructed in a manner similar (return to the ancestors, investigation of the sources, progressing through the generations to find an explanation for the worries and strains of an identity that was repressed and sometimes denied) to my own novel *Mestizo*, whose provisional title was *Family Tree* and which I had been writing since I was an adolescent, in the early sixties? It is possible to find "outside," sometime later, what one has been constructing "inside," convinced of its absolute originality and privacy of the narrative material. Am I, I, or am I the others?

To fill out this point, I believe it would be prudent to summarize some provisional conclusions:

1) The themes that preoccupy human beings are variations of a few great problems and joys—the mystery of love and death, the longing for the lost paradise, the initiation into maturity, moral profundities—essentials of the human being and permanent throughout history, with their logical spatial and temporal sequences.

2) What varies are the "forms" for expressing those "contents," the variations of development that occur in each place and time and in each artist or writer. At the same time, and I postulate this as a thesis, *the different forms chosen redetermine the contents*, they bring them new qualities and thicknesses, define them in a different way, modify and embellish them, give them meanings that remained invisible until they found their form of expression.

3) The creator who intuits and later matches diverse "forms" to those "contents" that he chooses to express doesn't create his works from nothingness, through a sudden illumination or through divine grace. On the contrary, he brings together—through a process that is indeterminate enough—facts and outflows, meanings and matrices that remain latent in the environment of their historical period or their most basic everyday situations, and those whose expressive antennas allow them to capture and synthesize (without excluding, certainly, the mathematics of the "law of probability"). In this manner, the artist would no longer be "one of God's enlightened ones"

but a kind of *medium*, "an intermediary spirit" who acts as a transmitter between forms and latent contents and their concrete expression in a poem, a painting, or a symphony.

4) This way of understanding the creative process doesn't invalidate individual effort and talent, needed to produce and accelerate this process of synthesis that leads to the completed work. Without the daily, craftsmanlike, and exhausting work of the literary trade, without the call to the fantasy and the hallucination, to the farthest limits of the imagination, the catalyzing process would not occur.

5) Nevertheless, the creator is not the only ruler of his truth. Other men, other artists, perceive similar signals in the distinct confines, collect with the fine-tuned radar of sensibility the anguish and expectations, the ideals and the fears, and channel them into forms that sometimes appear similar. Confronted with similar problems, the answers can coincide, approach each other. Intermediary between the spirit and the reality of his time, the artist comes to understand, with Plato, that "to learn" is to "remember." Nothing less.

"The search for one's self": a key decade.

Who, except the author himself, would be interested in this diversion about his own work? Is their anything more annoying than a literato puffed up with fatuousness, speaking of himself in the third person and talking about his books as if they were in the public domain and all were obliged to know them?

Another meaningful vision—no longer so humble—reveals that the writer possesses a minimal influence (and often a regressive one) on the social fabric. A few thousand readers, in general hurried and forgetful, don't guarantee any transcendence at all or authorial fidelity or recognition of the quotations to which reference is made in this type of analysis.

However, another point of view still exists: perhaps egotistical, doubtless productive. To study a posteriori the influences that illuminate a literary work constitutes an exciting adventure, not always (hardly ever?) at the reach of the author himself. Unconscious restrictions, self-satisfaction, childhood readings hidden in the folds of the memory, narcissistic negations, are some of the barriers that wall off the road to that objective. It has occurred, more than once, that the inquisitorial and objective view of a critic has made clear, with cool professionalism, motivations and variations that explain obscure zones of my own creations.

The objective of the following lines, therefore, is another concern: *the search for oneself in the body of one's literary creations.* To write about yourself, not so that someone will know you, but rather to know oneself though the process of writing. That burning desire is understandable: no one can be oneself without obtaining that knowledge.

Also, the possibility to experience again—as a substitute life, woven of disconnected pieces and disordered strands, a route of literary creation at the second power—the process of constructing a narrative puzzle, a frightening effort, if such a thing exists. The style is the man, what he signifies: I recognize myself in that mixture of personal adventure and excessive rationalization, as if the paragraphs and the silences of the page recall, laboriously, a slightly deformed mirror and with balsamic therapeutic action, on the way to exorcizing historic interior demons.

The construction, at times complex, of this narrative saga cannot be extracted from the period of cultural formation during which it was conceived: the decade 1960–70 in Argentina, a time especially significant for the sociology of art, for the close relationship among three simultaneous phenomena that included my own Jewish Argentinian generation:

1) The decade begins with the Cuban Revolution (Fidel Castro takes command the first of January, 1959) that profoundly moved all young Latin Americans; with its images of bearded faces and informal *guerilleros* defeating a corrupt army: *beginning* with a libertarian program that won the support of the most influential intellectuals of

the moment (Jean-Paul Sartre, Julio Cortázar, Leopoldo Marechal, etc.) and ended with Paris Spring (1968), when the French students propose "the imagination of power" and occupy Paris with slogans such as "Let's be realistic, let's ask the impossible."

2) The presence of the Jewish Question is added. It is understood—since the "Sirota case" (a young girl raped by a Nazi commando in 1963; he tortured her and tattooed a swastika on her breast) and the ultranationalist shock troops of Tacuara and Guardia Restauradora—as an emergency of particularized violence that brought back the horrible existence of the not-so-distant Nazi genocide in Europe and that didn't receive "specific" answers from the Argentinian political parties.

3) The lowest level is composed of the organic interrelationship between the economic positions in favor of development and the aesthetic ideology of the Argentine vanguards in that decade, between industrial development and the creation of better material and cultural conditions for artistic experimentation.

Thus the four novels written between 1972 and 1987—the trilogy *Sinfonía Inocente* and its river's mouth narrative *Mestizo*—encounter again and again the man that I was during the early decades of my life. The idea of a literary saga, conceived and then explicitly developed during those years, was to allow me to apply freely to the literary work the sublimation of my own tensions and personal experiences into an adventure on paper, with an uncertain and perhaps amusing finale—a proposition that could be summed up in the following four coordinates:

a) There exists the need "to tell the world" what the sixties were like for my generation. This adds an original variation to the *nonfiction* genre that I decided to employ in the novel cycle: the personal participation of the narrator/protagonist who would be the author himself (in the style of Hemingway and others).

Therefore, it is a *novel of initiation* that, starting from a private experience, reflects—to an extent that was only visible to the author, many year later—what was general in Argentine society, especially in the process of searching for identity in an immigrant country that is culturally mestizo.

b) There exists an incarnation of ideology; to bring banners and poetry declaimed in words to daily life would generate a feeling of adventure that inevitably created new technical problems for me: the relationship between truth and verisimilitude of the text, the necessity of a dramatic line, the selection of archetypical characters and their evolution, and, above all, a sufficient montage of reflections, actions, and crisscrossing experiences.

c) The two previous paths come together in my own experience as an architect and student of the theory of form and its relationship to content. So, as a variation of the *nonfiction* style, I brought together life and literature: the narrative transmission of that experience allowed for the combination of ambitious formal searches—already developed in earlier books and short stories—and a work with language that would be less acceptable in short stories or other forms.

These three paths produced four completed novels (a thousand pages) and the sensation of an autotherapeutic effort that greatly exceeds individual experience—because of its suggestions about ideology, human innocence, or cultural mestizaje—and permits a scenario for cardinal questions at this postmodern turn of the century with its "aesthetics of fragmentation" and its apparent impossibility of access to totalizing visions.

FINAL THOUGHTS

The idea of cultural—not ethnic—mestizaje recognizes the belonging to a generation, to the first litter of immigrants born in this country. In this fact appears, simultaneously, the following three dimensions: the European (village in Poland), the Latin American (Buenos Aires neighborhood) and the Israeli (the kibbutz, the childhood Arab friends, the Middle East Conflict). This mixture is found, but in a hybrid state, without having to give way to a new product.

In the "cultural mestizo," the three dimensions are still mixed and superimposed but not integrated; perhaps the coming generations will carry a new model of identity. But meanwhile the current world—not the dimpled protagonist of a narrative fiction—finds itself facing the option of choosing the improving mestizaje or fall into a fratricidal war between national or religious groups who definitely ought to coexist (the former Yugoslavia, the former USSR, European nations such as France, Italy, or Germany with immigrants from the starving Third World—or, in general, the entire "global village" that today constitutes the planet).

This point in time ceases to count this voyage historically. "There is no reading without a date," Ernst Fischer would say, while referring to the interpretations and writings of each of us. Somewhat more pragmatic, the Canadian poet Leonard Cohen prophetized, "All of those who marry the spirit of his generation will be a widower in the next."

In a manner that is perhaps ingenuous (innocent?), my novelistic saga pretends only to recover, at least understand, with affection and sensitivity that moment in which the world seemed better than that which resulted later: this difficult and vain present that we carry with us with exhausted hope.

Translated by Stephen A. Sadow

Ariel Dorfman
Chile/United States

Ariel Dorfman (1942–) has known exile, separation, and loss. While he does not generally write about Jewish themes, his life embodies much of the Jewish experience. He has been a highly politicized wandering Jew, trying to improve the lives of the poor and oppressed in several countries. He is prolific, using words as weapons, tricks, and confrontations. In many ways, he addresses the themes of good and evil, power and corruption, the horrible consequences of fascism and imperialism. Reading Dorfman is like entering the ring with a champ out of your weight class; you may get out alive, but you won't get out unscathed.

His first novel, *Moros en la costa* (Hard Rain), is an avant-garde work that explores the nature of good and evil; *La última canción de Manuel Sendero* (The Last Song of Manuel Sendero) is a complex portrayal of the experience of exile. His play *Death and the Maiden*, a political thriller about the transition from totalitarianism, was produced on Broadway and later in a movie directed by Roman Polanski.

Dorfman has also produced a prodigious amount of nonfiction. In his influential *Para leer el pato Donald: Comunicación de masa y colonialismo* (How to Read Donald Duck: Imperialist Ideology in the Disney Comic), he shows how American popular culture influences attitudes in Latin America. He turns to literary criticism in *Some Write to the Future: Essays on Contemporary Latin American Fiction.*

In this selection, from his *Heading North/Going South* (1998), Dorfman meditates on his background and his many initiations.

THE DISCOVERY OF LIFE AND LANGUAGE AT AN EARLY AGE

Ariel Dorfman

I was falling.

It was May 6, 1942, and the city was Buenos Aires and I had only just been born a few seconds ago and I was already in danger.

I did not need to be told. I knew it before I knew anything else. But my mother warned me anyway that I was falling, the first words I ever heard in my life, even if I could not have registered them in my brain, the first words my mother remembers being pronounced in my presence. Strange and foreboding that of all the many words attending the scattered chaos and delirium of my birth, the only shrapnels of sense my mother snatched from extinction and later froze into family legend, should have been that warning.

It was not intended as a metaphysical statement. My mother had been dosed with a snap of gas to ease her pain as she labored, and when her newborn baby had been placed on a nearby table to be cleaned, she thought, in her daze, that it was slanted and the boy was about to roll off and that was when she cried out: "Doctor," she called, and my uncomprehending ears must have absorbed the meaningless sound, "se cae el niño, se cae el niño." She told the doctor that I was falling, the boy was about to fall.

She was wrong about my body and right about my mind, my life, my soul. I was falling, like every child who was ever born, I was falling into solitude and nothingness, headlong and headfirst, and my mother, by her very words, by the mere act of formulating her fear in a human language, inadvertently stopped my descent by introducing me to Spanish, by sending Spanish out to catch me, cradle me, pull me back from the abyss. ⸱

I was a baby: a pad on which any stranger could scrawl his signature. A passive little bastard, shipwrecked, no ticket back, not even sure that a smile, a scream, my only weapons, could help me to surface. And then Spanish slid to the rescue, in my mother's first cry and soon in her murmurs and lullabies and in my father's deep voice of protection and in his jokes and in all the hum of love that would soon envelope me from an extended family. Maybe that was my first exile: I had not asked to be born, had not chosen anything, not my face, not the face of my parents, not this extreme sensitivity that has always boiled out of me, not the early rash on my skin, not my remote asthma, not my nearby country, not my unpronounceable name. But Spanish was there at the beginning of my body or perhaps where my body ended and the world began, coaxing that body into life as only a lover can, convincing me slowly, sound by sound, that life was worth living, that together we could tame the fiends of the outer bounds and bend them to our will. That everything can be named and therefore, in theory, at least in de-sire, the world belongs to us. That if we cannot own the world, nobody can stop us from imagining everything in it, everything it can be, everything it ever was. It promised, my Spanish, that it would take care of me. And for a while, it delivered on its promise.

It did not tell me that at the very moment it was promising the world to me, that world was being disputed by others, by men in shad-ows who had other plans for me, new banishments planned for me, men who were just as desperate not to fall as I had been at birth, des-perate to rise, rise to power.

Nor did Spanish report that on its boundaries other languages roamed, waiting for me, greedy languages, eager to penetrate my territory and establish a foothold, ready to take over at the slightest hint of weakness. It did not whisper a word to me of its own imperial history, how it had subjugated and absorbed so many people born into other linguistic systems, first during the centuries of its triumphant ascendancy in the Iberian Peninsula and then in the Americas after the so-called Discovery, converting natives and later domesticating slaves, merely because the men who happened to carry Spanish in their cortex were more ruthless and cunning and technologically practical than the men who carried Catalan or Basque or Aymara or Quechua or Swahili inside them. It did not hint that English was to the North, smiling to itself, certain that it would father the mind that is writing these words even now, that I would have to surrender to its charms eventually, it did not suggest that English was ready to do to me what Spanish itself had done to others so many times during its evolution, what it had done, in fact, to my own parents: wrenched them from the arms of their original language.

And yet I am being unfair to Spanish—and also, therefore, to English. Languages do not only expand through conquest: they also grow by offering a safe haven to those who come to them in danger, those who are falling from some place far less safe than a mother's womb, those who, like my own parents, were forced to flee their native lands. After all, I would not be alive today if Spanish had not generously offered my parents a way of connecting with each other. I was conceived in Spanish, literally imagined into being by that language, flirted, courted, coupled into existence by my parents in a Spanish that had not been there at their birth. Spanish was able to catch me as I fell because it had many years before caught my mother and my father just as gently and with many of the same promises.

Both my parents had come to their new language from Eastern Europe in the early years of the twentieth century, the children of

Jewish émigrés to Argentina—but that is as far as the parallel goes, because the process of their seduction by Spanish could not have been more different.

And therein lies a story. More than one.

I'll start with my mother: hers is the more traditional, almost archetypical, migratory experience.

Fanny Zelicovich Waisman was born in 1909 in Kishniev. Her birthplace, like her life itself, was subject to the arbitrary fluctuations of history: at that time Kishniev belonged to Romania, the Bolshevik Revolution would incorporate it into the Soviet Union—only to become, after the breakup of that country, the capital of the republic of Moldavia. If my mother had stayed there, she would have been able to change nationalities three times without moving from the street on which she had seen the first light of this world. Though if she had remained there she would probably not have lived long enough to make all those changes in citizenship.

Her maternal grandfather, a cattle dealer, had been murdered in the pogrom of 1905. Many years later, I heard the story from my mother's uncle Karl, in Los Angeles, of all places. It was 1969 and he must have been well over eighty years old but he cried like a child as he told us, tears streaming down his face, speaking in broken English and lapsing into Yiddish and being semitranslated by my mother into Spanish so Angelica and I would understand, his pain imploding like a storm into the mix of languages, unrelieved by the passing of time: how his mother had hid with him and his sisters and brothers in a church, how they had listened for hours while the Cossacks raged outside—those screams in Russian, those cries for help in Yiddish, the horses, the horses, my great-uncle Karl whispered—and how he had emerged who knows how many centuries later and had found his father dead, his father's throat slit, how he had held his father in his arms.

It was that experience, it seems, that had determined the family, after eons of persecution, to finally emigrate. Australia was considered and the United States, but Argentina was finally selected: Baron de Hirsch's Jewish Colonization Association had helped to open the pampas to Jews anxious to own land and till the prairies. Two brothers of my grandmother Clara set out, and when they wrote back that the streets of Buenos Aires were paved with gold, the rest of the family started making plans to leave as well. Only Clara's mother was unable to migrate: her youngest daughter would not have passed the tests of health authorities in Argentina, apparently because she had been taken ill with a meningitis that had left her seriously retarded. Which meant that both of them, mother and daughter, lived their lives out in Kishniev until they were killed by the Nazis. According to my mother, the old woman went out into the streets the day the Blackshirts drove into town and insulted them and was shot immediately; and though I would love this story to be true, love to have a great-grandmother who did not let herself be carted off to a concentration camp and forced her foes to kill her on the same streets where her husband had been slaughtered, I have often wondered if this version is a fantasy devised more to inspire the living than to honor the dead.

What is certain is that my mother was saved from such a fate by departing with her parents. At the age of three months, she found herself on a boat from Hamburg bound for an Argentina that, devoid as it might be of pogroms, nevertheless had enough Nazis and Nazi-lovers to force her, thirty-six years later, into her next exile. This ambivalent attitude of the host country toward the Jews was prefigured in two run-ins my mother had with the Spanish language at an early age.

When she was six years old, my mother recalls, she had been sent to her first school. In the afternoons, private piano lessons were offered and my grandmother Clara had insisted that her child take these, perhaps as a way of proving how genteel and civilized the family had become. On one of the first afternoons, my mother was by herself in the music room waiting for the teacher, when the door slammed shut. From its other side, a mocking chorus of Argentine children started shouting at her in Spanish. She tried to open the door but they were holding it tight. *"No podés,"* they taunted her. "You can't open the door, because you're a Jew," *"porque sos judía."* Definitely not the first words she ever heard in Spanish, but the first words she ever remembers having heard, the words that have remained in her memory like a scar. You talk funny, they said to her. You talk funny because you're a Jew.

She probably did talk funny. Yiddish had been the only language her family spoke in Argentina for years. It is true that my mom's father, Zeide, had forced himself to learn some rudimentary Spanish: a week after having arrived in Argentina, he was already peddling blankets house to house in Buenos Aires, starting with the Jewish community, and then soon enough knocking at the doors of Spanish-speaking goyim as well, prospering enough to eventually start a small shop. But his wife, at least during those first years, was inclined to stay away from the new life, from the new language: almost as if Clara feared, clutching her baby daughter to her, that out there the Cossacks were still lurking nearby, ready to attack.

But instead of the dreaded Cossacks, another military man passed briefly through the family's life and inadvertently convinced Baba Clara, several years before those anti-Semitic school brats refused my mother entry into the community, that Argentina was truly willing to welcome the immigrants.

One day, an Argentine colonel emerged from his brother's residence, next door to the Zelicovich house. He stepped into the torrid heat of the Buenos Aires summer and there, on the sidewalk, he saw his little niece playing with a pretty, blond-haired, foreign- looking girl—my mother, who was probably three years old, maybe four, and who had by then picked up a smattering of Spanish from the neighborhood kids. The colonel advanced toward them, reached out with one hand toward his Argentine niece and with the other one did not take out a gun and shoot my mother but clasped her small hand and trundled both of them off to the corner for some ice cream. An irrelevant incident, but not to Baba Clara: my mother's mother, on seeing the colonel go off with the children so amiably and then return with prodigal ice cream cones, was amazed beyond belief. She said she lifted her hands to heaven to thank the Lord. An army officer, any member of any army, was a devil, a potential Jew-killer: that such a man should invite a child from the tribe of Israel to share sweets with his niece was as miraculous as the czar quoting the Torah.

My mother does not remember the colonel or the little friend or the ice cream. What she has consigned to memory is the reaction of her mother. What she remembers is her mother's voice that very night, recounting in Yiddish the marvels of Argentina and its love of the Jews to her skeptical sister, Rosa. Or was it on a later occasion? Because Clara repeated the same story over and over again through the years. Paradoxical that it should have been in Yiddish because the story registers and foretells the defeat of Yiddish, how kindness forced it to retreat, her offspring's first tentative, independent steps into a world where Yiddish was not necessary. A world that would demand of my mother, like it demands of all immigrant children, that she abandon the language of her ancestors if she wanted to pass through that door those children would soon be trying to slam shut. I believe that story has abided in the family memory so many years because it is foundational: the prophetic story of how my mother would leave home and assimilate, escaping from that ghost language of the past into the Spanish-echoing streets.

Streets where my father, ten years down the road, was waiting for her.

By then, fortunately for me, they both spoke Spanish. I can almost hear him now convincing her to marry him in the one language they both shared, I try to eavesdrop so many years later on the mirror of their love-making, listening to how they conceived me, how their language coupled me out of nothingness, made me out of the nakedness of night, *la desnudez de la noche*. My father's trail to the wonders of the sleek Spanish he murmured in her ears had not been as direct and simple as my mother's. Rather than the normal relay race of one language replacing the other, he had taken a more convoluted bilingual journey.

To begin with, he had emigrated not once but twice to Argentina; though perhaps more crucial was that he came from a family sophisticated in the arts of language, a sophistication that would end up saving his life several times over.

Adolfo was born in 1907 in Odessa, now the Ukraine, then Greater Russia, to a well-to-do Jewish family that had been in the region for at least a century and probably more. As well as Russian, his father, David Dorfman, spoke English and French fluently, as did his mother, Raissa Libovich, who also happened to be conversant in German after three years of studies in Vienna. All those languages, but no Yiddish: they considered themselves assimilated, cosmopolitan, definitively European. If David and Raissa ended up in Argentina, it was not due to any pogrom. In fact, the 1905 pogrom where my mother's grandfather had died had been beaten back in Odessa by the Jewish riffraff and gangsters immortalized later in Isaac Babel's writings. Their expatriation derived from a more trite and middle-class problem: in 1909, at about the time my mother was being born across the Black Sea, David Dorfman's soap factory had gone bankrupt and he had been forced to flee abroad to escape his creditors. Of that venture, only a seal, used to stamp certain particularly fragrant epitomes of soap, remains in my father's possession: "Cairo Aromas," it grandly proclaims in Russian. But my grandfather, rather than head for the mythical Cairo of the seal, set off for the more distant and promising Buenos Aires of history. And one year later, his wife and three-year-old Adolfo followed him. Some years later—it was 1914 by then and the child was six—Raissa and her son were headed back to Russia, purportedly on a visit to see the family, though persistent rumors mention another woman who David might have been scandalously visiting. Whether or not the gossip is true, what is certain is that my grandmother and my father picked the worst time to go back: they were caught by the eruption of the First World War and then by the Russian Revolution. The reasons for their staying on have always been nebulous: "We were going to beat those Prussians in a matter of months, it was going to be a picnic," Pizzi told me half a century later, when she and the world knew that it had been anything but a picnic. "And," she added, "you always think it's about to end and then it doesn't and you wait a bit more and you've invested so much hope in believing that it'll all finish tomorrow that you don't want to give up that easily." Pizzi would tell me this in English on my visits to Buenos Aires, before I myself would experience what it is to believe that something terrible will end soon, before my own exile would teach me that we spend a good part of our lives believing things will get better because there is no way we can imagine them, wish to imagine them, getting worse. My exile—when I fled Buenos Aires after fleeing Chile; my exile—when the phone rang in Amsterdam with the news that Pizzi had died and I learned that banishment does not take from you only the living, but takes their death from you as well. Pizzi had died and I had not been there, I would never sit by her side again and ask her about the past, the steps of Odessa and the Potemkin, the Russian secret police raiding the house, never be able to ask her about the day my father brought my mother home to be introduced as his future wife, never again discuss with my favorite grandparent the difficulties of being a woman journalist in Buenos Aires, never again hear her painstakingly translate into English for my benefit the stories for children she published in the Argentine Sunday papers and had herself translated from Russian into Spanish, as she had translated *Anna*

Karenina for the first time into Spanish, never again hear from her lips the tales of how they had survived the hardships of the war, how she had spent those years alone with her son, preparing her return to the land where her husband awaited them.

And then the revolution had come. Like so many Jews at the time, she fervently supported it. But how to make a living with everything in turmoil? While her son went to school with the bullets flying and the walls splattered with red slogans and the city changing hands over night, she kept a home for him, and food on the table, and gave him a strict education, and it was all due to her languages, that's what kept them alive. And she was so proficient at them that she started working with Litvinov and ended up serving the most prominent Bolshevik Jew of them all, Trotsky, acting as one of his interpreters at the peace talks with the Germans at Brest Litovsk where the fate of the Soviet Union was decided. She remembered how he had paced up and down on the train as it sped through the Ukraine to the meeting: how much to give up, how much to concede, how much to pay for peace and the time to build a new army, a new society?

And while she was translating German into Russian in order to survive, her husband, half the world away, was patiently translating from Russian into Spanish in order to bring her and the boy safely to Argentina. When the revolution had broken out, it became almost impossible to get people out of the newly formed Soviet Union safely, but my grandfather had hit on a plan: there was a flood of immigrants streaming into Argentina and the police needed people who could interpret for them and help streamline the process, and David found a job with them, hoping that his new post would strengthen his contention that his faraway wife and son were de facto Argentine citizens and should be helped to exit from the Ukraine. Incredibly, he managed to convince some official in the Argentine government to intervene and, more incredibly, somebody in the frenzied Soviet Foreign Ministry listened and that is how Raissa and Adolfo managed to take the last ship—at least so goes the family legend—to leave Odessa at the end of 1920. My father remembers a stowaway who had hidden himself: the Red Army soldiers coming on board and the young man's fearful eyes when he was discovered, the stubble on his face, the look of someone who knew he would die—and then they hauled him away, dragged him back to that glorious Odessa of my father's youth, that Odessa now of danger and death. It's hard to be sure, but there's a good chance, my father says, that he and his mother would not have outlived the terrible year of 1921. The civil war, the famine, the plague, decimated Odessa and so many other cities in the country: most of Raissa's family, left behind, died. And among the dead was Ilyusha, Adolfo's elder cousin. To the fatherless boy, Ilyusha had been a protector, an angel, a brother for seven lonely years. That cousin of his had let my father tag along as he plunged into the turmoil and romance of the revolution. My father's participation had not gone beyond carrying a mysterious black bag that Ilyusha always wanted near him, a bag that contained nothing more dangerous, it seems, than poems and pamphlets, but it was the first social activism of my father's life and he was never to forget it. Ilyusha's memory was to haunt him through the turbulent twenties and into the thirties as Argentina itself began to be heading for what seemed a revolution of its own.

Spanish received my father with open arms, a smoother welcome than my mother's. Either because he had already had previous experience with the language as a child or because his parents were polylingual themselves, he was soon speaking and writing Spanish brilliantly, so well that, soon after graduating from the university, the Russian émigré Dorfman wrote and published the first history of Argentine industry and became, thereafter, his country's leading expert on the subject. More books, many articles and essays followed, all of them revolving around Argentina and its tomorrow, all of them in Spanish: apparently an absolute commitment to his new land and language.

And yet my father was bilingual and remains so to this day. That he kept his Russian intact can, of course, principally be attributed to having spent his formative years in Odessa, to the fact that Russian contained within its words the full force of its nationhood and literature and vast expanses—unlike the language that my mother discarded, a Yiddish that occupied no territory, possessed no name on the map of nations, had never been officially promoted by a state. And yet my father's retention of Russian may signal something else: a doubleness that did not plague my mother. She rid herself of Yiddish as a way of breaking with the past, adhering forever to the Argentina that had taken her by the hand that day she was three years old and had offered her an ice cream in Spanish. She could easily segregate her first, her original, language, relegate it to the nostalgia of yesteryear, a gateway to a land that no longer exists, except in the torn shards of hazy family anecdotes. Her monolingualism was a way of stating that Yiddish had become irrelevant to the present, to her present.

My father could never have said that of Russian. The language of his youth, the language his parents spoke with him at home, was to embody, for many in my father's generation—in Argentina and all over the world—the language in which the future was being built: the first socialist revolution in history, the first socialist state, the first place on the planet where men would not exploit men. Always vaguely leftist and rebellious, by the early 1930s, my father had joined the Communist party and embraced Marxism. Like many men and women his age, he saw no other alternative to what he was sure were the death throes of a capitalism reeling from the depression. It is one of the ironies of history, of course, that those ardent internationalists who were so suspicious of nations and chauvinism and proclaimed that only the brotherhood of the proletariat of all countries would free mankind, should have ended up subjecting their lives, ideas, and desires to the policies and dictates of one country, the Soviet Union. They perceived no contradiction: to defend real socialism in the one territory where it had taken power was to sustain a state that would, by its shining example—and later by its armed force—help bring freedom and equality and justice to every corner of the globe.

And the Moscow trials? And Stalin's purges? And the destruction and forced famine of the peasantry? And the Kronstadt massacre? And the gathering bureaucratic power of a new elite speaking in the name of the vast masses?

Few communists at the time protested or even seemed to care. My father was no exception. Though I have wondered whether my father's love affair with the Soviet Union was not also buttressed and even hardened by his romance with Russian, the circumstance that the language that had caught him as he fell into the abyss of birth happened to be the very language that he believed was destined to redeem the whole of fallen humanity. The language of his dead cousin, the language of the streets of Odessa, the language of the revolution: my father's past was not something to be thrown away, like my mother threw away her Yiddish. It could coexist with his Argentine present and inseminate it and bring together the two sides and periods of his life, Russia and Latin America, to create a nationless future, socialism in Argentina.

But there is, in fact, no need for this sort of pop psychology, no need to recur to linguistic explanations for my father's blind adoration of the Soviet Union. History was furnishing reasons enough: the consolidation of Mussolini and the rise of Hitler and then the Civil War in Spain convinced innumerable revolutionaries to swallow their doubts (if they had any) and embrace the one power ready to stand up to the Nazis. And even after my father was expelled from the party at the end of the 1930s—but not, I am sad to report, because of ideological or political differences but due to a slight divergence about some abstruse question of internal democracy—even then, even after the Hitler-Stalin Pact in 1939, he adhered steadfastly to Marxist philosophy and politics.

Up to the point that when I was born in 1942, my father gave me a name I would disclaim when I was nine years old for reasons that will be revealed: the flaming moniker of Vladimiro. In honor of Vladimir Ilyich Lenin and the Bolshevik Revolution, which, my father felt, was fast approaching the pampas.

Though what was really approaching those pampas was fascism— at least, a deformed and mild *criollo* version of it. A year after my birth, in June 1943, the military headed by General Ramírez toppled the conservative government of Castillo. It was a pro-Axis coup and behind it was the enigmatic figure of then Colonel Juan Domingo Perón.

My father would soon run afoul of these men. When the new military government took over the Universidad de la Plata where my father taught, he resigned indignantly, sending them a letter of protest, à la Emile Zola. A copy, unfortunately, does not remain extant: but I have been told that in it my father insulted the military, their repressiveness, ignorance, clericalism, extreme nationalism, and above all, their infatuation with Franco, Hitler, and Mussolini: the authorities reacted by expelling him from his position (a first in the history of Argentina) and then decided to put him on trial, demanding that his citizenship be revoked. I have taken out the old boxes in my parents' Buenos Aires apartment and leafed through the yellowed pro-government tabloids of the day, and there they are, the headlines calling for the "dirty Jew-dog Dorfman" to be shipped back to Russia "where he belonged."

History does repeat itself, first as tragedy and then as farce: years later, ultraconservative, anti-Semitic right-wingers in the United States would be suggesting that I do the same thing, following me around with signs screeching VLADIMIRO ZELICOVICH [sic] GO HOME TO RUSSIA whenever I gave a lecture about Chile at a university, waving copies of a twenty-minute speech Jesse Helms had delivered against me on the Senate floor, brimming with information provided to him by the Chilean secret police. But those people in America in the 1980s couldn't do anything to me. The men who were threatening my father in Argentina in 1943 were somewhat more powerful. Again, my father was falling.

But this time it wouldn't be Russian that would catch him, save him. Or the Russians, for that matter. It would be their archrivals.

Before he could be jailed, my father skipped the country on an already awarded Guggenheim fellowship. My pro-communist father fled in December of 1943, to the United States, the most powerful capitalist country in the world, protected by a foundation built with money that had grown out of one of the world's largest consortiums. Money that had come from tin mines in Bolivia and nitrate in Chile and rubber plantations in the Congo and diamonds in Africa saved my Leninist dad.

But the Americans were preparing Normandy and Stalingrad was raging and Auschwitz was burning Jews and homosexuals and gypsies and Roosevelt had created the New Deal and anyway, even if my father had not been able to offer himself all these expediently progressive reasons for journeying to the center of the empire, there was a more practical one: he had to escape. And America was the only place he could go.

And the place, therefore, where, over a year later, in February of 1945, the rest of the family joined him.

First, however, we hopped across Latin America, Santiago and Lima and Calí and Barranquilla and then finally Miami, each flight delayed for a day or two because of the war, as if Spanish was saying good-bye to me slowly, as if it were reluctant to let me depart on what would end up being a bilingual journey. Though what may have been most significant about that inaugural trip north was that the first night of my first exile should have been spent in the neighboring country just across the Andes, the place that still symbolizes the south for me, there, in that city of Santiago de Chile which was to become my home

The Discovery of Life and Language at an Early Age   135

so many years later. Wondrous may be a better word than significant: that my first night in that city should have been in a hotel, the Carrera, facing the Presidential Palace of La Moneda where I was to spend so many nights during the last days of the Allende revolution, looking out on the plaza and catching a glimpse of men behind the windows of that hotel looking back at me, perhaps from the very window of that room where I had slept as an infant. A mysterious symmetry which, of course, would have been even more amazing if I had died at La Moneda—because in that case, my first childhood voyage to Santiago could have been construed as truly premonitory, that two-and-a-half-year-old child visiting the site of the murder that awaited him twenty-eight years in the future.

If the gods existed and if they were inclined to literary pastimes, they would have organized precisely that sort of ending for their enjoyment, they would have taken my life and harvested one hell of a metaphor. Fortunately, in this case at least, nobody powerful enough to intervene was playing a sick practical joke on me. Instead, I was the one playing jokes—on my mother and elder sister, who spent most of the one afternoon they had for sightseeing shut up in that hotel room searching for the baby shoes, my only pair, that I had mischievously hidden inside a pillow case. With such skill and malevolence, according to my mother, that we almost lost the chance to tour the city before it grew dark. I like to think that the boy I used to be knew what he was doing, that he was in fact trying to intercept my innocent eyes from seeing Santiago for the first innocent time, from crossing the path of Angelica, the woman of my life, who was that same afternoon breathing those very molecules of air under those same mountains, I like to think he recognized Santiago, he had heard the city or its future calling quietly to him to wait, to reserve himself, to hide the shoes. Or maybe it was the city that recognized him.

New York, however, did not recognize me at all. Or maybe sickness is a form of making love, tact, contact, the winter of New York seeping into the lungs of that child still immersed in mind, if not body, in the sultry heat of the Buenos Aires summer, New York blasting that child inside his simulacrum of a snowsuit, inside the garments that had been hastily sewn together by his mother on the remote southern tip of the hemisphere to simulate a snowsuit, New York claiming that child, telling him that things were not going to be easy, no hiding shoes in this city, no guided tours: in this city we play for keeps, kid.

Our family descended from the train onto the platform in Grand Central Station, and there was nobody there to greet us but the cold. We had crossed the South of the United States during the night. I have no memory, again, of that trip, except that years later when I read Thomas Wolfe and his long shattering train ride to the home toward which the angel was fruitlessly looking, the home he said you could never return to, I felt a shudder of acknowledgment—I had been on that train, I had crossed that U.S. South leaving my own Latino South. So I do not remember the moment when I stepped for the first time in my life onto the concrete of the North, there in New York holding my mother's hand.

My father was not there, waiting for us.

He appeared fifteen minutes later, explained that he had made a mistake or the train had arrived at a different platform, but my mother felt something else was wrong, she felt the mix-up was ominous, because my dad was distant, unfamiliar, his eyes avoiding hers. What my father could not bring himself to tell her was that just before our arrival, at around the time I was hiding my shoes inside a Chilean pillow, he had been conscripted into the U.S. Army and that, unless he could defer or suspend his 4A classification, he would be off to the European Front and my mother, who didn't know a word of English, would be stranded in a foreign city with two small children and forced to live on a fifty-dollar-a-month G.I. salary. Four days later, still without telling his wife the truth, my father departed early from the hotel where we were lodged and reported for duty in downtown Manhattan, fully expecting to return in uniform to break the news to my mother, that the uniform would tell the news he dared not utter himself. He showered with dozens of other conscripts, he slipped into the army clothes, and then, at the very last moment, was informed that he had been reclassified because the sort of work he was doing at the newly formed Office of Inter-American Affairs had been deemed "essential." David Rockefeller, who had created that division in the State Department to fight the advance of fascism in Latin America, had intervened. Again, the tricks and treats of history: a Republican saved my philo-communist father from being sent to war against the allies of the fascists he had just escaped back home. But the point is that my father was able to make a cheerful trip back uptown and tell my mother the reason why he had seemed so remote since our arrival, assure her there was nothing to worry about, from now on happy days would be here again.

But they wouldn't, at least not for me, at least not immediately.

The first order of business was to move out of our prohibitively expensive hotel, not easy in a New York where no new housing had been built since the start of the war. A savvy Uruguayan friend suggested my parents read the obituaries of the newspapers, so as to speedily nab the vacated apartment. Implausibly, that stratagem worked. They rented what in the folklore of the family would always be called la Casa del Muerto, the Dead Man's House. It was, according to my mother, the most depressing, run-down joint she had ever inhabited: a two-room dump, airless under a weak dim bulb hanging like a noose from the ceiling, with small slits of windows gaping onto a grey desolate inner courtyard and three beds in each room, as if several people had died there, not just one.

That was the place, the house of death. That's where I caught pneumonia, one Saturday night in February of 1945, when my parents had gone out by themselves for the first time since we had arrived in the States—and I carefully use that verb, *to catch*, aware of its wild ambiguity, still unsure, even now, if that sickness invaded me or if I was the one who invited it inside. But more of that later. To save his life, that boy was interned in a hospital, isolated in a ward where nobody spoke a word of Spanish. For three weeks, he only saw his parents on visiting days and then, only from behind a glass partition.

My parents have told me the story so often that sometimes I have the illusion that I am the one remembering, but that hope quickly fades, like arriving at a movie theater late and never being able to discover what really happened, forever at the mercy of those who have witnessed the beginning: *"te internaron en ese Hospital,"* my mother says slowly, picking the words out as if for the first time, *"no nos acordamos del nombre,"* there is a large glass wall, it is a cold bare white hospital ward, my parents have told me that every time they came to see me tears were streaming down my face, that I tried to touch them, I watch myself watching my parents so near and so far away behind the glass mouthing words in Spanish I can't hear. Then my mother and my father are gone and I turn and I am alone and my lungs hurt and I realize then, as I realize now, that I am very fragile, that life can snap like a twig. I realize this in Spanish and I look up and the only adults I see are nurses and doctors. They speak to me in a language I don't know. A language that I will later learn is called English. In what language do I respond? In what language can I respond?

Three weeks later, when my parents came to collect their son, now sound in body but, in all probability, slightly insane in mind, I disconcerted them by refusing to answer their Spanish questions, by speaking only English. "I don't understand," my mother says that I said—and from that moment onward I stubbornly, steadfastly, adamantly refused to speak a word in the tongue I had been born into.

I did not speak another word of Spanish for ten years.

The Discovery of Life and Language at an Early Age   139

Isaac Goldemberg
Peru/United States

Isaac Goldemberg (1945–) writes with the ferocity of a biblical prophet. His search for truth, for identity, and for love takes on an intensity that cannot fail to stir, even disturb his readers. He seems unafraid of treating any issue. His novel *La vida a plazos de don Jacobo Lerner* (The Fragmented Life of Don Jacobo Lerner), presenting a darker picture of Jewish life in Latin America, is a *tour de force* that has influenced writers and intrigued critics. Novelist, poet, editor of *Brújula/Compass*, director of the Latin American Writers Institute—Isaac Goldemberg touches his readers' emotions as well as intellect. A tireless anthologist, Goldemberg brought together, in a work intended to present a collective voice, the literary production of several generations of writers in *El gran libro de la América Judía* (The Great Book of Jewish America). His ability to move among cultures allows him not only to create poetry and prose in a unique mixture of references but also to be a Latino editor in New York, a Peruvian poet, and, of course, a Jew.

Goldemberg revised this essay, in which he describes his struggles to become a Jewish Peruvian writer, for this anthology.

'LIFE IN 'INSTALLMENTS

Isaac Goldemberg

Nineteen forty-five: Born in Chepén, a small village in northern Peru, about an hour and a half from Trujillo. My memory of the town is rather hazy, made more so by the fact that time, distance, and my imagination have transformed it little by little. I think of it now as a lush area hemmed in by the desert, the ocean, and the Andes. What's certain is that Chepén wasn't on the coast, although it wasn't far from the sea. Our sea was the railroad tracks. And I'm also sure that the town was flanked by tropical vegetation. If it weren't, there would be no way to explain the sweltering heat, the vast amounts of fruits, and those downpours that were like fists beating on us. And the Andes? Cajamarca wasn't too far off; moreover, the Andes crisscross the whole of Peru both physically and spiritually.

Yes, I was born in Chepén in the bosom of a family that was questionably Catholic. From my maternal grandfather I inherited a bloodline whose roots were unclear: there was talk of English, Italian, and Basque ancestors who came to Peru in the middle of the nineteenth century, amassed a great fortune for the better part of fifty years, only to find themselves bankrupt by the twentieth century. As a result, my great-grandfather Carlo Bay Miani ended his life by putting a bullet in his head. From my grandmother, a native of the Andean town of Cajamarca and a folk healer by trade, I inherited a stream of blood no less confused: Andalusian on one side, Indian on the other. From my father, a Russian Jew who emigrated to Peru in the thirties, I only inherited—at least for the first eight years of my life—the weight of his shadow.

Here's one fact that may be of interest: my birthdate, November 15, and Cajamarca, the town where my grandmother was born, share a curious connection. According to history, on that very date four centuries earlier, the Spanish priest Valverde entered the town's main square, where the Spaniards and the Incas had gathered, and gave the Inca king the Bible saying: "Here is the word of God." Atahualpa took the book, put it to his ear, and tossed it into the air shouting: "I don't hear a thing." At that moment, the Spaniards opened fire, scattering the Indians in all directions, and captured Atahualpa, who, after he was granted the privilege of baptism, was condemned to the garrote.

1946: My family gives in to the parish priest's missionary zeal and has me baptized. Years later I would discover that, though my grandparents had ten children, I was the only person in my family ever baptized. From then on the parish priest becomes my father and the church a second home.

1948: One day an old man comes to the house claiming to have been sent from Lima by my father. He brings me a pile of gifts as if he were one of the Magi. One gift catches my eye: a six-pointed gold star. The old man ceremoniously places it around my neck while he says in a voiced choked with emotion: "Don't ever take it off. You're one of us now." A few days later, the star ends up at the bottom of a river. I weep over it all afternoon and I remember being plagued night after night by awful nightmares in which an old gypsy, eyes ablaze, comes into my room and asks me what happened to the star.

1950: I learn to read from two sources that, at first glance, seem contradictory: the Catholic missal and Hollywood movies. That's how I become the priest's helper during Mass and the cinematographic reader of the family. Practically illiterate, my aunts and uncles take me to the movies so that I can read the Spanish subtitles to them. A conflict develops: I'm not sure if I want to be a priest or an actor when I grow up. The Mass, as well as other rituals in the town, becomes, for me, a kind of small drama: town life is a chain of processions, funerals, festivals, births, carnivals in which we are all actors and audience at the same time. From that experience, I developed a liking for a special kind of literature: the type that celebrates the joys and sorrows of life. Literature as a collective experience. Literature not as the expression of a solipsistic "I" but rather as the universal expression that articulates the thoughts and feelings of a people.

1951: I read my very first book, the New Testament, and I also learn to write. I write my first book: I copy the Gospels word for word, letter for letter. My favorite is the Gospel according to John that starts off "In the beginning was the Word."

1952: For the first time in my life, I get a close look at death. After several days of painful agony, my aunt Amalia dies at the age of nineteen. Until the moment they place her in the coffin—three or four hours have passed—I stay at the foot of her bed watching her. A lovely smile lights up her face and I cannot accept her death. We hold a wake through the night, and the following morning we carry her to the cemetery. I "saw" her again twenty-two years later in New York's upper Manhattan when, as I was about to begin writing my first novel, she appeared at the foot of my bed one morning with the same smile with which she had died and wearing the same clothes she was buried in. That same day I begin working on *La vida a plazos de don Jacobo Lerner* (The Fragmented Life of Don Jacobo Lerner).

1953: First exile: I leave my village for Lima. My father awaits me there and 5,700 years of Judaism fall on me like a ton of bricks. In addition, my encounter with a large city takes place. The late night taxi trip to my new house is actually a journey through time: from the center of town, garbed in a baroque colonial style, we enter a long neoclassical avenue and then cross a wide nineteenth-century promenade that every ten minutes is interrupted by beautiful, small medieval-like plazas that house winged statues erected to commemorate national heroes. My house is in the Jesús María district and I walk into it knowing that my true home isn't here, but in the town I have left behind. (And now it occurs to me that I never lived in the same house in Lima for more than three years, a fact that has deeply affected the character of my work in which a recurring theme is the absence of roots and home.) Soon I discover that my father is a Jew and that his world stretches beyond Peru's borders. I begin to ask myself, who am I? what am I? I hunt around for mirrors to see if I can recognize myself. No luck. I am alone confronting my own fragmented image. I've got to be someone, I tell myself, and that someone is my father. I must become what he is: a Jew. But in order to be a Jew I must erase my past. Thus my second exile: from myself. I have to stop being in order to be. In my new environment, that of the Jewish community in Lima, I begin to discover that its members are living a marked schizophrenic existence. My new Jewish friends feel Peruvian, but also something else as well, something that in time I myself learn to feel. It so happened that we found ourselves, my friends and I, vacillating back and forth between Jewish and Peruvian culture. For that reason, a large part of my work deals with an attempt to reconcile both these roots and histories.

1954: I begin attending León Pinelo, a Jewish school. It's the first day of school for me. I know no one, and in comes the teacher. He picks up a piece of chalk, scribbles some very weird symbols on the blackboard, from right to left. Then he turns around and pronounces a few totally incomprehensible words. What's worse, the class then begins to repeat the teacher's words in a kind of litany. I sit there nailed to my chair wondering if I am going crazy. After four months of playing an invisible role in the class, I finally realize that they have been speaking Hebrew all along. That year I write my second book: an exact copy of a book of stories from the Old Testament in Hebrew. Writing those Hebrew letters placed me in a kind of trance—they were full of magic. I felt that a secret was hidden inside them, that these characters—and, by extension, all writing—could be used to decipher the world. I wasn't a bit surprised to discover many years later that the following three words have the same root in Hebrew: *sefer* means "book"; *sipur*, "narration"; and *mispar*, "number"—that which contains and measures all things.

That same year I began reading my fourth book, the Bible in Spanish. We read through it with the rabbi in my religion class. Those classes and my own reading of the Bible taught me that the history of a people is also its myth. This lesson has shaped my writing: I do not treat Judaism as a purely historical process, but as something from which to retrieve a series of myths still latent in Judaism.

1955: I join Betar, a club of young Zionists linked ideologically to Israel's Herut party, which advocates a Jewish homeland on both sides of the Jordan. Little by little Peru starts receding into the background: we study Peru's history, geography, and customs in school, but it's as if we were studying a foreign country. The Jewish community resembles a small Israeli ghetto nailed to the heart of Lima and, at the same time, it is also like a small Jewish village in Eastern Europe. For the first time in my life I suffer an identity crisis when both my Jewish as well as my Peruvian friends ask me: "If Peru and Israel went to war, who would you fight for?" I tell my Jewish friends for Israel and my gentile Peruvian friends for Peru. That year I write my first original work, a lengthy narrative poem that tells a story of love and abandonment. The autobiographical link is clearly there: an Inca king conquers a foreign land, falls in love with a princess, and then returns to his kingdom not knowing that the princess is carrying his child.

1956: My father and I move into the house of a friend of his who had emigrated with his family to Israel. It has an unbelievably huge library, full of books by French, Russian, and American authors. Peruvian writers stand out by their very absence; there are, however, an abundance of books by classical Jewish writers, especially those written by Sholem Aleichem.

Little by little I begin to learn what it means to be a Jew, what makes us different from other people. To begin with, I am told that the Jews are the Chosen People. There's an additional burden: the most important men in history, from Moses to Freud—so it seems— have been Jews.

1957: First rite of passage: I become an official member of the Jewish people by being circumcised in the clinic of my father's doctor. That same night, half a block from the clinic, the film *The Ten Commandments* premieres and almost all the Jewish community of Lima attends. My father and I miss the opening night. A week later, when I return to school, I no longer have to avoid my friends when I go to the bathroom. Now I can proudly show them that I, too, am a Jew.

1958: I am now a writer. I begin to write a novel entitled *El Ávaro* (The Miser), set in my hometown and based on my maternal grandfather. And yet the landscape I describe is Russian, not Peruvian, and Chepén is quite a faithful reproduction of Kasrilevke, the mythical town created by Sholem Aleichem. I don't get beyond chapter 3. That same year I discover César Vallejo's *Trilce* and Ciro Alegría's *El mundo es ancho y ajeno* (Broad and Alien Is the World), books written by writers born in La Libertad, my native province. I am particularly moved by those poems in *Trilce* that speak of family and home life. In Vallejo I find a familiar voice, a voice filled with echoes of my hometown. It is a voice—obviously, I wouldn't discover this until years later—that not only reveals the poet's innermost conflicts but actually extends to the very roots of the thoughts and feelings of his mestizo race. I'm also deeply influenced by one of the central themes of Ciro Alegría's book: the world is a huge place, there are many areas to explore, but it will always be a foreign land for the Indians. Couldn't the same have been said about the Jews of the Diaspora?

1959: My Bar Mitzvah is celebrated early one Thursday morning. No more than twelve very old, wrinkled, and somber men show up at the synagogue. The ceremony lasts five minutes, just enough time for me to stammer through the two prayers I had memorized.

In April of that year, my father takes me out of the León Pinelo school and puts me in the Leoncio Prado Military Academy. I'm the only Jew in the whole school and, for the first time in my life, I come face-to-face with anti-Semitism. There's no point in behaving like a good Peruvian Catholic from Chepén. My first and last name give me away, and I find myself forced to defend my Jewishness with my fists.

1960: I read for the first time José María Argüedas's novel *Los ríos profundos* (Deep Rivers). It's the story of a boy in search of his identity or, actually, in search of a way to reconcile his Western and Indian roots. The boy wanders through not a very clearly defined world, caught between two cultures that clash not only on the surface but in the very heart of every Peruvian. The story is told in a richly lyrical language and all sorts of mysterious and magical occurrences take place, the kind of writing that foreshadows what was later to be called "magical realism" and that pervades the work of García Márquez and Juan Rulfo. This book by Argüedas would be vitally important to me and would spur me to examine a similar problem in my own writings: the cultural and racial crossbreeding in Peru, incorporating history and myth.

1962: Third exile: I finish high school and my father sends me to Israel to study agronomy. Before leaving, I go back to Chepén to say good-bye to my past. My return forms part of the epilogue of *Tiempo al Tiempo* (Play by Play).

As I get off the boat in Haifa, I'm astonished to find that the dockworkers as well as all the people swarming around the piers are Jewish. An understandable reaction, if you consider that I was part of a community of barely five thousand Jews among fifteen million Peruvians. I live on a kibbutz for a year, and then I spend another six months in a Haifa boardinghouse run by an Argentine woman. In that house I discover Borges and Kafka, two contemporary cabalists and prophets living in a world devoid of memories.

1963: I leave for Barcelona to study medicine. A month late I receive word of my father's death in Peru; he died without me getting to know him, and from that moment on, he will only be a ghost in my memory. I give up medical studies, become an insurance salesman, and go back to work I had abandoned when I was twelve. It's still called *El Ávaro,* but now the book is actually set in Peru. Again, I get nowhere and I put it aside after writing three or four chapters. Eleven years later I would finally realize that if I wanted to write the book, I would have to make my father's world part of it.

1965: I return to Peru. All ties with my family, on both sides, have been broken. I'm married now and my wife, a girl from New York that I had met in Israel, is about to give birth. I'm unable to get any work, and I feel estranged from my native land. My trip to Israel and return to Peru, after a two-year absence, figures prominently in another poem, also entitled "Chronicles."

Our first child, David, is born, and our financial situation grows worse each day. Fourth exile: My wife convinces me that we should go live in New York. A month after our arrival, I enroll in college, and from 1964 until 1969 all I do is work and study. I do find time, however, to write two books of poetry. The first dies a quiet death at the bottom of a drawer. The second book, *Tiempo de silencio* (Time of Silence), is published in 1970 by a small press; the title is perfect, given the response it receives: not a word is written about it. That same year I begin teaching in New York University's Department of Spanish and Portuguese.

1969: Our second child, Dina, is born.

1973: My second book of poems, *De Chepén a La Habana* (From Chepén to Havana), is published in New York. I treat personal experiences in the book and I begin to explore Jewish themes for the first time. A few critics review the book, one of whom finds a strange, exotic voice in my poetry. "The poems in this book," he said, "comprise a kind of journey in search of a traveler: the father. The poet is a prototypical uprooted man, traveling against the current of history as he searches for his roots. How can this be done? By delving into the stranger that was the poet's father and changing the familiar Jewish myth into a personal story that is neither a fable nor an epic." Already in this book of poems was the seed that four years later would give fruit to my first novel.

1976: The mother of my children and I separate. A year later we divorce.

1977: My novel *La vida a plazos de don Jacobo Lerner* (The Fragmented Life of Don Jacobo Lerner) is published in an English translation. Using autobiographical material, it brings together the most important experiences of my childhood: my early Catholic upbringing, the experience of exile, the clash between Jewish and Peruvian culture. On the one hand, the novel establishes a sort of counterpoint between the short history of the Peruvian Jewish community and the much broader national experience. Yet, on the other hand, this reality plays against a much larger world: the five thousand or so years of Jewish history. To a large degree, the story of the novel—the Jewish immigration to Peru in the 1920s, the life of Jacobo Lerner, and so on—is only a backdrop for the re-creation of an experience that is at once historical and mythical: the Jewish exile. One critic claimed that I had written a documentary novel. Nothing could be farther from the truth: the novel does not depict the true history of the Peruvian Jewish community but instead fictionalizes a particular Jewish experience in which the historical is lived through certain remembered myths.

1978: *La vida a plazos de don Jacobo Lerner* is published in the original Spanish in Lima. The majority of readers, public and critics alike, claim that I have used an idiom, a mode of expression, and a "sensibility" that is foreign to Peruvian letters. Since this was also the reaction of my readers in English, I feel that I have been classified as the author of a Jewish novel written, as if by accident, in Spanish. Since I had not intended to write a Jewish novel, I ask myself the following questions: What makes a novel Jewish? What makes it Peruvian? Is it the subject matter? Is it the language in which it is written? If it is subject matter, then my novel is both Peruvian and Jewish, since it deals with both realities. But if the "nationality" of a novel is defined by the language in which it is written, then my novel is definitely Peruvian. Why, then, did Peruvian readers detect a mode of expression—both syntactical and cultural—that seemed alien to Peruvian Spanish? By way of explanation, I am only able to come up with more questions: Does culture exert an influence on language, or does language shape culture? Can a particular culture produce a sort of metalanguage even if that culture, as in the case of the Jewish experience, expresses itself in different and often unrelated languages? Is there such a thing as a Jewish collective unconscious with its own unmistakable mode of expression? I find myself unable to come up with adequate answers to these questions.

1981: *Hombre de paso/Just Passing Through*, my third book of poems, is published in a bilingual Spanish/English edition. It includes several poems from *From Chepén to Havana* and is a kind of poetic autobiography: the attempt to create an "I" through the process of self-examination. In a broad sense, these poems confront the human condition after it has been worn down by time; by examining Jewish and Peruvian roots, these poems manage to integrate the individual with the whole, memory with the future, and nostalgia with exile. The poetic "I" undertakes a journey that embraces a complex history, with many roots, times, and spaces. The protagonist is "passing through" at many levels: as someone subject to the world at large; as a victim of exile; and as the product of a process attempting to integrate his various cultural roots. Also, with this book, Peruvian critics began to notice the "Peruvian" quality of my writing, a discovery that forces them to reevaluate my first novel. "Goldemberg's novel," one of them suggests, "represents the start of a Judeo-Peruvian literary cross-breeding of special significance. The Peruvian Indian, as well as the Jew, is characterized by his submissive and nomadic nature. Goldemberg's poems reveal the same outlook: they are as clear and direct as verses from the Bible. These poems have an indisputable mystical foundation, a deep and unmistakable lyricism, religious feeling, and historical and cultural concerns found in another of our poets, César Vallejo." With these words I finally deserve Peruvian citizenship as a writer. And yet there still remains an unasked question: What is a Jewish Latin American writer? The answer, to paraphrase an Argentine Jewish writer, is simply: A Jewish Latin American writer is what he himself is, added to what Latin America is.

1984: My second novel, *Tiempo al tiempo* (Play by Play), is published; it reintroduces several themes that were developed in my earlier books. This novel also has an autobiographical foundation, but even I don't know where the autobiographical elements end and the fiction begins. I identify personally with the story that is being narrated because I can recognize certain events in it as real and because I've attempted to expand and unearth them, to *give* them meaning, significance. What survives all those events? What remains of the deeds that actually took place? Is there a faithful rendering of what took place? These are a few questions I've asked myself and tried to answer. A writer attempts to write an "autobiographical" novel and soon discovers that there is no memory—only what *is remembered,* and that's where the fiction bursts in. Memory, then, is that which I allow to exist and the only way to grasp it is by imagining it. Although the novel, any novel, happens to be autobiographical—even when the novelist identifies completely with the events—it is still the biography of an imagined being. Using one's own life to write a novel does not prevent the use of the imagination: to write a novel the writer must place himself right in the heart of the character, which implies that he has the character's intuitive imagination. Furthermore, underneath the plot line, *Play by Play* is a meditation on what it means or what it could mean to be Peruvian and/or Jewish. Throughout the whole book, characters and readers run up against the same question: What does it mean to be a Jew and/or a Peruvian?

1985–88: Four trips back to Peru. The full and undeniable reencounter with my past takes place: I renew the bonds with my family and friends, I fall in love with a childhood girlfriend, and I begin writing—for the first time—love poems. These poems form part of an unpublished manuscript entitled *De amor y sueños* (On Love and Dreams). I stop teaching and co-found the Latin American Book Fair (1985) and the Latin American Writers Institute (1987).

1992: My fourth book of poems, *La vida al contado* (Life Paid in Cash), is published in Lima. A Peruvian poet and critic had this to say about the collection:

> If the poems entitled *Chronicles* are nourished by collective history, both personal and familial, the texts entitled *Origins* grow out of the history of the Jewish people or any other kinds of history, to express the most basic of elemental situations, for example, the relationship between a man and a woman. There are other poems in the book entitled *Inventory* or *Just Passing Through* whose purpose we can define with two words: stillness and motion. Whoever is making the inventories doesn't want to go anywhere; on the other hand, the man just passing through, as defined, goes from one place to another, and is nowhere. These two signposts, corresponding on the symbolic level with two attitudes of Jewish people, both equally active, one can almost say genetically, in each individual: the crav-

ing for planting roots in a land that can be recognized as one's own and, on the other side, the need to be a traveler through this vast world. These two ways of being, both interconnected, has historically given the Jews the ability to adapt to any environment and, at the same time, together with an internal order of a religious nature, a firm will to return to sacred places.

My childhood friend Dina and I get married in New York. My life has come full circle.

1997: I finish working on *El gran libro de América Judía: Voces y visiones para el milenio* (The Great Book of Jewish America: Voices and Visions for the Millennium), an anthology of Jewish Latin American literature. Through the poems, stories, personal accounts and essays, interviews and testimonies of 155 writers, this book presents a panoramic vision of what Latin American Judaism has been in the twentieth century. With this book, and also with *La vida al contado*, I feel that I have completed my Jewish itinerary in Peru. Now, perhaps, I should begin to consider what it means to be a Peruvian Jew in New York. Something tells me, however, that I will only be able to relate this experience from the vantage point of Peru.

Translated by David Unger and Stephen A. Sadow

Mario Szichman
Argentina/Venezuela/United States
&

Novelist, newspaper editor, journalist, Mario Szichman (1945–) is often accused of distorting what he sees. The truth is the opposite. Szichman has a keen sense of the distortions and contradictions that keep life from being exactly what we want it to be. And he is funny. Szichman is a quiet man with brimstone inside. Parody and satire are his chosen weapons. Through his Pechof family novels, *Los judíos del mar dulce* (The Jews of the Freshwater Sea), *Crónica falsa* (False Chronicle), and *La verdadera crónica falsa* (The True False Chronicle), he skewered the Jewish community of Argentina. His putdowns, inside jokes, and multilingual banter are unrelenting. Later, in *A las 20:25 la señora entró la Inmortalidad* (At 8:25 Evita Became Immortal), he took on Eva Perón and her gang.

Mario Szichman left Argentina in 1976 and settled first in Caracas where he wrote for the tabloid *El comercial* and other newspapers and magazines. Married to a psychoanalyst, he now lives in New York where he is an editor in the Associated Press's Latin American bureau. His new fiction, dealing with Simón Bolívar's mentor Francisco de Miranda and Argentina in the twilight of the Perón era, retains the ferocity and black humor of his earlier work. Szichman's short story "The Dormant Father" shows a tenderer side of his writing as it examines the biblical injunction to honor thy father.

Szichman wrote this bittersweet essay about growing up Jewish in Buenos Aires expressly for this anthology.

DISTORTED WORDS, DISTORTED IMAGES, BROKEN LANGUAGES

Mario Szichman

For Ilan Stavans

I think I decided to start writing when I realized that every word could be either a lie or a misunderstanding. George Orwell speaks about "those wild, almost lunatic misunderstandings which are part of the daily experience of childhood,"[1] and if someone is patient enough, he, or she, can make a profession of it.

I remember my mother saying on one occasion that one of my friends fell on his head while riding his bike and that his right eye became the size of a soccer ball. (She didn't want to buy me a bike, so the accident of my friend was a good deterrent.) But the next day, when I was looking forward to seeing my friend transformed into a real freak—a small boy with a small head in which his eye protruded like a soccer ball—I felt totally disappointed. My friend's eye was a little bruised, but that was all. My mother had an excellent imagination but did not know how to make a lie stand. Maybe if she had talked about a small boy in another country, or in another era, one to whom I had no access at all, that would have been different.

But my mother's proclivity to exaggerate things, and let your faithful be disappointed after the encounter with the real article, was not something peculiar to her. It was in the atmosphere. People, institutions, had the tendency to look through both sides of the telescope, inflating or deflating threats, trends, reputations, or buildings, although only in the rarest of circumstances someone came forward to announce that he was seeing merely a bruised eye. Even if the truth was in front of our noses. I remember seeing the illustrations of El Cabildo, the municipal council of the colonial era, depicted in the schoolbooks. It was in El Cabildo where Argentinian patriots fought their first legal battles for independence, so in the illustrations it appeared as a mammoth building, huge as an Egyptian pyramid, and full of windows. Regretfully, we have the real thing in downtown Buenos Aires, opposite the Pink House, the government building. Well, it was really disappointing when I saw it in the flesh. It was a respectable building, but it could not be compared with the imposing illustrations. (I am sure Kafka felt as disappointed when he saw the real castles of Europe. Hence his description of a castle as a cluster of flat houses, indistinguishable from any village. The only grandeur left was in the magic word *castle*. And in the gap between the word and the thing, he constructed his own world.)

But every time a bruised eye of one of my friends deflated my expectations, I had a cherished recollection that helped me to look at things in an exalted way. Because before my friend's accident, I lived through the day of the Pampero, the wind of the pampas, which created the only hallucination I experienced in my life. (If it really was a hallucination, or a true fact that I had to accept as a hallucination in order to continue my life among sane people.) I heard many strange stories about that humid wind which brought dust and flying papers to the city. People went crazy, wells went dry, cows laid on the ground, as though struck by lightning, and chickens started to spin like propellers until they fell dead. So el Pampero had a built-in mythical quality to which I was able to add lately the story of the balloons and the wheels that went crazy. At that time I must have been three or four years old. I was playing with my tricycle near the door of my father's watchmaker shop when the Pampero materialized in our street. I first felt the dust in my eyes, then I saw papers flying all over the street, and after that the Pampero played exclusively for me. I saw a child holding a balloon on the end of a stick—a balloon inflated with the lungs, not with gas, because those fancy balloons, at least in the fifties, belonged solely to American children and American political conventions. Well, that balloon changed its shape. First it became elongated, then I saw some bulges in its skin, and finally it exploded. Well, that could have been a mere fluke. But after that, as if the god who was driving the Pampero wanted me to be a true believer, it took possession of a soccer ball that one of my talented friends was bouncing on his thighs, first on the left, then on the right, three, four, five times, without letting it fall to the ground. The soccer ball was not made of the same material as the balloon. It was a leather soccer ball, the kind used by professionals. But anyway, it acquired the same strange configuration of the balloon and exploded in midair, when my friend was making his seventh or eighth rebound on one of his thighs. And then, to show me that it meant business, the invisible force of the Pampero meddled with my tricycle. I saw one of the rear wheels starting to spin, then the tires getting bubbles, and at last, after an interminable time, it exploded. That was startling. And later on, a miracle occurred. And the miracle consisted in the fact that I did not tell a soul about the happening. I kept it to myself. I do not have any other fancy remembrance of my infancy. Contrary to what adults think, children are highly realistic. I remember once that I was walking along with my father and we saw a green disk in the sky. My father hadn't any explanation for the phenomenon and tried to dissuade me that I had seen something. And although I grew up listening to the stories of the Prophet Elijah and his chariot of fire, and of the image of Evita projected on the moon, I knew that what I saw was an explainable gimmick. I was sure that someone must have attached a neon light in the shape of a disk to the underside of a small plane.

So, with the same shrewdness, I decided not to tell a soul about the Pampero and its strange apparition. There was no advantage in informing my family or my friends about what I saw, because the last place I wanted to be was in a mental ward. I had kept the secret for almost half a century, until my dear friend Stephen Sadow asked me to write my own remembrances of things past, and if some reader has any reasonable explanation for that happening, please, don't tell me, because the worst thing a person can do is destroy a child's illusion.

And then another thing happened which showed me that there are more things in heaven and earth, Horatio, than are dreamt of in your philosophy. Let the reader imagine that a child grows up hearing that a man has the power of Samson, and suddenly, one day, Samson comes to the child's house and announces himself: "Hi, I am Samson, glad to meet you."

Well, that also happened to me when I was a child. A circus had come to Liniers, my Buenos Aires neighborhood. I saw the procession of elephants, each with its trunk grasping the tail of the one in front, the equestrians riding their horses, the tiger tamers inside the cages, cracking their whips to make the gentle, placid, ancient tigers roar—and believe me, their lashes were more scary than the tigers' roar—the still scarier clowns, who for me seem like the predecessors of the death squads, and finally Camacho the Giant. At that time, I did not know who Samson was, or Hercules. But Camacho was a household name. My father used to say of any big man (for instance, the bully who tried to make Charles Chaplin's life miserable): "He is a giant like Camacho." And then, one day, the legend crossed the threshold of my father's watchmaker shop. I think he did it with the humble purpose of changing his watchband, but for me it was as if my dream of Eliahu HaNavi, Elijah the Prophet, had materialized at last.

Camacho was faithful to his legend. He was the biggest man I ever saw in my life. And he was kind to the kids who had gathered outside the shop. While he was waiting for his watch, he did something for which I will always be grateful. He invited me to stand on his shoes to show my father, and the other kids, the difference between his feet and mine. (I would like to think that when in one of the *Godfather* movies Abe Vigoda allows a kid to dance on his own shoes, he is taking a cue from Camacho.) They were enough experiences to last a lifetime, and I thought that by combining them in different ways, I would be able to earn a living as a writer. (That was the only hallucination I was never able to overcome.)

But there was another fact that was as important as those incidents: the emergence of words that I could not understand.

"I don't understand Greek too well," said the giant in Voltaire's *Micromegas*.

"Nor do I," said the philosophic mite.

"Then why," retorted the Syrian, "do you quote a certain Aristotle in Greek?"

"Because," replied the scholar, "it is essential to quote what we do not understand at all in the language we understand the least."

This wonderful exchange helps to deflate a lot of egos, especially in our postmodern world, in which it seems that the only possible way to elaborate ideas is in dead languages—or at least in languages that seem as dead as doornails after they received the theoreticians' treatment. But it serves also to explain the schizophrenic world in which most of us Jews, children who belonged to families who packed hastily and left the Old World before the next pogrom surfaced, were raised.

The first impact was not only words but two kinds of words, the Spanish words that belonged to the place in which our families had the illusion that they would be accepted, and that which represented the world of guilt. The guilty words came in two brands, Yiddish and Hebrew. They informed us, even in our misunderstanding, or total ignorance, that we were set apart. We were walking through the Spanish language like marauders, feeling the pressure to speak correctly, even more than the natives or some prestigious strangers, like Englishmen or Frenchmen. A person who has to speak in a foreign tongue never takes that language for granted, as George Steiner, in his analysis of the works of Jorge Luis Borges, Vladimir Nabokov, and Samuel Beckett, stated. Those writers were perpetually trying to translate themselves into another language. Marcel Proust wrote, "Infirmity alone makes us take notice and learn, and enables us to analyse mechanisms of which otherwise we should know nothing. A man who falls straight into bed night after night, and ceases to live until the moment when he wakes and rises, will surely never dream of making, I don't say great discoveries, but even minor observations about sleep. He scarcely knows that he is asleep. A little insomnia is not without its value in making us appreciate sleep, in throwing a ray of light upon that darkness. An unfailing memory is not a very powerful incentive to the study of the phenomena of memory."[2] (In one of my novels, *A las 20:25 la señora entró en la inmortalidad* [At 8:25 Evita Became Immortal], one of the Jewish characters complains that a guest "talks worse than I do," and his brother, who tries to teach him good manners, answers, "He may. He may speak worse than you, but he does it with class," because the guest speaks in Portuguese.) And of course, at the same time, there was a built-in conflict with our parents and relatives due to their mispronunciation or their hesitation in using some words. Their uncertainty seemed to taint their status as role models.

But strangely enough, one of those foreign languages, Yiddish, could at times be a language of mirth. Because over that family, as in many Jewish families of such era, hovered the venerable ghost of Sholom Aleichem. It's hard to explain what Sholom Aleichem meant in Jewish culture. I don't think even Mark Twain comes closer.[3] It's, I presume, the triumph of life, in all of its manifestations, no matter the catastrophe, and his way to deflate the common proclivity of people to self-commiseration by way of some ironic or optimistic remark. (I don't think Sholom Aleichem would have ever dared to give the genocide of the European Jews the name Holocaust. By the same token, I don't think Elie Wiesel would have ever become a Sholom Aleichem character.)

I remember a skit played by two of my uncles, Leibel and Duveth—a skit, I suspect, that came from vaudeville. My uncle Leible, with a nasal twang, recited some verses that my uncle Duveth translated into some clipped prose. Everybody laughed at the double entendre, especially the children, who didn't understand a single word but suspected that there were some forbidden words or acts implied.

When I say that everybody laughed, I mean that sixty or seventy people laughed altogether. Because mine was a big family. For one of those infrequent miracles in Jewish history, my mother's side of the family was able to escape to Argentina between 1928 and 1933, the year in which the Argentinian government of General Agustín P. Justo decided to close the doors to immigration. The then minister of foreign affairs, Carlos Saavedra Lamas, who would later earn the Nobel Peace Prize—not precisely for saving Jews—said at that time that "Argentina needs immigrants, not refugees." (That decision left my father's side of the family, including his own parents, plus dozens of relatives, stranded in Poland until war came and they vanished from the face of the earth. I wasn't allowed ever to ask what happened to them, and that is another important reason why I decided to become a writer.)

Well, the Szylder family—that's my mother's maiden name—came to Argentina at the beginning of the Great Depression. Three generations altogether packed in one ship. I twisted that eventful voyage a little in two of my novels, *Los judíos del mar dulce* and *At 8:25 Evita Became Immortal,* when I wrote:

The Pechofs loaded two trunks and five children on a cart and fled towards Gdinia. There they boarded the *Titania,* and they arrived in

Buenos Aires after having made stops in Liverpool and Rio de Janeiro.

The *Titania* docked in front of the Immigration Building, with a horizon of gray buildings, rusty-hulled ships, cranes and trees.

Zeydeh Pechof became anxious because the harbor seemed a copy of Gdinia's. He had heard so many stories about Buenos Aires that he expected something less plausible.

His suspicions increased when the porter spoke to them in Polish and at the hotel they were greeted by *yidn*.

"A month at sea to get this. Once again in Poland," the zeydeh bitterly told his wife.

"You are crazy," said the bubbe.

"Believe me, we're still in Poland. Everybody speaks Polish. Don't they have to speak a different language in another country?"

"The one who stamped our papers spoke a different language," the bubbe reminded him.

"Big deal, because he belonged to customs. The customs officer in Gdinia also spoke a different language. In all customs they speak that way."

"I'm not going to move from here. God's will be done," the bubbe announced.

"You don't need to move, believe me. They're going to move you."

"Let them just try. If anyone touches me he will get a slap."

The next day was when the Tragic Week began, and all doubts were dissipated. They were still living in Poland.

But no, the zeydeh was wrong. The Pechofs had really arrived at the Promised Land of Argentina, although at an exceptional moment in the history of my country, when anti-Semitism was rampant. That was in 1919, when a strike in the Vassena metalwork factory, in Buenos Aires, exploded in bloody riots. The government of Constitutional President Hipólito Irigoyen was very afraid that the example set by the Russian Revolution would give Argentine workers exotic ideas, so it decided to teach them a lesson by killing an indeterminate number of people.[4]

Happily, the Szylder family arrived at a different moment in Argentinian history, in 1930, when anti-Semitism was not rampant, but dormant, and they were able to believe, as the Pechofs of *Los judíos del mar dulce* did, "In the country they had set up to fool the immigrant dupes, there were no Indians, no poison arrows, nobody down and out, short, fat, no anti-Semites." A country, which resembled the idyllic vision given by our great founding father, Alberto Gerchunoff, where the immigrants became great bronco busters, with the *criollos* looking on, the mockery in their eyes turning to wonder."[5]

They settled up, and a few of them even managed to prosper. But the most prominent feature of my extended family was not wealth but the proliferation of children. It seemed that two generations of women, altogether, were manufacturing babies at the same time. When I read recently that a woman in her sixties gave birth to a child through in vitro fertilization, I thought, Big deal. Because when my bubbe was fifty-seven years old—and my zeydeh the bon vivant sixty-five—she gave birth to her ninth child, Mendel. Do you remember the joke: "We keep our mother in an altar, so my father could not reach her?" Well, in the Szylder family *that* was not a joke. It's part of the family legend that some of my bubbe's eldest daughters were reluctant to invite their suitors to their homes because nobody would believe that the child who was crying in the crib was their youngest brother. (At that time, my eldest aunt, Dvoire, was the only one married and with two children, so Mendel became an uncle before he was born. The same thing happened to Sigmund Freud, with lasting impact on twentieth-century thought. Uncle Mendel didn't have the same lasting impact, but he did have some lasting virtues of his own, among them, a wonderful sense of humor.)

Of course, the only way to run such a big family is through hard work and longevity. My zeydeh started a new career as a *shochet* [ritual slaughterer] in Argentina at the time most people are retiring, and if I'm not wrong, he continued working until he was close to ninety. He was also the *shammes* [sexton] in a Mataderos synagogue and commanded enormous respect, whereas Manes Trachter, the millionaire, who gave the money to build the temple, was always slighted by the *kapzunim*, the bigshots, of the congregation, because he wasn't a learned man. (Talk about democracy!)

I remember that when my zeydeh was about ninety-three or ninety-four years old, he started to develop some problems with his legs, and the adolescent of the congregation, a Bessarabian Jew of about seventy-five, went daily to pick him up and take him to the shul. If Camacho was the tallest man alive, this Bessarabian Jew was the strongest. According to one legend, he used to work as a blacksmith in the Old Country and since the time he was twelve years old drank, before breakfast every day, a glass brimming with schnapps, instead of milk. Then, full of energy, he started his work. And when some horse didn't behave itself, he was able to knock it down with a punch and change its shoes. (Animal lovers must rest assured that he never caused any damage to his customers.)

But this Bessarabian Jew was not the exception when it came to drink. In the synagogue of Mataderos, when they sat down and wept, remembering Zion, and promised, *If I forget thee, O Jerusalem, let my right hand forget her cunning. If I do not remember thee, let my tongue cleave to the roof of my mouth*, the other thing they never forget, once they finished their prayers, was to celebrate life with a healthy drink. (Or better, make that several.) Anyway, they never got drunk, because, as the old song says, "Shiker is a goy." "A drinker is a goy."

In such a wordy, wordy world, it wasn't too difficult to spin stories. Moreover, it was almost impossible not to repeat them. And I decided it was worthwhile to pack some of them together. But I wasn't the only one. There are several members of the family who can do the same. And one day they will do it. That is why my favorite phrase, after I complete some writing, is not "The End" but "To Be Continued."

NOTES

1. George Orwell, *A Collection of Essays* (New York: Harcourt Brace Jovanovich, 1953) 81.

2. Marcel Proust, *Remembrance of Things Past*, trans. C. K. Scott Moncrieff and Terence Kilmartin (New York: Vintage, 1981) 2:675–76.

3. "Expostulate on Kafka or Dostoyevsky and people are fairly begging for your explanations and interpretations. Lecture on any other Yiddish writer—Mendel, Peretz, Asch, Grade, the brothers Singer—and your words will illumine, clarify, edify. But set out to discuss the 'narrative structure' or 'comic techniques' of Sholom Aleichem, and he undercuts your very best attempt. . . . He gives us no disquisitions on literature, no pen portraits of his contemporaries, no contemplative philosophy from the heights. . . . He deflates intellectual and artistic pretentiousness. . . . What confronts us, finally, is the quizzical smile of the author, compulsively skeptical about everything but the story." Ruth R. Wisse, in the introduction to *The Best of Sholom Aleichem* (New York: Touchstone, 1980) xxvii.

4. A cherished custom of many Argentine historians is never to give an exact or approximate account of people killed in massacres. Everybody knows that the Indian population was exterminated in the last two decades of the nineteenth century, but nobody knows exactly how many lie in common graves. Everybody knows also that thousands of people had been killed in the so-called Dirty War, between 1976 and 1983, but the official figure of 8,900, given by the National Commission of the Disappeared Ones, has been challenged by several human rights groups, who speak of 15,000 or 30,000 people killed by the military junta.

5. This passage was translated by Naomi Lindstrom.

Alcina Lubitch Domecq
Guatemala/Israel

The child of a father left deranged by the Holocaust, and born in
Guatemala, an outpost of the Diaspora whose community never exceeded one thousand members, Alcina Lubitch Domecq (1953–) looks
at writing as something she must do, as a way of handling her pain.
Her novels and stories are filled with sharp-edged images, are populated by the ghosts of her past, and possess a strong dose of the surreal. Every word, every comma is eked out. Putting enormous care
into each work, she has produced a number of veritable "jewels."

Experiences in a secular kibbutz and her profound encounters with
mystical teaching have heightened her already intense artistic sensibility. (In Mexico, under the tutelage of the writers Angelina Muñiz-
Huberman and Esther Seligson, she began an intense study of the
Cabala.) Lubitch Domecq's novels *El espejo del espejo: o, La noble
sonrisa del perro* (The Mirror's Mirror, or The Dog's Noble Smile) and
her stories in *Intoxicada* (Intoxicated) deal with a search for origins.

"Résumé Raisonné" was written expressly for this anthogoly.

RÉSUMÉ RAISONNÉ

Alcina Lubitch Domecq

1953–1961

I was born in Guatemala City. My father was a Holocaust survivor whose arrival in Central America was arranged by a distant cousin connected at some point to the Alliance Israélite Universelle. After the liberation of Auschwitz, Papa spent a few weeks wandering around in the Pale. He stayed briefly in Lodz (where he met an idol of mine, Isaiah Spiegel, at the time retrieving from memory the stories included in *Ghetto Kingdom*), then made his way to Lyon, worked a few weeks in a Paris shoe factory, and eventually sailed across the Atlantic. His arrival point was Havana, where he lived for three months toward the end of 1946. Then his cousin managed to bring him to Guatemala, where Papa's name changed from Ya' acov Yehoshua Lichtenshtein to Jacobo Lubitch and where, willy-nilly, he began working as an assistant in an optician's office. My mother, Josefina Domecq Pérez, a non-Jew, was from a wealthy Spanish family with ties to Mexico's wine industry. She was nineteen when she got pregnant with my brother Elías, twenty when I was born, and twenty-four when my youngest sibling, Nicolás, came into the world. By all accounts, Papa

173

met Mama at a *quinceañera* [Sweet Fifteen] party. She was immediately struck by the serial number tattooed on his arm. Their betrothal was not met with welcoming eyes by Mama's family. Thus the wedding was remarkably small: fewer than a dozen guests, mostly her friends; Papa's cousin refused to participate, accusing my father of betrayal. Up until his death in about 1969, he disapproved of *die goye*. The house I was raised in the first nine years of my life was a large, beautiful hacienda. I can still picture its endless corridors and exuberant gardens, manicured weekly by Don Lupe, the *portero*. The property belonged to the Domecq family, and we shared it with Abuela Clotilde and the strict Tía Refugio, whose changing moods the children learned to fear from early on. Papa changed jobs regularly. For several years, he worked at a hat factory in downtown Guatemala City—I remember its elevated shelves filled with elegant *sombreros de fieltro*. But he made little money. Still, we lived an opulent life, with servants and nannies, sponsored in full by Mama's family. My brother Elías and I had an English teacher, Señora Krieger, very strict in manners, who came to the house twice a week to give us private lessons. I also had a swimming teacher, Damián Pissá (his name will not abandon me, although the silhouette of his face has), whom we met every Saturday at an indoor swimming pool in a northern district of the city.

I spent my *niñez*—somehow the Spanish word rings truer—running up and down the hacienda alleyways, climbing trees in the yard, and frolicking in a river bend that crossed the southern section of the property. But my childhood was not happy. Ever since I can remember, Papa's sickness loomed in the background. The Holocaust had left a deep scar in him. He never talked about what he had gone through. But it was clear his suffering had been unbearable. He hardly ever smiled and detested seeing himself reflected in the mirror. He refused to shave. Mama would trim his beard in the garden every two or three months, while he sat in a reclining chair. He combed his hair in the kitchen. And his clothes were always disheveled and poorly matched. He was an outright nonobservant Jew, for he had lost all faith in G-d during the Holocaust; but in his physical appearance, he eerily resembled an orthodox Hasid, those I've come to despise since my *aliyah*. I always remember him as shadowy, erratic, waggish: though he wasn't severe, his facial gestures were always rigid; on occasion, he would smile at us children, but his smile would invariably come out as contrived, forced, unintended. For many years, I was sure his anger was directly targeted at me. And so did Elías. All photographs of his past vanished during the war—all except two. Someone in Israel sent them to us by mail, and somehow I ended up storing them in a bedroom drawer. I'm not sure he ever knew I had them. Alone at night, when he and Mama were away, I would study them carefully, figuring out the link between his calamitous past and his discomforting present. In one of these photos Papa, still a child of around eight or nine, is on a tricycle, smiling at the camera, without one of his front teeth; in the other, he stands next to one of his aunts—Pearl Lichtenshtein (1898–1944), I believe—and you can see in his expression the rascal he once might have been. But all this joyful spirit was lost forever. Lost many times over.

On one occasion, when I was about the same age as he is in the tricycle photo, I saw a portrait of Adolf Hitler in a history book. Mama explained to me he was the leader of the Nazi army that killed all of Papa's family. I was mesmerized. Somehow, it didn't seem possible that a man so gallant would perpetrate so much evil. Hitler's facial expression was enigmatic: he smiled at me. Was this smile stolen? Had he taken it away from Papa? I vividly remember telling myself that if I ever saw Hitler walking on a downtown street, I would first ask him. And if he refused to answer, I would call the police. My brother Elías laughed. His laughter hurt me.

"Hitler is dead, silly!" he would say.

"But what if he isn't? What would you tell him if you all of a sudden saw him on the sidewalk?"

"In Guatemala? Silly."

"Of course. Where else? Do you know how many Nazis fled to Brazil when the American soldiers were about to capture them?"

"How many?"

"Hundreds. Or perhaps more."

"To Guatemala?"

"Yes. Señora Krieger told me many speak Spanish now. Not German anymore . . ."

"Well . . ."

"Well what? Can you imagine Hitler stopping at our door? What would you do?"

"What would I do? I would kill him," Elías would answer.

And I got scared by his reply. "No, don't do that . . . Don't kill him! You would end up in jail! And I don't want you in jail. Jail makes people sad."

"And what would you do, Alcina?"

But I would fall dumb and have no answer. What would I *actually* do if I ever saw Hitler?

Shortly before we left Guatemala, Papa was placed in a psychiatric ward. We children were not told why, for we were supposed to be protected from such horrible endings. It took me many, many years to put the puzzle together. When I was born, he had begun talking to himself. At the hat store, he would stand alone for hours in his office, staring at the wall. He would see in his customers' faces a resemblance to his siblings and friends before the war, and would talk to them about incidents that had happened many years ago. His cousin tried to help. He recommended that Mama take him on a long vacation. She arranged a trip to Spain but Papa refused to go. "*No mientras Franco, el Mussolini español, nos dé la bienvenida*" (not while Franco, the Spanish Mussolini, is there to welcome us). He said—and often repeated—that everything was alright. And for a while things did seem okay. After a couple of brief psychotic incidents at the store, he returned to normal. Mama got pregnant again, this time with Nicolás. It was when Nicolás, barely two years old, was run over by a car and died in the hospital that Papa lost total control. He couldn't bear the tragedy. In his view, the driver had been a Nazi. He had been spying on our family and was ready to kill his children one by one. He asked Mama to move, and we did, to a small apartment in Calle Corregidor. But Papa's paranoia got worse. He was sure people were following us. He didn't want us to go out, to attend school. I didn't find out anything about the collapse of his partnership with his cousin. And I only remember slightly his erratic behavior. In my eyes, he had suddenly become alive, and I loved him more than ever for talking to me directly, for making sure I was fine, for not wanting me to go to school so that I could play with him at home. *Mi niña*, I remember him saying in Yiddish, *ales ken ich ton far dir, myn shayne, myn liebe*. Obviously, in my childhood mind only a small fraction of what he said and meant was understandable.

Why Mama married him is still a puzzle to me. The family legend has it that she got pregnant with Elías and her own mother, a devout Catholic, forced them to become husband and wife. But this explanation cannot quite satisfy me: as a young man, Papa might have been a caring lover; he might have wanted to stick to life by marrying such a wealthy and attractive woman; but there is an aspect in my mother's character, one I can easily trace in my own behavior, that serves as a key to the enigma: her messianism. She was obsessed with the way in which Jews had been treated by the Nazis. Spain's expulsion of the Jews was a constant theme in our family conversations—what a mistake it was, how much Spaniards had lost, how the nation's "ticket to becoming modern" had thus been delayed for centuries. In her view, the Holocaust and the 1492 expulsion were symmetrical events in history, and at least in her life she wanted to set the record right. So she married Papa to amend the world. In doing so, of course, she lost her only chance to happiness and pushed us all into an abyss.

Nicolás—Nicolasito—died in June 1961, and Papa was finally declared "incapable of civil conduct" at the end of that year. Abuela Clotilde and Tía Refugio capitalized on the occasion and forced Mama into a divorce. Enraged, she took Elías and me to Mexico, where we settled in the Polanco district. We never saw Papa again. I wish we had, though. Guatemala for me is a sad country.

1962–1981

We lived in Mexico until 1972, but I never learned to love it. Mexicans are friendly and warm, but I arrived at a time of enormous spiritual upheaval in my life and had little interest in my surroundings. Mama was reticent, uncommunicative. She felt she had betrayed Papa and was in constant struggle with my grandparents about returning to Guatemala. They forbade her to do so. Instead, they sponsored her lavish trips abroad—to Europe, Asia, the Middle East—while Elías and I were left with an endless number of nannies and enrolled in day schools where teachers struggled hopelessly to integrate us into the classroom. Mama insisted that we attend Jewish school, and so my grandparents sent us to Escuela Yavneh, where Elías stayed until his graduation. I, instead, was a more troublesome case and was transferred to various other schools. My last two years of high school were at Colegio Israelita, in Colonia Narvarete.

My adolescence was thoroughly influenced by what I lived through in Mexico. We lived in the Polanco district, not far from Chapultepec Park, where the wealthy Jewish community ostentatiously parades its riches. As a result of Papa's breakdown, I felt a deep need to understand his past—and my Jewishness. But my surroundings offered me few clues. Those who surrounded me were not inclined to intellectual reflection. Even the holiday of Yom Kippur was performed in a theatrical, treacherous fashion: it was more about high fashion than about atonement and repentance; in the main synagogue of Acapulco No. 70, where Mama took me and my brother, Jews would show up in fancy leather jackets and expensive cars. I was thirsty for knowledge about the Holocaust, but since Mexico had only marginally participated in World War II, there was no serious debate about its tragic consequences. As a result, my longing to unravel Papa's dementia only deepened.

In my late teens, I began to socialize only with non-Jews, especially with a dance troupe I got acquainted with, whose rehearsals took place in the Teatro de la Danza, behind the Auditorio Nacional. I also got involved in a theater workshop directed by Hugo Hiriart. (He first introduced me to Ilan Stavans). My first literary attempts were sophomoric poems I published in a magazine put out by a small group of Jewish dissidents, Odradek, a title inspired by an imaginary animal invented by Franz Kafka.

Then I traveled to London, Spain, Rome, and, eventually, Israel. Mama had by then remarried—a non-Jew, a mechanic whose overwhelming love for her made him go through a painful conversion to Judaism that included the ritual of circumcision at thirty-seven years of age—and Elías was enrolled in engineering school at the Universidad Nacional Autónoma de México. I had saved some money while working at a multimedia company, putting together audiovisual shows for big companies like Coca-Cola and Kodak. In London I stayed at a friend's apartment. My friend's mother was a high-powered set designer in the West End, and she took us to parties and cocktails and introduced me to Harold Pinter and Eugène Ionesco. I was so impressed by Ionesco, a Romanian absurdist, that I began reading everything he had ever written. I even memorized The Bald Soprano in full.

I had the good fortune, during one of his short stays in London, to work for him as an assistant for a couple of summer weeks, organizing his papers and correspondence. Thanks to Ionesco I came to understand the true purpose of art: to fluster and disturb, to do what reality had forced on Papa—an explosion!

I stayed a total of fifteen months in Europe. In Las Ramblas of Barcelona, I became reacquainted with my mother's family. And by sheer accident I met Ilan Stavans again, first in Toledo and then in Salamanca, at the home of a mutual friend whose name I again cannot invoke but whose generosity is long-lasting. On my departure, he gave Stavans and me a copy of the same book, Enrique de Murger's *Escenas de la vida de Bohemia* (Scenes of Bohemian Life). I still have my copy, with its solid red hardcover and embossed golden title and the following Spanish inscription:

!*Adios, Cruel Tierra Inconstante!*
Azote humano, sol helado
Cual solitaria alma errante
Inadvertido habré pasado.

Good-bye, Cruel Inconstant World!
Human scourge, frozen sun
A solitary errant soul
I will have passed unnoticed.

At that time Stavans and Zuri Balkoff, a BBC correspondent, had begun to conceive their collaborative novel, *Talia in Heaven*, and we talked about the plot and its ramifications in detail. When I left them, Stavans promised to send me a copy in six months, but he took over three years. I was dumbfounded by it: much of what we had jointly imagined had materialized, described in a meticulous, almost mathematical prose. With lightning speed, I wrote a preface, and the volume was finally published in 1989.

In Italy I wandered around from one museum exhibit to another, adding to my diary, drafting possible short stories, without a goal in sight. I wandered until my money ran out. It is at that point that I decided that, rather than return to Mexico, where no one waited for me, I would wander a bit more. And so I took a boat across the Mediterranean to Greece and on to Haifa. I arrived in 1975, shortly after the spaceship *Voyager* was launched into orbit and before Israeli commandos rescued a hijacked Air France plane in Entebbe, Uganda. Israel for me was a revelation. Papa had considered making *aliyah*, immigrating to Palestine, but changed his mind and instead traveled to Central America. Thus from my arrival on, I was struck by what his life would have been had he opted for the first choice. For one thing, I wouldn't have been alive; fate is nothing but a chain of accidents. This casualty concerned me far less, though, than the landscape I was witnessing: natural and human. The soil felt as if it was mine; I sensed that I had belonged to it long before I had arrived. At a volunteer office, I was placed in Ma'ale ha-Chamisha, a kibbutz not far from Jerusalem, where I began cleaning the kitchen and milking cows. These menial jobs would have been unacceptable to me in Mexico, but in Israel I was prepared to do them without complaint. After all, the kibbutzniks immediately embraced me as one of theirs; they realized I was a wandering soul in need of permanent shelter. And that, precisely, is what they gave me.

I lived in the kibbutz almost seven years, becoming part of the larger family. Mama and Elías came to visit me on occasion. I kept writing in Spanish while, at the same time, I immersed myself in an Ulpan to learn Hebrew. This made my redemption all the more complete. Hebrew for me is a tongue of spirituality, much more solid than Spanish or any other Diaspora language. Recently, at the request of my friend David Grossman, I have begun writing in it—a piece for *Ma'ariv*, a story, not much. I've learned its syntax well, but I confess to still feeling alien to it. The tongue became more pedestrian, less elevated in

1979, with my brief three-year marriage to a kibbutz member. My daughter Yael Bathya was born in 1980. I brought her to Mexico with me when she was two. My divorce was painful, if anything because my ex-husband was always around—working the fields, chatting at breakfast in the cafeteria, organizing the self-defense squads. Grossman, although not a kibbutznik, has been quite supportive. Hearing him talk about Jewish literature in the privacy of an afternoon walk, particularly about the work of Eastern Europeans, is a source of inspiration.

It is during those difficult months that most of my novel *El espejo del espejo: o, La noble sonrisa del perro* was written. The fragmented plot circles around the misadventures of a girl lost in a battlefield. The ubiquitous public images of Israeli independence and the Six-Day War stuck in my mind. But the mood of the volume is much more introspective and reflexive. I conceived it as the search for a lost father figure, a meditation on pain and desolation. It was released in 1983. I had sent it to Salomón Laiter, a novelist friend in Mexico. He embraced it from the beginning and persuaded the publisher Joaquín Diez Canedo to bring it out. My gratitude is immense.

1982–1995

I returned with Yael to Mexico to promote it and stayed with Mama and her new husband in the Tecamachalco district. I had intended my visit to be brief, but it ended up lasting half a decade. Money was not an issue since my maternal grandfather had died a year before, and both my brother Elías and I had each inherited a large sum of money. With it I bought an apartment in Colonia Hipódromo, not far from my grandmother, and a pied-à-terre in Jerusalem. I began to socialize with Esther Seligson. And I tried to write more.

Literature for me is a most strenuous, painful endeavor. It takes me months, at times years, to complete a short story. Thus as I look back at *The Mirror's Mirror* I am astonished by how quickly it was born— thirteen months all together. Critics have compared it to Borges and Calvino, but I trust it is closer to the oeuvre of Isaiah Spiegel, the inimitable Ida Fink, and Lamed Shapiro, in particular, the scene in which Teresa is raped and "savaged" by an enemy soldier. The novel was born during an in-between period sparked by inspiration, one from which I've never been able to recuperate. I suffer from a terrifying inferiority complex: as soon as I finish a tale, I'm convinced of its worthlessness; and so, I tear it up. Each word, each comma emerged out of a deep struggle with forces within that I'm unable to control. As a result, I have often tried to give up writing, but I can't; I need literature as much as I need food and love. I write to explain the ghosts of my past, to come to terms with Papa's tragic existence and its aftermath; I write to understand the coincidences that have made me who I am. My fiction, consequently, is always about origins and about the magic that surrounds us. In 1987, after a long struggle and just before I resettled in Israel, I finished *Intoxicada*. Many of the stories in this volume began as novels, but I simply gave them up: their images were too excruciating, too sharp. That readers can identify with them puzzles me but also satisfies me: What ought we to do with pain if not transform it into art? Isn't that the only way to overcome suffering? What does silence mean for a writer? When Primo Levi is told by a Gestapo soldier at Auschwitz, "There is no 'why' here!" what ought the survivor do if not turn the why into a statement on the possibilities of life? I have returned to Guatemala once or twice in my adulthood. My only purpose: to look for traces of Papa. Elías had a vague recollection of the name of the ward he had been sent to: Florista or Floresta; but it proved to be mistaken. I returned to our hacienda: it had been abandoned since the late seventies, when a guerrilla group had kidnapped an important businessman in the neighborhood and dropped his body a few blocks away. I wandered from one psychiatric hospital to another looking for clues. But I found none. Not only had he abandoned me, he had been swallowed by anonymity.

I began studying the *Sefer ha-Zohar* with Esther Seligson. She introduced me to Angelina Muñiz-Huberman, whose teaching opened my eyes to Mexico's Sephardic ancestry. Her volume *Enclosed Garden* opened my eyes to a universe inside me. In 1989 I brought Yael back to Ma'ale ha-Chamisha. Soon after, I began studying Cabala in earnest at various yeshivas. Judaism has a derogating approach to women: we are wise when it comes to earthly knowledge but inept in intellectual matters. Time and again my studies were interrupted by obstructing rabbis refusing to allow me to sit at their learning rooms. But orthodox women are not as passive as secular Jews want to believe; they organize themselves, and so I got involved in a number of marginal learning groups. As I immerse myself in religious matters, I realize how literary the Jewish religion is: the written word is sacred, and the mysteries of the universe are all hidden in it. Not only is the Bible filled with extraordinary tales, but so is the work of G-d's progeny— the Talmud and Gemara. My own books are filled with anecdotes, but they are deficient in style and structure. I often wished I had not written them. Silence, I often think, is my true language.

And yet, I write . . . Alone, to myself. I write in spite of all the suffering it unravels. And I will continue to do so even if I don't ever show the product to others. In all honesty, I might never bring out another book again. Still, literature places me firmly on the ground. It gives weight to my being. Not surprisingly, I find it quite difficult to stay in a single place for long: in 1993, after Mama died of breast cancer, I sold my apartment in Mexico; and since then I've also sold the pied-à-terre in Jerusalem. Only in literature I find a home—silent, eclipsed, but a home nonetheless. Last time I saw Angelina Muñiz-Huberman in Israel, in 1991, I asked her: Is writing worth the effort?

"Perhaps not," she replied. "But do we have a choice?"

"Silence," I responded.

"Nature is silent . . . words are human. And only words can be *personalized*."

She is right: To write is to erupt.

Translated by Ilan Stavans

Marjorie Agosín
Chile/United States

Marjorie Agosín (1955–) is fierce, and she is caring. With great courage, she personally aided those who challenged the Pinochet dictatorship in Chile, and she worked to support the Mothers of the Plaza de Mayo in Argentina. She uses her poetry as a weapon in the struggle. In other poems, Agosín deals with love: sensual, filial, maternal. Her poetry is built from memory and dream. She has the easy ability to move from reality to a dreamlike state, to remember bits and fragments that are infused with meaning and mood. The poems of *Querida Anne Frank* (Dear Anne Frank), *Hogueras/Bonfires,* and many other collections and the stories of *La felicidad* (Happiness) are written with a scorching intensity.

A devoted feminist, Agosín has actively fought for women's rights on two continents; she writes and is an anthologist of Latin American women's literature. She has written autobiographies of both her mother and her father. These fictionalized prose works are filled with warmth but do not downplay the pernicious anti-Semitism of the transplanted Nazis who controlled life in isolated Osorno, Chile, where they lived. While not religious, she is dedicated to Judaism.

Marjorie Agosín is a fireball of energy, amazingly prolific, and also helpful to other writers: she has edited several anthologies of their work. Her own writing, which is difficult to characterize, is found in anthologies of Jewish writers, Latin American writers, Jewish Latin American writers, women writers, feminist writers, and many more. She is professor of Spanish at Wellesley College.

Looking back at moments both shocking and uplifting, Marjorie Agosín wrote this lyrical essay expressly for this anthology.

THROUGH A FIELD OF STARS, I REMEMBER

Marjorie Agosín

In the mornings the sparrows encircle a sky that fills me with wonder. Through beloved objects I greet the Andean mountain range as well as the mutterings of Carmencita with her shawls as grey as the smoke that emanates from her freckled and beautiful skin. Carmen Carrasco gathers the golden leaves with a broom and frightens away the sparrows, omens of uncertainties, with her jet-black braid, while I get dressed to attend the school for English girls on the first day of class.

The school is only four blocks from my house. We lived in Nuñoa, one of the oldest districts in Santiago, a modest neighborhood across from the meat market that my father detested. The butcher, however, took care of us whenever we got sick, by always giving us the best cut of meat. This was in the year 1960, in my country, Chile, a long, strange, and beautiful piece of land.

Perhaps Ms. Stewart chose to have a school on Coventry Street because it reminded her of the cathedral of the same name and also of one of those elegant districts in her beloved England. Ms. Stewart spoke like a refined lady from the upper class, and on that first day of school the sky seemed like a great lightning bolt confusing itself with the late afternoon.

My mother decided to bring us to school through those endless city blocks filled with old grandmothers buying bread and dreaming about lost youth. What I most remember and loved were the almonds and chestnuts scattered on the ground. Whenever I would get sad or frightened by the deep physical grief of absence, I remembered the almonds, the aromas and life on those four streets, and the ladies singing *boleros* while they swept the sidewalks dressed in black and oblivion. When we finally arrived at the immense iron door that said "Welcome to the Union School," a very skinny woman with a voice that was both devilish and angelic received us and asked us all sorts of questions. Her legs were very close together and I wondered if she needed to pee. She wanted to know what our religion was, and my mother, with her usual composure and grace, said, "Jewish." The very thin lady fidgeted and asked again, "Jewish?" as if to assure herself that we indeed belonged to that accursedly "chosen" race. Then she looked at us and said, "But you are so blond and your noses are so small!" My mother in turn responded, "Yes, even Hitler would confuse us and mistake us for Aryans." The woman wrote the word "JEW" in enormous red letters and said that I was excused from religious class. This saddened me because I wanted to hear the stories about that gentleman who rose to heaven. These were the last words spoken by that thin lady. Afterward my mother left me alone and at that English school, where my neighbors also attended, they taught us to carefully raise our skirts and curtsey.

Time passed haphazardly with a sweet tedious rhythm. At first the other children played with me, but gradually, as I stayed behind in the school's only playground, the girls began to whisper, since I wasn't allowed to attend religious class. I heard them say a multitude of things, among them, a painful chorus of "'She is Jewish. She is Jewish. She is Jewish."

One afternoon they made up a chant and said that Jews could not participate in it. They began to sing: "Who ate the bread in the oven? The Jewish girls, the Jewish girls. Who is the rotten thief? The Jewish dog, of course, the Jewish dog." For many afternoons that song was like a stinging wound in my young girl's ears. When they sang, my head felt like it was ablaze with flames and evil omens. Sometimes I looked at them incredulously, asking myself if dogs could have a religion.

I thus returned home crestfallen and dreaming about the almonds and chestnuts that I would gather along the way, hoping to find Carmen grumbling because we had arrived late or had stained our clothes with dirt and acted like mischievous children. One afternoon when my mother was combing the long hair of my Viennese grandmother, Helena, the one who never learned to speak Spanish and who sang and prayed in beautiful Yiddish and German cadences, I told my mother about the song and about the girls who mocked me on their way to Catechism.

My mother didn't say a word. Instead, she decided to go to the school to speak with the director. There she was received coldly. After all was said and done, it was a well-known fact that I was the only Jewish girl in the English school, the only one who didn't eat pork, who didn't make Christmas cards, and the only one who didn't have a First Communion.

Oh, how I dreamed about that white dress with angel wings! I didn't have any of these things. I did, however, possess a past, a history and the dates of sacred rituals that commemorated the lives of dead sisters without graves, with only imaginary stones and imaginary relatives.

The director of the school made my mother sit on a small, cracked wooden bench that wasn't in the living room, where she received important visits. When my mother asked her how she could allow the girls to sing that perfidious song, the director said that it was a part of Chilean lore, that it was sung in all the schools throughout the nation and that this was how things were, impossible to change! My mother asked why they didn't sing about the Christian or Moslem dogs. The director wrinkled her brow and then showed her the exit. Dismissed from school, I despondently followed my mother. She dried my tears and arranged my hair the way all mothers do with their children. She also rinsed my cheeks with her kisses and I suddenly sensed a smell of almonds and chestnuts in the air as we returned home listless, silent, and certain about our heritage.

The next day I went to another school. This time all the children were Jews, and for sure their dogs were also Jewish but not because of this, thieves who stole bread from the oven. I was happy at the Hebrew Institute where there were no iron gates or young ladies teaching us how to curtsey. Ms. Stewart was the true beginning of my Jewish education and of anti-Semitism in Chile. She taught me that I would always have to defend myself for not participating in religious classes, in the Order of Saint Teresa, or in those activities or groups to which good upper-class obedient girls belonged. But wasn't I also a good girl? Why couldn't I be like the others? Why did they spit at me whenever I waited outside? I carried my religion like a question, and I also carried within me the names of my dead relatives and of those who arrived in my country on freighters. One of them was my grandfather Joseph, Helena's son, who fled from a cabaret dancer, and others were refugees like my uncle Mordecai who had fled from the Gestapo. Whenever I would rush to my grandmother Helena's side, she would tell me that it was necessary to say sweet words in order to ease the hollowness of the grief.

The Hebrew Institute was established in the fifties by the small Jewish community of Santiago. It was always outstanding because of the wisdom and high intellectual standards of its teachers. The time that I attended the school, it was truly "liberal" in the broadest sense of the term (progressive Christians also went there). We didn't learn about the miracles of Zionism but rather about life in the kibbutz. We also learned about social justice, prudence, and the benefits of socialism.

My years at the Hebrew Institute were happy ones. My sister and I would wake up cheerfully very early to go to school. We would drink coffee with milk and eat toast with avocado pear jelly. At that time, happiness for us consisted in waking up to the joys and rigor of everyday life, to the sounds of Carmencita or the sparrows. Our father would bring us to school at daybreak, around seven o'clock because his chemistry classes at the medical school at the University of Chile began before eight. On the way to school, he would talk to himself out loud and repeat equations and strange formulas. In the backseat of the car my sister and I would spend the time counting the houses and imagining the lives of the men and women who lived in them.

The Hebrew Institute was in the neighborhood of Macul, a modest district of Santiago, very close to the Pedagogical Institute, which had one of the country's most politicized student centers. I liked looking at the sixty or so bearded men and the women dressed in black making peace signs and marching through the plush avenues. On numerous occasions we stayed late at the school because there were disturbances at the center, and the police exercised their usual violence against the young idealistic students, many dreamers among them.

Political action, denunciation, and apprenticeship were the sacred lessons of my childhood. The despicable Union School had been left behind. Now I was among Jews like myself and together with everyone I studied the Talmud, the Torah with its charms and wise advice, the poetry of Bialik and Sachs, and the stories of Selma Legerloff. In elementary school, I was an avid reader of poetry and fantasies, exploring the rich world of the imagination. Perhaps I always wanted to retain the illusion and sense of permanence in the world and of ways to dwell in it. Poetry was my closest companion. I loved words, those in Spanish as much as Hebrew, and I spoke both languages fluently.

My first great literary acknowledgment occurred when one of my poems was published in Jerusalem in the Sephardic newspaper, *Aurora Sfarad*. Another poem was published in a newspaper on Easter Island and a leper wrote me a letter after reading it. Poetry was like fate. It saved me. Words for me were like rituals, always sweet and generous. Mathematics betrayed me and numbers danced in my head. I was only interested in the number seven, in the principles of the Cabala and in alchemy. Logical and official symbols never entered my world. I let myself be guided by fantasy and intuition. This is why I survived by writing. What was the outside world like, where I existed as a thirteen-year-old Jewish girl in a Hebrew school? The truth is that the outside world did not at all appear strange to me. My Jewish education gave me an identity and life, but more than anything it gave me the possibility to love those of my neighbors who differed from me. The diversity emerging from Catholic, Protestant, and Jewish cultures was an integral part of my childhood. Refugees from the Nazi Holocaust and from Central America frequently arrived at my door, both in Chile and in the U.S.A. Among them were biochemists, beggars, and people of royal blood, like the famous and honorable Baron von Brand, my father's teacher. I remember that when he visited us I curtsied as I had learned to do at the Union School, but afterward I sang to him in Hebrew.

The great upheaval of my adolescent life occurred when we left Chile in the early seventies. Totalitarianism was looming on the horizon. My father's laboratory was shut down in 1971 because despite his being a man of profoundly liberal ideas and a true socialist, he received money from the Rockefeller Foundation, a Yankee enterprise, to finance his magical investigation of enzymes and mellifluous formulas. Unable to work because of the threatening phone call he received for being Jewish or for supposedly "selling out to Yankee Imperialism," we felt obliged to leave the country. We traveled to another southern American region, Georgia, where I learned to speak with a drawl and

I also discovered that the majority of North Americans, southerners in particular, were terrified by strangers and "communists." I was a stranger and my entire family fulfilled the eternal tradition or curse of the diasporic Jew.

If my experience as a Jew in Chile was both disquieting and luminous, in the United States, I felt more and more an outsider and not a kindred spirit to those who belonged to the Jewish community in Georgia. During the first years after our arrival as poor immigrants, when we lived in empty houses with loaned furniture, we weren't even greeted by other Jews in the synagogue because everyone was obsessed with Russian Jews and we were from Latin America.

At that time I remembered how we had been treated by Ms. Stewart. Now in our new home in North America, I was not only a Jew but a Latin American Jew, which implied to others, less dignity. Gradually my parents kept a respectful distance from the Jewish community of Georgia. To this very day they still do not belong to the temple in their city. They have found comfort and solidarity among Colombian and Puerto Rican Catholics who share friendship and faith with goodwill.

I also distanced myself from that community, and I missed not being able to speak Hebrew, the language of my first poems and passions. Nevertheless, I understood that now I was a Latina and not that Jewish girl that they had called me in Chile. I also learned that oppression and pain go much further than the color of one's skin.

The years in Georgia passed by aimlessly, and I quickly found myself speaking in English and reading Shakespeare in a language I grew to love. I was also lonely because in school they would say: "Don't talk to her. She is a Latina and also a Jew." The horrors of discrimination marked my childhood in Chile and adolescence in the U.S.A, but I wore both my Judaism and my *latinismo* like a deep blue shawl. I wore it with peace and dignity. My education at the Hebrew School was my most powerful weapon for defending myself against universal prejudice. Judaism and the diasporic condition of my family became an emblematic metaphor for lost and irrecoverable things. They also came to represent all that was worthless, because the gift of wisdom was in the ability to understand and forgive the ignorance of others. From the United States, I passionately and profoundly began to love my country, to know her and embrace her. Perhaps I loved Chile even more than when I was living in it. It was akin to recognizing the love one feels toward a mother only after abandoning her. This is how my country became part of the baggage of lost things that I carried to other places. Many times in other lands and mist-laden cities, I wrote her name in territories that also didn't belong to me. My human rights activism in Chile coincided with my passion for always forming alliances with marginal beings. I sensed myself as one of them. In the United States, in spite of my being blond and white, I had a Hispanic accent, and I was Jewish, which made things difficult. I became a fragile and vulnerable being. However, from this other America I had the most exquisite opportunity of my life—to develop intellectually and to go to libraries, to explore, to learn and to be aware.

I was accepted at many universities and behind their doors I found young people who shared an alliance with those Chileans who fought with pencils and paper and disappeared and died for wishing to be free. The experience of not having been one of "them," of not having disappeared, had an immense impact on my conception of the world. I was a survivor who must not succumb to a silence of complicity. Nor could I ever say, "I don't know anything about this. I don't want to say anything about this." Not doing anything was as good as being guilty. It was like being part of that amalgam of ordinary people who perform evil acts.

I spoke through my writing. This was the site of my identity. I refused to feign the grief of others and also refused to imagine the torture, the terror, the slashed body. I only wanted to hear so that I could tell. Many of my verses and poetry collections, like *Zones of Pain/Las zonas del dolor* and *Circles of Madness/Círculos de la locura,* arose from the experience of hearing the testimonies of victims or of the disappeared or of the relatives of disappeared citizens. Their voices accompany me in the heavy insomnia of the night or in the luminosity of peaceful days.

When I reached so-called maturity and my voice began to change, my walk became more deliberate and my anger transformed into a map of hope, I finally understood what my grandfather naturally showed me in actions but never told me in words: the fact that one must live at the service of others as well as with them. My political activism for the voiceless had certain resonances in the work of my beloved grandfather, Joseph Halpern, in southern Chile and also in Santiago during the years 1938–43. At that time he devoted himself to gathering refugees who would come to our humble house in the south where the Sabbath candles were always lighted. This is how Kurt Goldshmild, Annie and Sharie Brinner, and Emma Weiss arrived. Their names are already a part of my history, of my life here in Wellesley where I also open the doors of my home to others in search of refuge.

It is difficult being a Jew and a Latina, but it is also quite marvelous to belong to a people with a long and wise history, a people who believe in the passion of memory and who carry the Torah and do everything possible to act justly. Perhaps I am following in the footsteps laid down by the Ten Commandments delivered by Moses, the patriarch, and also those of my father, Moses. Above all else, I have tried to fight against all types of foolish fanaticism. I have also tried to fight against the commercialism of certain Jewish communities, making Judaism a metaphor of human life that struggles against intolerance.

My son has the name of his great-grandfather Joseph, who saved refugees and met them at the station, and my daughter has the names of her great-grandmothers, Sonia from Odessa and Helena from Vienna. By naming my son and daughter after the patriarch and the matriarchs of the family, I sense their presence like a fragrance, a thread of memories in our lives.

Although my early years were defined by that ominous incident at the Union School, today the planet seems more gentle and benevolent. I wear my Star of David not so that others will point at me but so that I can share my identity with a courageous and persecuted people who left the smoking forests behind and made life flourish in the desert.

Sometimes, at my home in Wellesley, I go out at night and look at the sky. I don't see the stars of the Southern Hemisphere, but I imagine them close to my soul as I hear a voice that says, "Your people will multiply like the stars in the heavens." This planet is inhabited by my people. I am a Latin American Jewish woman among many other things. I know the *Our Father* and the *Shema*. Above all, I am a woman who delights in thinking that it is through words that I can reach the stars.

Translated by Celeste Kostopulos-Cooperman

Ruth Behar
Cuba/United States

Ruth Behar (1956—) is a poet and a professor of anthropology at the University of Michigan, and so practices two methods of studying the human spirit. She has been enormously successful in both areas: she has won major fellowships for her academic work and wide admiration for her poetic insights about everyday life and Jewish identity. Behar is an acute observer who appreciates what she sees while also watching herself. She has won both a MacArthur "Genius" Fellowship and a Guggenheim Fellowship. Her studies have focused on village life in Spain and Mexico and on relations between Cubans in the United States and Cuba.

With an Ashkenazi mother from Eastern Europe and a Sephardic father from Turkey, Ruth Behar embodies both halves of the Jewish Diaspora. She is a Cuban-American who came to the United States as a child and grew up in a kaleidoscope of cultures: Jewish (both European and Turkish versions), Cuban, and American. Though a native speaker of Spanish, she tends to write her poetry as well as her scholarly work in English. Her poetry, not surprisingly, deals with the experience of exile from a country that she hardly knew but to which so many of her family friends want to return, as well as the difficulty of fitting into (and being accepted into) a society so different from that of her childhood.

Ruth Behar's essay on family, exile, and adjustment was published previously in *Poetics Today*.

JUBAN AMÉRICA

Ruth Behar

Shortly before his death in Miami Beach in 1987, my maternal grandfather, Maximo Glinsky, stapled an old photograph to a small piece of cardboard. On the cardboard, by way of explanation, he wrote, *"Recuerdo de Linka de a donde yo nació en 1901, esto era nuestra casa y atras un jardin verde."* His words were intended for his descendants, now living English-speaking lives in North America: "Souvenir of Linka, where I was born in 1901, this was our house with its garden in back." The picture, indeed, shows a house, or something rather more like a homestead. Three boys in knickers and hats, their faces dim and indistinct, cluster together just off-center; perhaps one of them was my grandfather. The ground is covered with snow.

As a good archivist and granddaughter, I have had this image carefully mounted on acid-free cardboard, put under glass and framed with simple, etched wood. Naturally, I removed the staples, which were beginning to rust. The picture now hangs in a quiet domestic space, above our used, $150 mahogany piano, where I sit almost every night with my kindergarten-age son, Gabriel, begging him to practice his lessons. I had wanted terribly to learn piano as a child during the years after we arrived in the United States from Cuba, but my parents told me they didn't have the space or the money; besides, they thought it wiser for me to learn to play a more portable instrument like the accordion or the guitar, an instrument you could take anywhere. I could not understand then how for my parents, who were in their late twenties when they decided to leave Cuba in 1961, all sense of permanence had been ruptured. Although they were themselves children of immigrants, they had never expected to have to leave Cuba, *nunca me ha ido*, I have never left. A piano in the drawing room— that, for me, is the epitome of a settled, bourgeois existence: the life of people whose citizenship documents are in order and who therefore have no reason to harbor an immigrant's fears, the life of people who don't expect a revolution to occur overnight and challenge their hold on the things of the world. And yet, what if, at a moment's notice, I had to leave? What would I take with me? I think of the picture above the piano, which traveled through two exiles, from Russia to Cuba and from Cuba to America. That picture, which by itself would have said very little, became, with the addition of my grandfather's words, an image of displacement, of deterritorialization.

The image-text harks back to a lost home in Byelorussia, the old country. That this home is undeniably lost is evident not only in my grandfather's use of the past tense, but in the fact that he tells the story of its loss in Spanish, which became the language of his reterritorialization in the New World. The brief, seemingly uncomplicated statement that my grandfather inscribed under the photograph of his birthplace, in which he locates himself as a minority speaker of Spanish, is redolent with politics and history. His Spanish embodies too many contradictions of territoriality and deterritorialization.[1]

As any educated speaker of Spanish knows, my grandfather's text reflects a nonstandard use of the language. Following the Yiddish usage, he disregarded the difference between the first and third person, using the grammatically incorrect "yo nació" instead of the proper "yo naci." It seems eerie to me that he placed himself in the interface between the first person and the third person, as if already imagining himself no longer here in the world of the living, no longer speaking as "I" but being spoken of, by someone else, as "he," already edging toward the third person of biography, of the narrator, of his own granddaughter's text.

Spanish was not my grandfather's "mother tongue." He was a stepson of the language, yet he claimed it as his own. He spoke Spanish to his children and grandchildren; the Yiddish that he spoke with my grandmother and others of their generation failed to get passed on, while English, learned in a second exile, never entered his veins. My relationship with my grandfather, a man of the Jewish European Old World, was lived entirely in Spanish. To be more exact, it was lived in a combination of Spanish and silence. My grandfather did not talk very much. He was suspicious of people who talked too much. He spoke telegraphically. His most memorable utterances were his jokes, tellable only in Spanish, a Spanish that showed a stepson's tenuous kinship to the language. His jokes were really questions, such as "*¿Cómo ando?*" to which he would answer, "*Con los pies*"; or "*¿Cómo te sientes?*" to which the reply was, "*En la silla.*" These jokes—which were also the actual replies that he'd give when asked the Spanish equivalent of "How are you?"—encoded his refusal to say how he was "doing," his refusal to admit that he was "fine, thank you."

It is these refusals, so characteristic of how he spoke and didn't speak, that make me think my grandfather was acutely conscious that his was a colonized voice. The "sound" of a colonized voice, it seems to me, carries traces of the effort to resist speaking, to resist speaking "as usual." The locus of enunciation is challenged before any speaking can even occur. For the colonized speaker, language is never taken for granted; you cannot go into automatic drive. My grandfather's literal enunciations served as a continual brake on our becoming too comfortable in the language of our colonization, and yet, curiously, these enunciations were so thoroughly rooted in Spanish idiomatic phrases as to be untranslatable. *Después de todo,* Spanish was my grand-father's language, in much the same convoluted way that it is mine now.

As a Russian, Yiddish-speaking immigrant, my grandfather learned Spanish in his early twenties after arriving in Cuba in 1924. He was one among thousands of Jews from Southern and Eastern Europe who were fleeing the legacy of pogroms and the difficult economic conditions that arose in the aftermath of World War I and the collapse of the Hapsburg and Ottoman empires, then the rise of nationalist ideologies increasingly threatened, and undermined, Jewish life. After the United States severely limited Eastern European emigration with its 1924 Immigration and Naturalization Act, a growing number of Jews were forced to imagine a future for themselves in the other America south of the border (Elkin; Elkin and Merks). Some Latin American countries, such as Argentina, seeking to whiten their population and find agricultural settlers to make their lands productive, had encouraged Jewish emigration since the turn of the century. But as conditions worsened in Europe, especially by the late 1930s, the U.S. government acted with supreme hypocrisy, pressuring Latin American countries to absorb the thousands of desperate Jewish emigrants who were being systematically prevented from entering the America north of the border.

Cuba, then a backyard colony of the United States, came under particularly strong pressure to take in Jews and, by 1938, had a Jewish population of about 16,500, most of whom settled in Havana, but with about 3,500 scattered among provincial cities and rural towns. In the years when Nazi power was being consolidated and Jews were attempting to flee Europe to any country that would have them, Cuba became the center of a lucrative traffic in visas, landing permits, and other immigration papers. Travel agents bought permits from Cuban officials and then resold them in Europe for three and four times the amount they had paid. Most of these permits left their holders in limbo, allowing them only to land in Cuba and remain there until they had secured a visa to the United States. As the traffic in Jewish cargo intensified, some xenophobic American observers became concerned that too many Jews were illicitly entering the United States via Cuba. In a strictly confidential document on "European Refugees in Cuba" written in 1939, a consular official warned the authorities in Washington that "Cuba has long been a base from which aliens are smuggled into the United States." These "aliens," he explained, gained entrance into the country "by means of false visas, Cuban citizenship documents, passports, and birth certificates; by smuggling as stowaways on vessels, by smuggling in small boats hired for the purpose; and attempts have been made to smuggle by airplane" (qtd. in Levine 60).

Many Jewish emigrants had initially viewed Cuba as a way station, the route to the United States. After all, wasn't America only ninety miles away. Yet that America which was so omnipresent as a colonial power was, when it pleased, so conveniently distant. By the late 1930s, the goal of gaining entrance to the America across the border became less and less urgent for the many Jews who had made tropical lives for themselves, after awakening to the realization that Cuba was to be their America. Jewish Cuban intellectuals came to identify not only with José Martí's stance against racism, but with his dialectics of "Our America" versus "the America which is not ours," the America of the U.S. empire (Martí; Fernández Retamar; Saldívar). The Cuban Hebrew Cultural Society even sponsored a forum on Martí, as seen from a Jewish perspective (Matterin). When the outlook for Jews in Europe had grown dim, those who found a second home in Cuba, even if it was not quite the America of their expectations, had reason to be grateful. The Jews who stayed in Cuba became "Jewish Robinson Crusoes" (Elkin 88 [quoting Sander M. Kaplan]), stranded by a twist of fate on an island that many years later, from their second exile in the United States after the Cuban Revolution, they would remember nostalgically as a paradise lost. In the words of the Jewish Cuban poet Sarah Luski:

> Will I again one day, dear Cuba
> Or will I spend the rest of my life in exile
> Longing for your sky, your beautiful beaches
> Oh Cuba! My native land. (qtd. in Oberstein 4)

As a result of the Cuban Revolution, those same Jewish "aliens" whom the consular official in 1939 had feared would smuggle themselves into the United States, concealing their "true" Jewishness behind the mask of a "false" Cuban identity, crossed the border into America after all. History repeated itself in an ironic way: the second time around, the Jews of Cuba gained entrance into America as Cubans, not as Jews. Fidel Castro called the Cubans who deserted the island, rather than work to build the revolutionary state, *gusanos*. The Cuban Jews in the United States were doubly "wormy": not only had they abandoned the Revolution, as earlier, in the 1940s and 1950s, many had abandoned their Jewish-Communist ideals when they ceased being peddlers and became deproletarianized members of the Cuban middle class (Bejarano),[2] but they had also made their way into the U.S. body politic as Cuban refugees. Once in America, they would always have to explain that they were Cubans who also "happened" to be Jewish.

I need to interrupt this third-person historical interlude to speak, again, as "yo," at least momentarily. Like my grandfather, I keep wanting to situate myself somewhere between the third-person plural and the first-person singular. Indeed, "yo nació" seems exactly right for getting at the peculiar confluence of identity that is implied in the idea of being Jewish-Cuban, or "Juban," as they say in Miami. It has taken me a long time to reach an obvious conclusion: I am *cubana* because I am Jewish. I am *cubana* because my grandparents were unwanted cargo that could not be delivered to the United States. I am *cubana* because the border between "our America" and "the America which is not ours" is a real border guarded by guns and decorated with ink. If I am now welcome in the America which is not mine, it is because of my value as symbolic capital, as one of the human spoils of the victory of U.S. capitalism over impudent Cuban socialism. My parents taught me to be grateful that we ended up with the *yanquis* because in Cuba I'd be wearing clunky shoes and being told what to study. *Hay que dale, gracias a este país* (we have to thank this country) was the incantation I heard all the years I was growing up. So I can't claim too much *cubanidad* for myself. My feet have worn out plenty of good leather, and I've studied what I've pleased. My documents are in order. I'm a legal alien, and I have an American passport that warns me, "Certain transactions involving travel to Cuba are prohibited."

On the day I swore my allegiance to the United States, the woman who had examined me on my knowledge of American presidents while chain-smoking in a dingy office offered me a tempting proposition: I could change my name. It wouldn't cost anything extra. No easier time to change your name than when you're being "naturalized," she told me. I was eleven at the time and felt as though this woman had bestowed immense power upon me. I didn't even consult my parents; I immediately told her to erase that other name of mine, my middle name. I was a child who had been plopped into a New York public school without knowing a word of English, and there was nothing that filled my soul with as much fear as the thought of being ridiculed. I was terrified that one of my schoolmates would discover my middle name on some official slip of paper and make my life insufferable. That name was a deep, dark secret that the insecure immigrant child felt compelled to hide in feeble protection of her dignity. And so, whenever I'm asked my middle name, I always say I don't have one. This name that I refused, I learned much later, was my grandfather's mother's name. She had been killed in her bed in Byelorussia by Nazi soldiers;

that was the story that reached my grandfather in Cuba years afterward. Her name was Fiegele, which means "little bird" in Yiddish, and in Cuba that name became Fanny, pronounced with a soft vowel sound. But for a chubby immigrant girl in America, that name was unredeemable. I'd become Fay-with-the-fat-fanny, forever and ever. It was already bad enough that I'd been made excessively conscious of that part of my body by *el grupo,* whose home movies of Castro's triumphal procession into Havana were punctuated with flashes of female backsides. On the edge of adolescence, I was only too glad to be able to strip myself of a name that would have made me even more distressingly aware of my budding sexuality. There seemed no way to liberate the name Fanny from its embarrassing American translation and fly with it—so I clipped my wings. In Mexico there are those candy skulls on sale for the Day of the Dead, with names like Vicente, Alfredo, Antonia, Catalina, and Esperanza taped onto their foreheads. When I have the blues, I start to imagine myself as a skull with the name Fanny engraved on my forehead.

The question of my name was on my mind because I was preparing to visit Cuba in 1991, and in order to be able to make that trip I had to acquire a Cuban passport listing my full name as it appears on my Cuban birth certificate. According to Cuban law, you cannot stop being Cuban. Even if you have been "naturalized" by another nation, you must obtain a Cuban passport to return to Cuba, at a cost of about $300. I suppose that the purpose of this law is to keep track of the flow of *gusanos* returning to the country while drawing some revenue from them. But I don't feel at all cynical about my Cuban passport; I want to pay my dues for having been spared the clunky shoes and having been allowed to study for a career of dubious social value. So I now have a valid Cuban passport, in which I have recovered both a lost middle name and a lost surname. In Cuba I will be Ruth Fanny Behar Glinsky, I will regain the names that link me back to my maternal grandfather. I was named Ruth because my great-grandfather, Abraham Levin, my grandmother's father, who did make it to Cuba with my great-grandmother, was reading the Book of Ruth when I was born. I am not surprised that my mother, who was only twenty when she had me, agreed to name her baby girl to satisfy the literary whims of her maternal grandfather. My great-grandfather, the only truly practicing Jew on my mother's side of the family, was highly respected both for his knowledge of the Torah and for his unwillingness to force his religious views on others. The Levin family became a clan in Cuba. After my grandmother married my grandfather in 1929, they worked, together with my great-grandfather, to bring my great-grandmother and the remaining six children from Poland. Reunited in Cuba, the extended household settled in the small town of Agramonte, in the sugar province of Matanzas, where they ran a general store that sold everything from pins to mattresses. For many years, until another family arrived, they were the only Jewish family in Agramonte, and my aunt Silvia remembers, as a child, that the curtains would be drawn on Passover. But if they were Jews in the wilderness, known to local people as *los polacos*, they were not unhappy. In Agramonte, my grandfather belonged to the Lion's Club and grew roses and *guayabas* in the backyard, while my aunt Silvia and my mother played with the mayor's children. On many a quiet day, my grandmother would dress up and take her two young daughters to the station to watch, along with everyone else, as the train from Havana made its daily stop in Agramonte.

Eventually, my great-aunts and great-uncles moved out of Agramonte as they married, and left for more urbane destinies in Matanzas and Havana. For years my grandparents lingered in Agramonte. Only after my grandfather won the lottery in 1946 did they move to Havana, where they opened up a lace shop called Casa Máximo in the old part of the city. This little store on Calle Aguacate, which still had its original sign with my grandfather's name when I visited Cuba in 1979, never brought in enough money for my grandparents to become more than insecurely middle class.

It was in Havana that my mother met my father. Their relationship was a cross-cultural encounter, for my father was a *turco* who came from a traditional Turkish Sephardic background, in which Ladino, the old Spanish of the expelled Jews, was still spoken at home. He had grown up street-smart near the docks of Havana, and, though a first-generation Cuban like my mother, his black hair and *habanero* style allowed him to pass more easily as a Cuban. His father was a peddler who worked only half the day and spent the afternoons playing dominoes with his buddies. If my mother's family were doing only moderately well, my father's family were barely making it. Some time in the late 1930s, when my father's family had gone hungry for several days, my grandfather brought home an excellent cut of beef. It had been given to him by one of his clients, and he presented it with enormous satisfaction to my grandmother. She refused to accept it because it wasn't kosher meat. My grandfather insisted she take it, saying it was a gift and that they were too hungry to be choosy. My grandmother kept refusing. My grandfather kept insisting. Finally, my grandmother took the meat from him. Holding it in her determined hands, she lifted the package high above her head and flung it out the window. The argument that ensued must have been momentous because the story about the beef that ended up in the street has never been forgotten in my father's family.

My father has often claimed that it was my mother who taught him to eat the prohibited foods that his mother had so vehemently kept out of her house. Not that my mother allowed unkosher meat in her house, either. At home she translated recipes from her Cuban cookbook, *Cocina Criolla*, itself a creole culinary mix, making kosher *tamales* and kosher *caldo gallego* by substituting chicken and Hebrew National beef fry for the pork that was supposed to be in these dishes.

But in the street, *en la calle*, it was different; there, Leviticus gave you license to taste more of the world. Keeping kosher stops at your doorstep. That has been our primary dietary rule, our culinary semiotics, our way of forging a Cuban identity we could lie in.

When we were recently at El Rincón Criollo, a Cuban restaurant in New York where my parents eat almost every weekend, my father adamantly refused to let me bring home what was left of my *pollo a la plancha*. "But it's just chicken," I protested. "I don't want it in my house, *y se acabó*, okay?" replied my father. "Case closed," as he likes to say. And yet he and my mother, like their friends in *el grupo*, will rush over to El Rincón for *frijoles* (black beans) and *bistec de palomilla* (fried steak) the day after the fast of Yom Kippur. I hope my mother will forgive me for remembering forever that late night summer outing in Puerto Rico when her front tooth, which I had no idea was false, fell out as she swooned *qué rico está este sandwich*, this sandwich is fabulous! while biting into the sweetly pickled ham-and-cheese Cuban special that bears the nostalgic name of *una media noche* (midnight).

In Cuba my mother would have remained a *polaca*, and my father a *turco*; at the very least, they would always have been the children of *polacos* and *turcos*. It is in the United States that they have settled into their Cubanness. In this America that is not theirs, they are viewed as Latinos, quirky Latinos, to be sure, but Latinos nonetheless.

My mother says to me, "With my accent, all I have to do is open my mouth and people ask me, 'Where are you from?' When they want to be nice, they say, 'Where are you from originally?'" She works in an overcrowded basement of New York University, checking that people's names are spelled correctly on their diplomas. In her office she's now the only Latina, and she finds herself having to straddle between her white American and black American female co-workers. She's neither white nor black in that context, but certainly a little more black than white. It doesn't help her much that she's white and Jewish because a white Jewish woman in America doesn't usually speak the kind of "broken English" that Latinas and Latinos speak. Her accent and her ongoing struggle with the English language are an ever-present reminder that she is an immigrant in an America that is not hers, that she is "originally from "elsewhere." She realizes she's being "othered" all the time, and she notices how the black women in the office get the same treatment. And so, as she tells me, "I'm with them, with the women of color." And I say to her, "Ma, don't you see? Here you are a woman of color too."

I was speaking to my mother from my own experience. I was denied a position at my university as a "minority" because it was decided that, given my Jewish heritage, I was not a racially pure Latina. And yet even this impure Latina gets counted as a "minority" or as a woman of color when the statistics are looking bad for affirmative action hirings. So I've decided that if I'm going to be counted as a "minority," if I'm going to be on the margin, if I'm going to be a woman of color, I'm going to claim that space and speak from it, but in the interests of a politics that challenges the language of cultural authenticity and racial purity. I'm going to be a Latina, *no a las buenas, pero a las malas,* the hard way, because that's the identity that, exactly inverse to my mother, they're always trying to take away from me, because "I'm white like you, English-speaking like you, right-thinking like you, middle-class living like you, no matter what I say" (Morales 148).

My father gets Latinized not just because of his accent but because of his García Márquez eyebrows and moustache that come from his Sephardic origins. And he responds with *rumbero* humor, purposely mispronouncing words in English while parading about in a U.S.A. baseball cap and T-shirt. But some of his responses are also tinged with bitterness and an internalized racism that chills me. This past summer, as we cleared up our poolside snacks at an undistinguished Holiday Inn on the northern outskirts of Philadelphia, he said, "Don't leave a mess, okay? *Porque si no van a decir, que somos puertorriqueños.*" "So they won't say we're Puerto Rican." My father has often been mistaken for Puerto Rican and this bothers him. Being Puerto Rican represents, to him, not making it in America, staying poor, not being a reasonable, white, middle-class, right-thinking person just like you. Yet it is as a Latino that my father earns his living. As the Latin American sales representative of a textile firm in New York City, it is his job to sell closeouts and other fabric that no one wants to buy on this side of the border to clients in Panama, the Dominican Republic, and Mexico. And, indeed, he is remarkably successful at selling what the gringos could never sell, for he's an expert border crosser. But when his humor becomes self-deprecating, he says he's a junk salesman, a peddler of *basura*, of *shmates*. He's the Latino smuggled into a company where all the bosses are third-generation American Ashkenazi Jews, who drive Jaguars. They're nice enough to my father, but he knows he's not one of the boys. So he takes their smugness with a grain of salt. Each boss, for example, has gotten a nickname. Mr. Sachs, pronounced "socks" with a Latino accent, is La Media. When things get rough at the office, my father phones my mother at NYU and says, "*Está La Media hoy que apesta*" (The Sock sure stinks today).

Lately it is Mr. Wolf, El Lobo, who is being difficult. And I am to blame. "*El Lobo está que aulla*" (The Wolf is about to start howling), my father tells me, as I hold a three-way conversation with him and my mother on the phone from Michigan. And my mother adds, "*Le vira la cara a tu padre. Se lo quiere comer—crudo*" (He refuses to look your father in the face. He wants to eat him—raw). El Lobo is angry, you see, because he asked my father to ask me to write a letter of recommendation for his daughter to help her get into the University of Michigan. El Lobo himself describes his daughter as indistinguishable from all the other girls at her suburban Long Island high school, telling my father that she needs a little extra something to get her into a place like Michigan. A letter from a professor at Michigan is just the mark of distinction she needs; surely I will understand. My father dutifully calls me and relays the order from El Lobo. I try to explain that I have no special power to get El Lobo's daughter accepted by the university. I try to explain that the university is not totally like the business world yet, and that merit still counts for something. I try to explain that it's not a good idea to fake it. And then I flatly say that I will not do it. I will not write a letter on behalf of a young woman on Long Island whom I have never met in my life. I don't care if she is the daughter of a werewolf who drives a Jaguar. My father starts to get upset, but my mother, who has been hovering around waiting to hear my response, gets on the phone and says, "*Te lo dije. Yo sabía que Ruty no lo iba a hacer*" (I told you, I knew, Ruty wouldn't do it).

So El Lobo is getting ready to howl. But, fortunately, it's still La Manzana, Mr. Applebaum, who signs the paychecks. And La Manzana adores my father. As my mother tells me so I won't feel too guilty, "*Me llama tu padre y me dice, 'La Manzana me tiene loco hoy dándome besos'*" (Your father calls and says to me, "The Apple is driving me crazy today kissing me so much").

To join together Latin American and Jewish, terms that are not "normally" joined together, creates a shock effect; as Saúl Sosnowski puts it, one encounters "astonished gazes and conflicting images of the accepted and simple clichés for both" (299). And, as Kenneth Kemble, an Argentine painter, once noted, "They say of Linnaeus that when he found an insect which resisted classification, he would crush it immediately" (qtd. in Noe 146). A Jew is not expected to have Spanish as a mother tongue, or to be from Latin America. But in the Cuban-Jewish milieu that I have known firsthand, these uncommon expectations exist in a common reality, a Cuban-Jewish sense of identity, of being-in-the-world. It is essential, Sosnowski feels, to "protect the hyphen" in the Latin American-Jewish sense of identity. The hyphen highlights the unease produced by the importation, even smuggling, of the Jew into the monolithic territory of Latin America. It also signals "the inability of language to produce a composite word and of beings to give birth to a gay, melted self" (Sosnowski 307). And yet, in the Cuban-Jewish case, there's a composite word, "Juban," that gets at a sense of *mestizaje* rooted in a creative amalgam that is different from assimilation. Such an amalgam is possible because of the criollism at the center of Cuban culture.

In Latin America, where the traces of the great Nahua and Inca civilizations are in permanent tension with the struggles for survival of post-Conquest indigenous people, the "other" as well as the "native" has always been the Indian. Cuba, like the other islands of the Caribbean, has only a vague "prehistoric" connection to the indigenous substratum because its smaller native populations were quickly destroyed by the Spanish conquest, leaving hardly any traces. Positioned at the entrance to the New World much more prominently than the other Caribbean islands, Cuba became a unique crossroads, bustling with the movement of people and goods, but also vulnerable over the centuries to "invasion, depredations, and harassment," which have not yet stopped (Pérez 12). Cuban culture was shaped by the exogenous, the foreign. The absence of "aboriginality," as Gustavo Pérez-Firmat has pointed out so insightfully, has given to Cuban culture an "originality" that "subsists in and through translation" (4–12). Like an *ajiaco,* a hearty stew of heterogeneous ingredients, Cuban culture has been concocted from diverse migrant displacements and resettlements.

At the beginning of *The Cuban Condition,* Pérez-Firmat gives an example, which touches directly upon the theme of this essay, of what he calls the Cuban "translation sensibility." His example is a Cuban-Jewish wedding that took place in Miami, where the Cuban singer Willie Chirino performed a version of the Jewish song "Hava-Nagilah" in *guaguacó* rhythm, creating a "Havana-gilah" to which people danced "a *horah* with *salsa* steps." For Pérez-Firmat, there was something peculiarly Cuban in that irreverent, creole translation of this Hebrew son" (1). And I agree with him. But there was also, I would add, something peculiarly Juban in that irreverent, creole acceptance of Willie Chirino's "Havana-gilah" as something to which you could dance a *horah con salsa*. If only a Cuban could have done the kind of translation that Chirino did, only a Juban would have had the bicultural fluency to make sense of that creole language—and invent a way to dance to it. Jubans have outdone the *ajiaco* sense of identity. They don't just have a translation sensibility; they are themselves translated people.

Sometime after I began writing this piece, I came across Salman Rushdie's essay "Imaginary Homelands," which also begins with an account of an old family photograph. Rushdie's photograph is of the house where he was born in Bombay, which he visited again after living in London for most of his life. Seeing the red roof tiles, the cactuses, and the bougainvillaea creepers made him vividly aware of the home and the homeland he had lost. (Yet none of these things is "native" to Bombay: the red tiles come from Portugal, the cactuses and bougainvillaea from Mexico.) Writers who are exiles, emigrants, and expatriates are haunted by the desire to "reclaim, to look back, even at the risk of being mutated into pillars of salt," notes Rushdie. Yet the real distance from the places left behind "almost inevitably means," Rushdie is careful to add, "that we will not be capable of reclaiming precisely the thing that was lost; that we will, in short, create fictions, not actual cities or villages, but invisible ones, imaginary homelands" (9–10).

This essay has been a first effort on my part to begin to imagine Juba, a Juba that I want to build, salt pillar by salt pillar, from both family stories and my own struggle to reclaim all the little forgotten villages of my mestiza identity. Villages, *pueblos,* mean a good deal to me. I went into anthropology because I thought that a discipline rooted in the foreignness of other worlds would help me to solve the puzzle of my identity. Instead, I ended up spending years of my life in two forgotten villages, one in northern Spain and one in northern Mexico. The village in Spain, called Santa María del Monte after the Holy Mother, lived up to its name, and everyone went to church, without fail, for Sunday Mass. In Santa María I learned to say the rosary and recite the Apostles' Creed, to get down on my knees at the appropriate parts of the service, and to cross myself. Yet I never forgot that I was a Jew. In the village in Mexico, just 500 miles from the U.S.-Mexican border, everyone needed something from *el otro lado,* "the other side." Could we bring back a tape recorder, a television, basketball sneakers, a stethoscope? Could we line up some work, any sort of work, over there? I wasn't allowed to forget that I was in Mexico as a gringa with gringa privileges and gringa money. But neither could I forget that I had wormed my way into Gringolandia as a *cubana.* When I refused a *compadre's* request that I claim him as my next of kin to help him get across the border, he said to me in a pained voice, "But didn't you tell me that you and your family aren't from there, that you also had to fight to get in?" I was prohibited from forgetting that to become a gringa I would have to be legally alienated by the United States.

In addition to these villages, whose dust I have eaten, there is, of course, my grandfather's Linka, the village where he was born, a village that is beyond tasting, beyond remembering. And then there is Agramonte, where I imagine no one any longer remembers *los polacos viejos* that had the general store, but where my grandfather's *guayabas* are still fragrant nonetheless and people continue to wait for the train from Havana that comes through once a day. Then there are the cities—Havana, New York, Miami Beach, Ann Arbor. In my Juba, there is room for all these villages and cities, and many other places for which I do not yet have names. In Juba there are no aliens. Only people like Lot's wife, who just won't listen.

I had the Cuban passport, but as 1991 drew to a close I wasn't sure I would make it to Cuba. In the weeks before my trip I became ill with what appeared to be a mysterious flu. I was beside myself with exhaustion and yet I couldn't sleep. I became jittery, my heart raced constantly, I was dizzy and could barely eat. I cried, I was overcome with fear. My entire life had curled up into a ball that stuck in my throat. Classic anxiety symptoms, I later learned. All I wanted to do was retire to my bed and forget everything. Why was I so concerned about going to Cuba, anyway? Me, this inauthentic Jubana who had been unhinged from Cuba at the age of five, what did I think I would find?

Sure, it didn't help much that I would be leaving Gabriel behind with my parents in New York. They had told me that in case I didn't come back I should leave them all the *papeles* (papers). My mother said, "*Me dejas todo lo del niño, Ruty, por si acaso Fidel Castro no te deja salir*" (Leave me everything pertaining to your child, Ruty, in case Fidel Castro doesn't let you leave). Castro himself, she felt certain, had a vested interest in my not returning to the United States. And my father: "*Ruty, no hables nada nada de política con nadie. Ni una palabra.*" Don't talk politics—yes, I had grown up hearing that, had learned early on that talking politics led to arguments, to veins throbbing in the neck, and finally to those two words, "case closed," and silence. I tried to let this paranoia wash over me, but scenarios kept unfolding in my imagination of dear Gabriel being raised by my parents, watching cartoons on television all day, being served breakfast, lunch, and dinner in bed, surrounded by a complete set of Ninja Turtles and Swamp Things. Me, his mother, I'd be stuck in Cuba, maybe in jail for talking about politics, or maybe in an insane asylum for doing something crazy like screaming in the street, saying the unsayable. And his father, the *griguito* from Texas, he'd be running around Cuba, wondering how to save me—that is, if he didn't just get on a plane and leave me there alone, turned into a pillar of salt for daring to look back.

My body turned into a boulder that I dragged all the way to Miami. And then the next day, when we were supposed to leave for Cuba, I learned that my visa had not arrived. I felt a touch of disappointment, wondering whether the Cubans had somehow looked into their crystal ball and learned I was too neurotic to deserve to be let in. But mostly I felt great relief, I thought to myself, oh, well, it wasn't my *destino* to go to Cuba, after all. Now I could relax, take a vacation. Yet we kept our suitcases by the door. Just in case. And four days later, just after we had given up hope and unpacked our bags, word arrived from Cuba that the visa was ready and I could leave the next morning. I had been warned to adopt a Zen attitude if I wanted to work in Cuba, and I now understood why. Arriving at the airport at the crack of dawn, there was already *la cola* of people waiting to check in for the daily flight to Havana. There was a man with sad eyes who said in a sad voice that he was going to visit his dying mother whom he hadn't seen in years; there was a woman carrying an oversized shopping bag stuffed with a frilly pink parasol and matching lace basket who was begging the clerk to let her take it on board; there was a man wearing three hats on his head; there was a woman stuffing beans and sausages under her clothes because, this time, she was going to get these things through Cuban Customs; and some people were carrying portable pharmacies, stocked with enough aspirin for several lifetimes of headaches. In the midst of this mixture of tenderness and zaniness, I lost all fear of crossing the border into Cuba. Waiting in the airport to board the plane, I knew I was already inside the belly of the beast when I found myself forced to listen four times, twice in English and twice in Spanish, to a U.S. government statement reminding us of the trade embargo against Cuba and restrictions on the number of dollars that could be given to the enemy.

Entering Cuba with dollars in my purse, I immediately forget the rules of the embargo and rent a spanking new car, red as blood. And in that car I go to Agramonte—a village of one long street, just the way my Aunt Silvia described it, And I learn that they still call the store on one corner *la casa de los polacos nuevos* and the store on the other corner *la casa de los polacos viejos.* You see, there were two Jewish families in Agramonte; but my family got there first, so they became "los polacos viejos," while the others were merely "nuevos."

"Does anybody remember *los polacos viejos?*" I ask, and as we stand outside the mint green store entrance, a little circle forms around us, and older men begin to utter the names of my great-grandparents, my grandparents, my great-aunts and great-uncles: Abraham, Hannah, Esther, Máximo, Jaime, Dora, Irene . . . Just hearing the names coming from the lips of these men, I feel my lifeline extending, the ball in my throat uncurling. They pose for a photo, and a woman who's been standing nearby yells to one of the men to roll down his pant legs, which are folded to the knee, and then she looks at me and says, "*Viniste a retratar los viejos más feos del* pueblo!"(You came to photograph the ugliest old men in town!). A man who says that he's known as El Chiquito tells me to give his regards to my great-uncle Jaime and to ask if he doesn't remember all the devilish things they did together. Doctor Pablito, the town doctor, who is now ninety, tells me that my great-aunt Dora fell in love with his brother, the lawyer, but the family quickly whisked her away to Havana, fearing she'd marry a gentile. Dora is dead, I tell him; and my brother too, he replies.

I forget to ask about the *guayabas* and the train from Havana, but expecting to return soon, I don't worry about it. Having said my last good-bye for now, I am heading toward the car when a young man wearing a baker's hat calls to me. At first I think he's asking me for something, maybe to change dollars like the *jineteros* who now trail after tourists in the hotel zones of Havana, but no, I have gotten my guard up too quickly, It turns out that he simply wants to know if I'd like some *dulces*. There's nothing I desire more at that moment than a sweet ending to my story, so I say yes and he brings out, on a sheet of brown paper, several chunks of glittering rum cake. The drops of sugary rum meander down my chin and linger and onto the camera hanging from my neck that will die two days later while I am trying to photograph the tomb of a cousin in Havana's Jewish cemetery. With the taste of that rum cake in my mouth, I begin to know why my family made Cuba their promised land. I begin to know, too, that I must keep reconnecting with the Cuba that my family refused, the Cuba they are afraid of and that I believed I also should fear, the Cuba that dawdled on my visa and almost didn't let me in, but also the Cuba of the young baker in Agramonte who offered me rum cake because I *happened* to be walking by. To imagine it all is not enough. This Jubana will have to taste the salt of memory and of loss, but she will also have to make a *rinconcito*, a small place, for herself in the Cuba of the present.

NOTES

For help with references, I thank Judith Elkin, Robert Levine, and Gustavo Pérez-Firmat. For comments, I thank Anton Shammas. My writing and travel were supported by the MacArthur Foundation.

1. His Spanish seems to be dressed in "a Harlequin costume in which very different functions of language and distinct centers of power are played out, blurring what can be said and what can't be said" (Deleuze and Guattari 26). For a feminist rereading of Deleuze and Guattari that has informed my interpretation, see Caren Kaplan (1990).

2. Some Jews did remain members of the Communist party and later participated in the Cuban Revolution, staying on in Cuba even after the mass exodus of the Jewish community. There are now about 1,000 Jews left on the island. Most have intermarried, and those with high-ranking positions tend not to identify themselves as Jewish. During my visit to Cuba in 1991, I was told that there are currently only fourteen families in which both the husband and wife are of Jewish origin.

REFERENCES

Bejarano, Margalit. "The Deproletarianization of Cuban Jewry." *Judaica Latino-americana: Estudios históricos-sociales.* Ed. AMILAT. Jerusalem: Editorial Universitario Magnes, Universidad Hebrea, 1988. 57–67.

Deleuze, Giles, and Félix Guattari. *Kafka: Toward a Minor Literature.* Minneapolis: U of Minnesota P, 1986.

Elkin, Judith Laikin. *The Jews of the Latin American Republics.* Chapel Hill: U of North Carolina P, 1980.

Elkin, Judith Laikin, and Gilbert W. Merks, eds. *The Jewish Presence in Latin America.* Boston: Allen & Unwin, 1987.

Fernández Retamar, Roberto. *"Caliban" and Other Essays.* Minneapolis: U of Minnesota P, 1989.

Kaplan, Caren. "Deterritorializations: The Rewriting of Home and Exile in Western Feminist Discourse." *The Nature and Content of Minority Discourse.* Ed. Abdul R. JanMohamed and David Lloyd. New York: Oxford UP, 1990. 357–68.

Levine, Robert M. *Tropical Diaspora: The Jewish Experience in Cuba.* Gainesville: UP of Florida, 1993.

Martí, José. [1891]. *Nuestra América.* Comp. Roberto Fernández Retamar. Havana: Casa de las Américas, 1974.

Matterin, Abraham Marcus. *Martí y las descriminaciones raciales.* Havana: Ediciones de la Agrupación Cultural Hebreo-Cubana, 1953.

Morales, Aurora Levins, and Rosario Morales. *Getting Home Alive.* Ithaca: Firebrand Books, 1986.

Morales, Rosario. "I am the Reasonable One." Morales and Morales 147–49.

Moschkivich, Judit. "But I Know You, American Woman." *The Bridge Called My Back: Writings by Radical Women of Color.* Ed. Cherrie Moraga and Gloria Anzaldúa. New York: Kitchen Table, Women of Color Press, 1981. 79–84.

Noe, Luis Felipe. "Does Art from Latin America Need a Passport?" *Being América: Essays on Art, Literature and Identity from Latin America.* Ed. Rachel Weiss, with Alan West. New York: White Pine Press, 1991. 142–51.

Oberstein, Alicia. "Cuban Jewish Writers and the Immigrant Experience." *Latino Stuff Review* (Winter 1991): 4.

Pérez, Lou A., Jr. *Cuba: Between Reform and Revolution.* New York: Oxford UP, 1988.

Pérez-Firmat, Gustavo. *The Cuban Condition: Translation and Identity in Modern Cuban Literature.* New York: Cambridge UP, 1989.

Rivero, Eliana S. "(Re)Writing Sugarcane Memories: Cuban Americans and Literature." *Americas Review* 18.3–4 (1990): 164–82.

Rushdie, Salman. "Imaginary Homelands." *Imaginary Homelands: Essays and Criticism 1901–1991.* New York: Viking Penguin, 1991. 9–21.

Saldívar, José David. "The Dialectics of Our America." *Do the Americas Have a Common Literature?* Ed. Gustavo Pérez-Firmat. Durham, NC: Duke UP, 1990. 62–84.

Sosnowski, Saúl. "Latin American-Jewish Writers: Protecting the Hyphen." Elkin and Merks 297–307.

Ilan Stavans
Mexico/United States

Ilan Stavans (1961–) produces ideas and constellations of thoughts at the speed of light. He possesses seemingly unlimited energy, able to develop numerous projects at the same time. He writes, edits, and schmoozes in a myriad of tongues, including Yiddish and Hebrew. His publications in Spanish and English appear in the most prestigious periodicals and publishing houses. In addition, he is the editor of *Hopscotch: A Cultural Review*, a quarterly addressing Hispanic issues—politics, history, the arts—from a cosmopolitan viewpoint. Yet with all of his endeavors, Stavans retains a sense of his own limits.

A self-styled Jewish Mexican American, Stavans emigrated from Mexico to New York in search of freedom and to find an audience. Now at Amherst College, he teaches his favorite Jewish writers—Sholem Aleichem, Isaac Beshevis Singer, I. J. Singer—and American masters such as Jorge Luis Borges and Herman Melville. Besides writing fiction, such as the novel *Talia y el cielo* (Talia in Heaven), and social commentary, such as *The Hispanic Condition*, he has edited two important anthologies of Jewish short stories, *Tropical Synagogues* and *The Oxford Book of Jewish Short Stories*.

In this essay, previously published as an epilogue to *The One-Handed Pianist*, Stavans writes of the tribulations and joys of a Jewish-Mexican childhood and of a lifelong fascination with language. It forms the seed of his memoir *On Borrowed Words*.

LOST IN TRANSLATION

Ilan Stavans

My heart is in the East and I am at the edge of the West. Then how can I taste what I eat, how can I enjoy it? How can I fulfill my vows and pledges while Zion is in the domain of Edom, and I am in the bonds of Arabia?

JUDAH HALEVI

Work of good prose has three steps: a musical stage when it is composed, an architectonic one when it is built, and a textile one when it is woven.

WALTER BENJAMIN

I was born in Mexico City, April 7, 1961, on a cloudy day without major historical events. I am a descendant of Jews from Russia and Poland, businessmen and rabbis, who arrived by sheer chance in Veracruz, on the Atlantic coast next to the Yucatán peninsula. I am a sum of parts and thus lack purity of blood (what proud Renaissance Iberians called *la pureza de sangre*): white Caucasian with a Mediterranean twist, much like the Enlightenment philosopher Moses Mendelssohn and only marginally like the Aztec poet Ollin Yollistli. My idols, not surprisingly, are Spinoza and Kafka, two exiles in their own land who chose universal languages (Portuguese and Hebrew to Latin, Czech to German) in order to elevate themselves to a higher order, and who, relentlessly, investigated their own spirituality beyond the reach of orthodox religion and routine. Ralph Waldo Emerson, in *Essays: Second Series* (1844), says that the reason we feel one man's presence and not another's is as simple as gravity. I have traveled from Spanish into Yiddish, Hebrew, and English; from my native home south of the Rio Grande far and away—to Europe, the Middle East, the United States, the Bahamas, and South America—always in search of the ultimate clue to the mysteries of my divided identity. What I found is doubt.

I grew up in an intellectually sophisticated middle class, in a secure, self-imposed Jewish ghetto (a treasure island) where gentiles hardly existed. Money, and comfort, books, theater and art. Since early on I was sent to Yiddish day school, Colegio Israelita de México in Colonia Navarete, where the heroes were Sholom Aleichem and Theodor Herzl, while people like José Joaquín Fernández de Lizardi, Agostín Yáñez, Juan Rulfo, and Octavio Paz were almost unknown; that is, we lived in an oasis completely uninvolved with things Mexican. In fact, when it came to knowledge of the outside world, students were far better off talking about U.S. products (Hollywood, TV, junk food, technology) than about matters native—an artificial capsule, our ghetto, much like the magical sphere imagined by Blaise Pascal: its diameter everywhere and its center nowhere.

Mother tongue. The expression crashed into my mind at age twenty, perhaps a bit later. The father tongue, I assumed, was the adopted alternative and illegitimate language (Henry James preferred the term "wife tongue"), whereas the mother tongue is genuine and authentic— a uterus: the original source. I was educated in (into) four idioms:

Spanish, Yiddish, Hebrew, and English. Spanish was the public venue; Hebrew was a channel toward Zionism and not toward the sacredness of the synagogue; Yiddish symbolized the Holocaust and past struggles of the Eastern European labor movement; and English was the entrance door to redemption: the United States. Abba Eban said it better: Jews are like everybody else except a little bit more. A polyglot, of course, has as many loyalties as homes. Spanish is my right eye, English my left; Yiddish my background and Hebrew my conscience. Or better, each of the four represents a different set of spectacles (nearsighted, bifocal, light-reading, etc.) through which the universe is seen.

THE ABUNDANCE OF SELF

This multifarious (is there such a word?) upbringing often brought me difficulties. Around the neighborhood, I was always *el güerito* and *el ruso*. Annoyingly, my complete name is Ilan Stavchansky Slomianski; nobody, except for Yiddish teachers, knew how to pronounce it. (I get mail addressed to Ivan Starlominsky, Isvan Estafchansky, and Allen Stevens.) After graduating from high school, most of my friends, members of richer families, were sent abroad, to the U.S. or Israel, to study. Those that remained, including me, were forced to go to college at home to face Mexico tête-à-tête. The shock was tremendous. Suddenly, I (we) recognized the artificiality of our oasis. What to do? I, for one, rejected my background, I felt Judaism made me a pariah. I wanted to be an authentic Mexican and thus foolishly joined the Communist cause but the result wasn't pleasing. Among the *camaradas*, I was also "the blondy" and "the Jew." No hope, no escape. So I decided to investigate my ethnic and religious past obsessively and made it my duty to really understand guys like Maimonides, Arthur Koestler, Mendelssohn, Judah Halevi, Hasdai Crescas, Spinoza, Walter Benjamin, Gershom Scholem, Martin Buber, Franz Rosenzweig, Abraham Joshua Heschel. It helped, at least temporarily—nothing lasts forever.

Years later, while teaching medieval philosophy at Universidad Iberoamericana, a Jesuit college in downtown Mexico City, during the 1982 Lebanon invasion, a group of Palestinian sympathizers threw rotten tomatoes at me and my students (99 percent gentiles). Eager to manifest their anger, and protest, they had to find an easy target and I was the closest link to Israel around. The whole thing reminded me of a scene that took place at age fourteen, while sitting in Yiddish class at Colegio Israelita. Mr. Lockler, the teacher, was reading from I. J. Singer's *The Family Carnovsky*—a story of three generations in a German-Jewish family enchanted with the nineteenth-century Enlightenment, slowly but surely becoming assimilated into German society until the tragic rise of Nazism brought unthinkable consequences. The monotonous rhythm of the recitations was boring and nobody was paying much attention. Suddenly, a segment of the story truly captivated me: the moment when Jegor, eldest son of Dr. David Carnovsky's mixed marriage to Teresa Holbeck, is ridiculed in class by Professor Kirchenmeier, a newly appointed principal at the Goethe Gymnasium in Berlin. Singer describes the event meticulously. Nazism is on the rise: the aristocracy, and more specifically the Jews, are anxious to know the overall outcome of the violent acts taking place daily on the city street. Racial theories are being discussed and Aryans glorified. Feverishly anti-Jewish, Kirchenmeier, while delivering a lecture, calls Jegor to the front to use him as a guinea pig in illustrating his theories. With a compass and calipers, he measures the length and width of the boy's skull, writing the figures on the board. He then measures the distance from ear to ear, from the top of the head to the chin, and the length of the nose. A packed auditorium is silently watching. Jegor is then asked to undress. He is terrified and hesitates, of course; he is ashamed and feels conspicuous because of his circumcision. Eventually other students, persuaded by Kirchenmeier, help undress the Jew, and the teacher proceeds to show in the "inferior" Jewish strain the marks of the rib structure. He finishes by calling attention to Jegor' genitals whose premature development shows "the degenerate sexuality of the Semitic race."

Astonishment. What troubled me most was Jegor's inaction. I suppose it was natural to be petrified in such a situation, but I refused to justify his immobility. So I interrupted Mr. Lockler to ask why didn't the boy escape. A deadly silence invaded the classroom. It was clear I had disturbed the other students' sleep and the teacher's rhythm. "Because he couldn't, he simply couldn't," was the answer I got. "Because that's the way lives are written." I don't know or care what happened next. As years went by I came to understand that concept, the almighty Author of Authors, as intriguing, and the scene in Yiddish class as an allegory of myself and Mexican Jews as an easy and palatable target of animosity. At the Jesuit college almost a decade later, I was the marionette-holder's Jegor Carnovsky—God's joy and toy: the Jew.

KALEIDOSCOPE

Bizarre combination—Mexican Jews: some 60,000 frontier dwellers and hyphen people like Dr. Jekyll and Mr. Hyde, a sum of sums of parts, a multiplicity of multiplicities. Although settlers from Germany began to arrive in "Aztec Country" around 1830, the very first synagogue was not built in the nation's capital until some fifty-five years later. From then on, waves of Jewish immigrants came from Russia and Central and Eastern Europe. Ashkenazim whose goal was to make it big in New York (the Golden Land), but since an immigration quota was imposed in the United States in 1924, a little detour places them in Cuba, Puerto Rico, or the Gulf of Mexico (the Rotten Land). Most were Yiddish-speaking Bundists: hardworking peasants, businessmen, and teachers, nonreligious and entrepreneurial, escaping Church-sponsored pogroms and government persecution whose primary dream was never Palestine. Hardly anything physical or ideological differentiated them from the relatives that did make it north, to Chicago, Detroit, Pittsburgh, and the Lower East Side—except, of course, the fact that they, disoriented immigrants, couldn't settle where they pleased. And this sense of displacement colored our future.

Migration and its discontents: I have often imagined the Culture Shock, surely not too drastic, my forefathers experienced at their arrival: from *mujik* to *campesino*, similar types in a different milieu. Mexico was packed with colonial monasteries where fanatical nuns prayed day and night. Around 1910 Emiliano Zapata and Pancho Villa were making their Socialist Revolution, and an anti-Church feeling (known in Mexico as La Cristiada and masterfully examined in Graham Greene's *The Power and the Glory*) was rampant. Aztecs, the legend claims, once sacrificed daughters to their idols in sky-high pyramids, and perhaps were cannibals. Undoubtedly this was to be a transitory stop, it had to. It was humid, and at least in the nation's capital, nature remained an eternal autumn. I must confess never to have learned to love Mexico. I was taught to retain a sense of foreignness—as a tourist without a home. The best literature I know about Mexico is by Europeans and U.S. writers: Italo Calvino, André Breton, Jack Kerouac, Greene, Joseph Brodsky, Antonin Artaud, Katherine Anne Porter, Malcolm Lowry, Harriet Doerr . . . I only love my country when I am far away. Elsewhere—that's where I belong: the vast diaspora. Nowhere and everywhere. (Am I a name dropper? Me, whose name no one can pronounce?)

OUT OF THE BASEMENT

When the Mexican edition of *Talia in Heaven* (1989) came out, my publisher, Fernando Valdés, at a reception, talked about the merits of this, my first (and so far only) novel. He applauded this and that ingradient, spoke highly of the innovative style, and congratulated the author for his precocious artistic maturity. Memory has deleted most of his comments. I no longer remember what he liked and why. The only sentence that still sticks in my mind, the one capable of overcoming the passing of time, came at the end of his speech, when he said: "For many centuries, Latin America has had Jews living in the basement, great writers creating out of the shadow. And Ilan Stavans is the one I kept hidden until now." A frightening metaphor.

In the past five hundred years, Jews in the Hispanic world have been forced to convert to Christianity or somehow to mask or feel ashamed of their ancestral faith. Their intellectual contribution, notwithstanding, has been enormous. Spanish letters cannot be understood without Fray Luis de León and Ludovicus Vives, without Fernando de Roja's *La Celestina* and the anti-Semitic poetry of Francisco de Quevedo, author of the infamous sonnet "A man stuck to a nose." (*Erase un hombre a una nariz pegado, érase una nariz superlativa, érase una alquitara medio viva, érase un peje espada mal barbada . . .*) In the Americas, a safe haven for refugees from the Inquisition and later on for Eastern Europeans running away from the Nazis, Jewish writers have been active since 1910, when Alberto Gerchunoff, a Russian immigrant, published in Spanish his collection of interrelated vignettes, *The Jewish Gauchos of the Pampas*, to commemorate Argentina's independence. He switched from one language to another to seek individual freedom, to validate his democratic spirit, to embrace a dream of plurality and progress: Yiddish, the tongue of Mendel Mokher Sforim and Sholem Aleichem, was left behind; Spanish, Cervantes's vehicle of communication—Gerchunoff was an admirer of *Don Quixote*—became the new tool, the channel to entertain, educate, and redeem the masses. Like Spinoza, Kafka, Nabokov, and Joseph Brodsky, he was the ultimate translator: a bridge between idiosyncrasies. The abyss and the bridge. Many decades later, some fifty astonishing writers from Buenos Aires and Mexico to Lima and Guatemala, including Moacyr

Scliar, Clarice Lispector, and Mario Szichman, continue to carry on Gerchunoff's torch, but the world knows little about them. The narrative boom that catapulted Gabriel García Márquez, Carlos Fuentes, and others from south of the Rio Grande to international stardom in the sixties managed to sell a monolithic, suffocatingly uniform image of the entire continent as a Banana Republic crowded with clairvoyant prostitutes and forgotten generals, never a multicultural society. To such a degree were ethnic voices left in the margin that readers today know much more about Brazilians and Argentines thanks to Borges's short stories "Emma Zunz" and "El milagro secreto" (The Secret Miracle), and Vargas Llosa's novel *El hablador* (The Storyteller), than to anything written by Gerchunoff and his followers. Sadly and in spite of his anti-Semitic tone, my Mexican publisher was right: in the baroque architecture of Latin American letters, Jews inhabit the basement. And yet, *la pureza de sangre* in the Hispanic world is but an abstraction: native Indians, Jews, Arabs, Africans, Christians . . . the collective identity is always in need of a hyphen. In spite of the "official" image stubbornly promoted by governments from time immemorial, Octavio Paz and Julio Cortázar have convincingly used the salamander, the *axolotl*, as a symbol to describe Latin America's popular soul, always ambiguous and in mutation.

AMERICA, AMERICA

I honestly never imagined I could one day pick up my suitcases to leave home once and for all. And yet, at twenty-five I moved to New York, I was awarded a scholarship to study for a master's at the Jewish Theological Seminary and, afterwards, perhaps a doctorate at Columbia University or elsewhere. I fled Mexico (and Spanish) mainly because as a secular Jew—what Freud would have called "a psychological Jew"—I felt marginalized, a stereotype. (Little did I know!) A true chameleon, a bit parochial and nearsighted, a nonconformist with big dreams and few possibilities. Like my globe-trotting Hebraic ancestors, I had been raised to build an ivory tower, an individual ghetto. By choosing to leave, I turned my past into remembrance: I left the basement and ceased to be a pariah. *Talia in Heaven* exemplifies that existential dilemma: its message simultaneously encourages Jews to integrate and openly invites them to escape; it alternates between life and memory. Paraphrasing Lionel Trilling, its cast of characters, victims of an obsessive God (much like the Bible's) who enjoys ridiculing them, are at the bloody crossroad where politics, theology, and literature meet. To be or not to be. The moment I crossed the border, I became somebody else: a new person. In *Chromos: A Parody of Truth*, Felipe Alfau says: "The moment one learns English, complications set in. Try as one may, one cannot elude this conclusion, one must inevitably, come back to it." While hoping to master the English language during sleepless nights, I understood James Baldwin, who, already exiled in Paris and quoting Henry James, claimed it is a complex fate to be an American. "America's history," the black author of *Nobody Knows My Name* wrote, "her aspirations, her peculiar triumphs, her even more peculiar defeats, and her position in the world—yesterday and today—are all so profoundly and stubbornly unique that the very word 'America' remains a new, almost completely undefined, and extremely controversial proper noun. No one in the world seems to know exactly what it describes." To be honest, the rise of multiculturalism, which perceives the melting pots, a soup of diverse and at times incompatible backgrounds, has made the word "America" even more troublesome, more evasive and abstract. Is America a compact whole, a unit? Is it a sum of ethnic groups unified by a single language and a handful of patriotic symbols? Is it a Quixotic dream where total assimilation is impossible, where multiculturalism is to lead to disintegration? And Baldwin's statement acquires a totally different connotation when one goes one step beyond, realizing that "America" is not only a nation (a state of mind) but also a vast continent. From

Alaska to the Argentine pampa, from Rio de Janeiro to East Los Angeles, the geography Christopher Columbus mistakenly encountered in 1492 and Amerigo Vespucci baptized a few years later is also a linguistic and cultural addition: America the nation and America the continent. America, America: I wanted to find a room of my own in the two; or two rooms, perhaps?

ON BEING A WHITE HISPANIC AND MORE

Once settled, I suddenly began to be perceived as Hispanic (i.e., Latino)—an identity totally alien to me before. (My knowledge of spoken Latin is minimal.) To make matters worse, my name (once again?), accent, and skin color were exceptions to what gringos had as the "Hispanic prototype." In other words, in Mexico I was perceived as Jewish; and now across the border, I was Mexican. Funny, isn't it? (In fact, according to official papers I qualify as a white Hispanic, an unpleasant term if there was ever one.) Once again, an impostor, an echo. (An impostor, says Ambrose Bierce in *The Devil's Dictionary,* is a rival aspirant to public honors.)

Themselves, myself: Hispanics in the United States—some 22,254,159 according to the 1990 census: white, black, yellow, green, blue, red . . . twice Americans, once in spite of themselves. They have been in the territories north of the Rio Grande even before the Pilgrims of the *Mayflower;* and with the Guadalupe Hidalgo Treaty signed in 1848, in which Generalísimo Antonio López de Santa Ana gave away and subsequently sold half of Mexico to the White House (why only half?), many of them unexpectedly, even unwillingly, became a part of an Anglo-Saxon, English-speaking reality. Today after decades of neglect and silence, decades of anonymity and ignorance, Latinos are finally receiving the attention they deserve. The second fastest-growing ethnic group after the Asians, their diversity of roots—Caribbean, Mexican, Central and South American, Iberian, and so on—makes them a difficult collectivity to describe. Are the Cuban migrations from Holguín, Matanzas, and Havana similar in their idiosyncratic attitude to those of Managua, San Salvador, and Santo Domingo? Is the Spanish they speak their true lingua franca, the only unifying factor? Is their immigrant experience in any way different from that of previous minorities—Irish, Italian, Jewish, what have you? How do they understand and assimilate the complexities of what it means to be American? And where do I, a white Hispanic, fit in?

Nowhere and everywhere. In 1985 I was assigned by a Spanish magazine to interview Isaac Goldemberg, a famous Jewish-Peruvian novelist who wrote *The Fragmented Life of Don Jacobo Lerner*. When we met at the Hungarian Pastry Shop at Amsterdam Avenue and 110th Street, he told me, among many things, he had been living in New York for over two decades without mastering the English language because he didn't want his Spanish to suffer and ultimately evaporate. Borges says in his short story "The Life of Tadeo Isidoro Cruz (1829–1874)": "Any life, no matter how long or complex it may be, is made up essentially of a single moment—the moment in which a man finds out, once and for all, who he is." That summer day I understood my linguistic future lay in the opposite direction from Goldemberg's: I would perfect my English and thus become a New York Jew, an intellectual animal in the proud tradition celebrated by Alfred Kazin. And I did. In just a single moment I understood who I could be.

THE DOUBLE

To write is to make sense of conditions in and around. Didn't somebody already say this? Jean Genet, John Updike? I am a copy, an instant replay, a shadow, an impostor. Everything is an echo. To live is to plagiarize, to imitate, to steal. I have always had the feeling of living somebody else's life. When I first read Felipe Alfau's *Locos: A Comedy of Gestures*, I was possessed by the idea that, had I been born in

1902 in Barcelona, as had its author, I would have written his book. The exact same sensation was repeated when discovering Pinhas's "Der Nister" and Kahanovitch's *The Family Mashber*, a masterpiece of Soviet Jewish fiction by a writer who died in a Russian hospital in 1950 as a result of Stalin's purges. And my mother keeps a yellowish school photograph I once gave her. It was taken when I was eight or nine: although smiling, I really don't look happy; and in the back it has a brief line written: "With love from a non-existent twin brother." Furthermore, I am often sure I am being observed by an omniscient Creature (with a capital "C"), who enjoys inflicting pain and laughs at the sorrow of His creatures. I cannot but equate the act of writing to God's impact on Nature: He is simultaneously absent and present in His creation, granting birth and death—the Absolute Novelist, a marionette-holder with a vivid imagination and a bad sense of humor (even if I-He laughs).

"TOTAL FORGETERY"

Acting was my father's trade.

As I was growing up, I remember feeling amazed by his incredible talent. I adored him. Watching his performances, I would be pushed to what Søren Kierkegaard regarded as "an existential vacuum—a mystery." Was he really the man I knew or, instead, a mask-carrier? I was particularly fond of him taking me along on Sunday afternoons. We would leave home alone after lunch. While driving an old Rambler, he would ask me about school and friends, about ideas and books, masturbation and a girl's sexuality. He was a hero, a man of integrity like few others, the only guy I knew who was actually happy, very happy, a few minutes every day: on stage. Then, as my father would park the car, I would begin noticing a slow change of attitude, a metamorphosis, as if a veil, an abyss was now setting us apart. Another self would graciously descend to possess him, to take the man I knew and loved away from me. A few minutes later, I would witness how, without shame, he would undress in front of a mirror, put on a bathrobe, and begin to hide his face in cosmetics. He was becoming somebody else, a stranger, a ghost: today a hotel owner, next season a boxer, a cancer patient, a Jewish prisoner in Germany. His breathtaking masks were infallible: they always hid my dad's true self, deformed it. As a result of that transformation, I felt totally alone.

Alone and lonely. The whole phenomenon inspired in me mixed feelings: I was astonished by the magic and frightened at the same time; I hated the whole thing and yet would literally do anything to return tomorrow and witness it anew. My father would then ask a handyman to seat me behind the stage, next to a curtain, in order for me to watch the show. And that, oh God, was his and my greatest moment on earth, the one we awaited even more eagerly than the facial and physical change he underwent to become a character. With a difference: In front of an audience, he was happy; I, on the other hand, was scared to death—invaded by the kind of fear that simultaneously generates joy and sorrow. What did others think of his "new" self? Could they recognize the true face behind the mask? Was he an impostor?

Alone and lonely and full of envy, I would feel an overwhelming sense of profound and disturbing jealousy toward the audience. They received all of his attention, which, in normal circumstances, I would keep for my own, or at most, share with my brother and sister. They would be manipulated, seduced by his talents. Why was he so eager to become other people and take a rest from himself? And hide behind a mask? Even more suspiciously, why did the viewers pay to have him taken away from me? How could people pay for my father to cease being himself? The Author of Authors, the Impostor of Impostors: God as playwright. In my eyes the entire universe was a vast and mysterious theater in which he (Yahweh, Adonai, Elohim, the Holy Spirit, the Father of Fathers) would capriciously establish what people, the actors, are to do, to say, to think, to hope. My dad's actual stage was a microcosmos that inspired me to philosophize about religion and eschatology, about freedom and determinism. I wondered: while acting, was my father free to refuse pronouncing a certain line of the script? Could he talk to me at least once during the performance? (Through his real and unimported self?) I also wondered if I, Ilan Stavans (aka Ilan Stavchansky Slomianski), was free to stop being his son? Could I also become other people—like Shakespeare, be one and many? To answer these questions, I became a novelist. To write is to make sense of confusion in and around. (It was me who said that.)

To write, perchance to dream. (Or vice versa?) Not long ago an interviewer asked me why I didn't follow his footsteps and enter the stage. My response was short and somewhat condescending. Deep inside, I dislike actors. I find their vulnerability, their trendiness and exhibitionism disturbing. I would rather live in the shadow than in the spotlight. I love the theater of the mind and have a terrible fear of dying. It might sound absurd, but I see literature as brother to memory and theater as symbol of the ephemeral present. I write in order to remember and be remembered. Death is the absence of recollection—what Luis G. Rodríguez calls "total forgetery." Theater, on the other hand, is *performance art*, a transitory game. It is only alive during a night show, afterwards it's gone . . . forever. Nothing remains, nothing. Except perhaps a handful of yellowish photos and (luck permitting) an award or two. And if the theater is like a vanishing photograph, writing is signing one's name on concrete: a proof of existence ("I was here . . ."). But, incorporating past and present images, a narrative plays with Time (with a capital "T") in an astonishing fashion: it makes reality eternal. Marcel's desire for his mother's goodnight kiss in Proust's *Remembrance of Things Past* is not a pre–World War I scene alone but unquestionably an image for the ages. When death turns me into a ghost, at least something, one ingenious thought or a breath of life, will remain a written page like those of Virgil, Dante, and Cervantes. Perhaps and perhaps not. The only certainty is that a library is a triumph over nothingness. And yet, the warm human contact my dad encounters while performing is always reinvigorating. Literature, on the other hand, is a secluded activity. Isolation, silence, detachment, escape. You hope someone will read you someday, although nothing (not even the timing of God's laughter) is certain. Thus decades away from those Sunday afternoons when my father would take me along to his show, I still confess I feel envy: he can be happy, I cannot. I honestly wish I could at times take vacations from myself—like him, have another self. It must be refreshing. Isolation, silence.

Before death and after. Literature, I'm perfectly sure, is no palliative to cure spirit's suffering. The day I die, people will not interrupt their routines, why should they? They will make love, eat, defecate, smoke, and read. They will smile and cry and kiss and hate. It will matter to no one (not even my dearest ones, really) that my life has ceased to be and all is over. The show will go on. Grief—a strange and dishonest feeling. When Calvino and Danilos Kiš, two mentors, died, did I cry? (Albert Camus's protagonist in *The Stranger* is incarcerated for not crying during his mother's funeral.) I did pray for their souls and after that . . . nothing. Only through literature, I feel, can I transcend myself. To write is to overcome the imperfections of nature. I do it every day, every day, every day, every . . . otherwise, I sense that a day's 86,400 seconds are meaningless and in vain.

THINGS TO COME

A future encyclopedia, to be published in Brussels in 2087, states that at age thirty-one I wrote a book, *Imagining Columbus*, about the Genoese admiral's fifth and final voyage of discovery, one not across the Atlantic but through the human imagination. That I was the author of a controversial reflection on the identity of Hispanics in the United States, and a volume of early short stories, collectively called in English, *The One-Handed Pianist*. It mentions the fact that sometime after 1995, I published a novel about a Belgian actor of Jewish descent, who has trouble distinguishing where reality ends and fantasy begins (poor Konstantin Stanislavsky! Or is it Konstantin Stavchansky?)— inspired, obviously, by his dad's trade; translated into numerous languages, the volume was enthusiastically received by critics and readers. Afterwards, I wrote another novel, this one in the style of Vargas Llosa, about the exiled family of a Latin American dictator, after which I won numerous grants and prizes, was internationally applauded and commemorated.

It discusses my multilingualism. After a literary beginning as a Yiddish playwright and short fiction writer, I moved first into Spanish and then into English, translating and reinventing myself. (Although I wrote English with ease and distinction, I spoke like a tourist.) If, as Nabokov once claimed, our existence is but a brief crack of light between two eternities of darkness, why not take advantage and be two writers at once? The entry also states that I left an echo, an echo, an echo. Critics praised my oeuvre, comparing it to precursors and successors like Kafka, Spinoza, and Borges. Because of my dual identity, in Mexico, I was considered a "bad citizen." My themes always dealt with God as manipulator of human conscience and my existential journey could be reduced to a verse by the Nicaraguan *modernista* poet Rubén Darío: "To be and not to know . . ." My style is very precise and direct, akin to religious insights. Cyril Connolly says in *Unquiet Grave:* "The more books we read, the sooner we perceive that the only function of a writer is to produce a masterpiece. No other task is of any consequence." The encyclopedia claims that toward the end of life, I wrote extraordinarily lasting short stories, as if everything that preceded them was a prophecy. Finally, it states that I died on August 18, 2033, with some twenty-two original books to my credit.

After a consuming sickness, I contemplated suicide but a sudden attack impeded me from arriving at a nearby New York hospital and nothingness took over. That was also a rainy day without major historical events. God witnessed my death and pretended to suffer, although His was of course an actor's gesture. In fact, He laughed: I was (am) his joy and toy.

BIBLIOGRAPHY

MARJORIE AGOSÍN

Always from Somewhere Else: A Memoir of My Jewish Father. New York: Feminist Press, 1998.

Ashes of Revolt: Essays on Human Rights. Fredonia, NY: White Pine Press, 1996.

Brujas y algo más/Witches and Other Things. Trans. Cola Franzen. Pittsburgh: Latin American Literary Review Press, 1984.

Circles of Madness: Mothers of the Plaza de Mayo/Círculos de la locura: Madres de la Plaza de Mayo. Trans. Celeste Kostopulos-Cooperman. Photographs Alicia D'Amico and Alicia Sanguinetti. Fredonia, NY: White Pine Press, 1992.

Conchali. New York: Senda Nueva de Ediciones, 1980.

A Cross and a Star: Memoirs of a Jewish Girl in Chile. Trans. Celeste Kostopulos-Cooperman. Albuquerque: U of New Mexico P, 1995.

Council of the Fairies. Washington, D.C.: Azul Editions, 1997.

Dear Anne Frank: Poems. Bilingual ed. Trans. Richard Schaaf. Washington, D.C.: Azul Editions, 1994. Hanover, NH: UP of New England, 1998.

A Dream of Light and Shadow: Portraits of Latin American Women Writers. Albuquerque: U of New Mexico P, 1995.

La felicidad. Santiago, Chile: Cuarto Propio, 1991.

Happiness. Trans. Elizabeth Horan. Fredonia, NY: White Pine Press, 1993.

Hogueras. Santiago, Chile: Universitaria, 1986.

Hogueras/Bonfires. Trans. Naomi Lindstrom. Tempe, AZ: Bilingual Press/Editorial Bilingüe, 1990.

"A Huge Black Umbrella." Trans. Lori M. Carlson. *Where Angels Glide at Dawn: New Stories from Latin America.* Ed. Lori M. Carlson and Cynthia L. Ventura. New York: HarperCollins, 1990. 99–104.

La literatura y los derechos humanos. San José, Costa Rica: EDUCA, 1989.

Melodious Women: A Poetic Celebration of Extraordinary Women. With Monica Galmozzi. Pittsburgh: Latin American Literary Review Press, 1997.

Memory and Passion: Jewish Women Writers in Latin America. Albuquerque: U of New Mexico P, 1998.

The Mothers of Plaza de Mayo (Línea Fundadora): The Story of Renée Epelbaum 1976–1985. Trans. Janice Molloy. Stratford, Ont., Canada: Williams-Wallace Publishers, 1989.

"My Stomach," "Where We Are," "Penis." Trans. Daisy C. de Filippis. *Pleasure in the Word: Erotic Writings by Latin American Women.* Ed. Margarite Fernández Olmos and Lizabeth Paravisini-Gebert. Fredonia, NY: White Pine Press, 1993. 46–49.

Pablo Neruda. Trans. Lorraine Ross. Boston: Twayne, 1986.

Sargazo = Sargasso: Poemas. Trans. Cola Franzen. Fredonia, NY: White Pine Press, 1993.

Scraps of Life: The Chilean Arpilleras: Chilean Women and the Pinochet Dictatorship. Trans. Cola Franzen. Trenton, NJ: Red Sea Press, 1987.

Silencio e imaginación: Mátaforas de la escritura femenina. México, D.F.: Katún, 1986.

Starry Night. Trans. Mary G. Berg. Fredonia, NY: White Pine Press, 1996.

Tapestries of Hope, Threads of Love: The Arpillera Movement in Chile, 1974–1994. Albuquerque: U of New Mexico P, 1996.

Toward the Splendid City. Trans. Richard Schaaf. Tempe, AZ: Bilingual Press/ Editorial Bilingüe, 1994.

Violeta Parra: Santa de Pura Greda. With Inez Dolz Blackburn. Santiago: Planeta, 1988.

"When She Showed Me Her Photograph," "Memorial," "The Most Unbelievable Part," "Disappeared Woman V," "Seven Stones," "Language." Trans. Celeste Kostopulos-Cooperman and Cola Franzen. *These Are Not Sweet Girls: Poetry by Latin American Women.* Ed. Marjorie Agosín. Fredonia, NY: White Pine Press, 1994. 239–44.

Women in Disguise: Stories. Trans. Diane Russell-Pineda. Falls Church, VA: Azul Editions, 1996.

Women of Smoke/Mujeres de humo. Trans. Naomi Lindstrom. Pittsburgh: Latin American Literary Review Press, 1988.

Women of Smoke: Latin American Women in Literature and Life. Trans. Janice Molloy. Trenton, NJ: Red Sea Press, 1989.

Zones of Pain/Las zonas del dolor. Trans. Cola Franzen. Fredonia, NY: White Pine Press, 1988.

MARCOS AGUINIS

Brown. Buenos Aires: Delegación de Asociaciones Israelitas Argentinas, 1977.

Cantata de los diablos. Barcelona: Planeta, 1972.

Carta esperanzada a un general: Puente sobre el abismo. Buenos Aires: Sudamericana/Planeta, 1983.

El combate perpetuo. (New edition of *Brown.*) Buenos Aires: Planeta, 1981; Buenos Aires: Sudamericana, 1995.

La conspiración de los idiotas. Buenos Aires: Emec, 1979.

La cruz invertida. Barcelona: Planeta, 1970.

La cuestión judía vista desde el Tercer Mundo. Río Cuarto: Librería Superior, 1974; Buenos Aires: Centro Cultural I. L. Peretz, 1986.

Diálogos sobre la Argentina y el fin del milenio. Buenos Aires: Sudamericana, 1996.

"De la legitimación apologética a la crítica reparadora." *Hispamérica* 14.42 (1985): 57–64.

Elogio de la culpa. Buenos Aires: Planeta, 1993.

La gesta del marrano. Buenos Aires: Planeta, 1991.

"The Homage." *Present Tense* 2.4 (Summer 1975): 42.

"Hopeful Letter to a General: A Fragment." Trans. David William Foster. *Massachusetts Review* 27.3–4 (1986): 712–21.

Importancia por contacto. Buenos Aires: Planeta, 1983.

Judaísmo y psicoanálisis. Buenos Aires: Fundación Tzedaka, 1993.

Maimónides: Sacerdote de los oprimidos. Buenos Aires: Ediciones Biblioteca Popular Judía, 1976.

Maimónides, un sabio avanzado. Buenos Aires: Editorial Iwo, 1963.

La matriz del infierno. Buenos Aires: Sudamericana, 1997.

Nuevos diálogos. With Justo Oscar Laguna. Buenos Aires: Sudamericana, 1998.

Operativo siesta. Buenos Aires: Planeta, 1977.

Un país de novela: Viaje hacia la mentalidad de los argentinos. Buenos Aires: Planeta, 1988.

"La perpetua tensión entre institución y creador." *El imaginario judío en la literatura de América Latina: Visión y realidad.* Buenos Aires: Grupo Editorial Shalom, 1990. 172–73.

"Profeta en Ninive." *Cuentos judíos latinoamericanos*. Ed. Ricardo Feierstein. Buenos Aires: Milá, 1989. 114–33.

Refugiados: Crónica de un palestino. Buenos Aires: Losada, 1969, 1970, 1976.

"Short Story Contest." Trans. Norman Thomas di Giovanni and Susan Ashe. *Celeste Goes Dancing and Other Stories: An Argentine Collection*. Ed. Norman Thomas di Giovanni. San Francisco: North Point Press, 1990. 75–84.

Todos los cuentos. Buenos Aires: Sudamericana, 1995.

El valor de escribir. Buenos Aires: Sudamericana/Planeta, 1985.

Y la rama llena de frutos. Buenos Aires: Sudamericana/Planeta, 1986.

RUTH BEHAR

Bridges to Cuba/Puentes a Cuba. Ann Arbor: U of Michigan P, 1995.

"Juban América." *Poetics Today* 16:1 (Spring 1995): 151–70.

Santa María del Monte: The Presence of the Past in a Spanish Village. Princeton: Princeton UP, 1986, 1991.

Translated Woman: Crossing the Border with Esperanza's Story. Boston: Beacon Press, 1993.

Las visiones de una bruja guachichil en 1599: Hacia una perspectiva indígena sobre la conquista de San Luis Potosí. San Luis Potosí, México: Centro de Investigaciones Históricas de San Luis Potosí, 1995.

The Vulnerable Observer: Anthropology that Breaks Your Heart. Boston: Beacon Press, 1996.

Women Writing Culture. Ed. with Deborah A. Gordon. Berkeley: U of California P, 1995.

The Wrath of a Woman: A Mexican Life Story. East Lansing: Michigan State UP, 1990.

Ruth Behar's poetry has been published in *Tikkun, Witness, Michigan Quarterly Review, Brújula/Compass, The American Voice, Latino Stuff Review, Bridges: A Journal for Jewish Feminists and Our Friends,* and in the anthologies *Little Havana Blues: A Cuban American Literary Anthology* (Houston: Arte Público Press, 1996) and *Sephardic American Voices: Two Hundred Years of Literary Legacy* (New York: Brandeis UP, 1997).

ARIEL DORFMAN

El absurdo entre cuatro paredes: El teatro de Harold Pinter. Santiago de Chile: Universitaria, 1968.

Con sangre en el ojo. With Marcelo Montecino. México, D.F.: Nueva Imagen, 1981. [Texts by Dorfman and photographs by M. Montecino.]

Cría ojos. México, D.F.: Nueva Imagen, 1979; Buenos Aires: Legasa, 1978.

Cuentos casi completos. Buenos Aires: Ediciones Letra Buena, 1991.

Cuentos para militares ("La batalla de los colores" y otros cuentos). Santiago de Chile: Emisión, 1986.

Culture et résistance au Chili. Grand-Saconnex: Institut d'Action Culturelle, 1978.

Death and the Maiden. New York: Penguin, 1991.

Dorando la píldora. Santiago de Chile: Las Ediciones del Orntiorrinco, 1985.

De elefantes literatura y miedo: Ensayos sobre la comunicación americana. La Habana: Casa de las Américas, 1988.

The Empire's Old Clothes: What the Lone Ranger, Babar, and Other Innocent Heroes Do to Our Minds. Trans. Clark Hansen. New York: Pantheon, 1983.

Ensayos quemados en Chile (Inocencia y neocolonialismo). Buenos Aires: Ediciones de la Flor, 1974.

Going North/Looking South. New York: Farrar, Straus, and Giroux, 1997.

Hacia la liberación del lector latinoamericano. Hanover, NH: Ediciones del Norte, 1984.

Hard Rain. Trans. George Shivers and Ariel Dorfman. New York: Readers International, 1990.

How to Read Donald Duck: Imperialist Ideology in the Disney Comic. Trans. David Kunzle. New York: Readers International, 1975.

Imaginación y violencia en América Latina: Ensayos. Santiago de Chile: Universitaria, 1970. Barcelona: Anagrama, 1972.

Konfidenz. Buenos Aires: Planeta, 1994.

Konfidenz. New York: Farrar, Straus, and Giroux, 1995.

The Last Song of Manuel Sendero. Trans. George R. Shivers and Ariel Dorfman. New York: Viking, 1987.

Last Waltz in Santiago. New York: Viking Penguin, 1988.

Mascara. New York: Viking Penguin, 1988.

Máscaras. Buenos Aires: Sudamericana, 1988.

Missing. Trans. Edith Grossman. London: Amnesty International, 1982.

Moros en la costa. Buenos Aires: Sudamericana, 1973.

La muerte y la doncella. Buenos Aires: Ediciones de la Flor, 1992.

My House Is on Fire. Trans. George Shivers and Ariel Dorfman. New York: Viking, 1990.

Nuestro que estás en la tierra: Esayos sobre el imperialismo cultural. México, D.F.: Nueva Imagen, 1980.

Para leer al pato Donald: Comunicación de masa y colonialismo. With Armando Mattelart. México, D.F.: Siglo Veintiuno, 1972.

Pastel de choclo. Santiago de Chile: Sinfronteras, 1986.

Patos, elefantes y héroes: La infancia como subdesarrollo. Buenos Aires: Ediciones de la Flor, 1985.

Pruebas al canto. México, D.F.: Nueva Imagen, 1980.

La rebelión de los conejos mágicos. Buenos Aires: Ediciones de la Flor, 1987. Barcelona: Ediciones B, 1988.

"The Rebellion of the Magical Rabbits." *Where Angels Glide at Dawn: New Stories from Latin America.* Ed. Lori M. Carlson and Cynthia Ventura. Introd. Isabel Allende. New York: HarperCollins, 1990. 7–25.

The Resistance Trilogy. London: Nick Hern, 1998.

Sin ir más lejos. Santiago de Chile: Pehuén, 1986.

Sobre las artes de espectáculo y fiestas en América Latina: Documento de información y trabajo para la reunión de expertos organizada por la Unesco en Bogotá. La Habana: UNESCO, 1976.

Some Write to the Future: Essays on Contemporary Latin American Fiction. Trans. George Shivers and Ariel Dorfman. Durham: Duke UP, 1991.

Los sueños nucleares de Reagan. Buenos Aires: Legasa, 1986.

Superman y sus amigos del alma. With Manuel Jofré. Buenos Aires: Galerna, 1974.

Travesía. Montevideo: Banda oriental, 1986.

La última aventura del Llanero Solitario. San José de Costa Rica: EDUCA, 1979.

La última canción de Manuel Sendero. México, D.F.: Siglo Veintiuno, 1982.

Viudas; Lector. Buenos Aires: Ediciones de la Flor, 1996.

Viudas (novela). México, D.F.: Siglo Veintiuno, 1981.

Widows. Trans. Stephen Kessler. New York: Vintage, 1984.

RICARDO FEIERSTEIN

"Amigos." *40 cuentos breves argentinos-siglo XX.* Ed. Fernando Sorrentino. Buenos Aires: Plus Ultra, 1977, 1981. 89–93.

"Argentina 1983." Trans. J. Kates and Stephen A. Sadow. *Minnesota Review* 30–31 (1989): 36.

Bailáte un tango, Ricardo. Buenos Aires: Centro Editor de América Latina, 1973.

La balada del sol. Buenos Aires: Indice, 1969.

"El Camino." *39 cuentos argentinos de vanguardia.* Ed. Carlos Mastrángelo. Buenos Aires: Plus Ultra, 1985. 172–78.

El caramelo descompuesto. Buenos Aires: Pardés, 1979.

Cien años de narrativa judeoargentina: 1889–1989. Buenos Aires: Milá, 1989.

Contraexilio y mestizaje. Buenos Aires: Milá, 1997.

Cuentos con rabia y oficina. Buenos Aires: Stilcograf, 1965.

Cuentos con un gris absurdo. Buenos Aires: Editores Dos, 1970.

Cuentos para hombres solos. Buenos Aires: Instituto Amigos del Libro, 1967.

"Diptich." Trans. J. Kates and Stephen A. Sadow. *Plum Review* (Winter 1994): 55–57.

Entre la izquierdisa y la pared. Buenos Aires: Pardés, 1983.

Escala uno en cincuenta. Buenos Aires: Pardés, 1984.

Historia de los judíos argentinos. Buenos Aires: Planeta, 1993.

Homicidios tímidos. Buenos Aires: Galena, 1996.

Integración y marginalidad: Historias de vidas de immigrantes judíos en Argentina. Ed. Ricardo Feierstein, Sara Itzigshon, Leondardo Senkman, and Isidro Nicorski. Buenos Aires: Editorial Pardés and the American Jewish Committee, 1985.

Inventadiario. Buenos Aires: Tiempo de Hoy, 1972.

Judaísmo 2000. Buenos Aires: Lugar Editorial, 1988.

"The Last Charge of the Polish Cavalry." Trans. J. Kates and Stephen A. Sadow. *Stand.* Forthcoming.

Letras en equilibrio. Caracas: Ediciones Arbol del Fuego, 1975.

Lucy en el cielo con diamantes. Buenos Aires: Ediciones Papiro, 1972.

Mestizo. Buenos Aires: Milá, 1988. Rev. ed. Buenos Aires: Planeta, 1994.

"*Mestizo* de Ricardo Feierstein (Selection)." *Anthologie de la littérature hispanoaméricaine du XXe siècle.* Ed. Jean Franco and Jean Lemogodeuc. Paris: Presses Universitaires de France, 1993. 371–73.

"Nostalgia." Trans. J. Kates and Stephen A. Sadow. *Literary Olympians II: A Crosscurrents Anthology.* San Diego: Crosscurrents, 1987. 134.

El pequeño Kleinmentch ilustrado. Buenos Aires: Pardés, 1980.

Sinfonía Inocente. (Reprint in one volume of the trilogy *El caramelo descompuesto, Entre la izquierdisa y la pared,* and *Escala uno en cincuenta.*) Introd. Andrés Avellanda. Buenos Aires: Pardés, 1984.

La vida no es sueño. Buenos Aires: Ediciones de la Flor, 1987.

"Vital Statistics (Selections)." Trans. J. Kates and Stephen A. Sadow. *International Poetry Review* 17 (1991): 58–69.

We, the Generation of the Wilderness. (Bilingual edition in Spanish and English.) Trans. and introd. J. Kates and Stephen A. Sadow. Boston: Ford-Brown, 1989.

"We, the Generation of the Wilderness (Selections)." Trans. J. Kates and Stephen A. Sadow. *Pig Iron Review Anthology of Third World Literature.* Youngstown, OH: Pig Iron Press, 1988. 96.

ALICIA FREILICH DE SEGAL

Cláper. Caracas: Planeta, 1987.

Cláper. Albuquerque: U of New Mexico P, 1998.

Colombina descubierta. Caracas: Planeta, 1991.

Cuarta dimensión. Caracas: Biblioteca Nacional, Síntesis Dosmil, 1975.

Entrevistado en carne y hueso. Caracas: Librería Suma, 1977.

Legítima defensa. Caracas: Seleven, 1984.

"El misiú: Interview with Máximo Freilich, Her Father." *Echad: An Anthology of Latin American Jewish Writings.* Ed. Robert Kalechofsky and Roberta Kalechofsky. Marblehead, MA: Micah Publications, 1980. 274–79.

"Prólogo." *Cinco novelas de Guillermo Meneses.* Caracas: Monte Avila, 1972. 1–9.

Triálogo. Caracas: Tiempo Nuevo, 1973.

La venedemocracia. Caracas: Monte Avila, 1978.

ALBERTO GERCHUNOFF

Los amores de Baruj Spinoza. Buenos Aires: BABEL, 1932.

Argentina, páis de advenimiento. Buenos Aires: Losada, 1952.

La asemblea de la bohardilla. Buenos Aires: Manuel Gleizer, 1925.

Autobiografía. Buenos Aires: Libreros y Editores del Polígano, 1983.

Buenos Aires: La metrópoli de mañana. Buenos Aires: Cuadernos de Buenos Aires, 1960.

La clínica del Dr. Mefistófeles: Moderna milagrería en diez jornadas. Santiago de Chile: Ercilla, 1937.

Comedia de pequeños burgueses. A three-act play serialized in *Nosotros* (Buenos Aires) 38 (1912): 193–206; *Nosotros* 39 (1912): 278–95. Act 3 was never published.

Cuentos de ayer. Buenos Aires: Ediciones América, 1919.

Enrique Heine, el poeta de nuestra intimidad. Buenos Aires: BABEL, 1927.

Entre Ríos, mi país. Buenos Aires: Futuro, 1950.

Figuras de nuestro tiempo. Buenos Aires: Vernácula, 1979.

Los gauchos judíos. La Plata: Talleres Gráficos Joaquín Sese, 1910.

Historias y proezas de amor. Buenos Aires: Manuel Gleizer, 1926.

El hombre importante. Montevideo/Buenos Aires: Sociedad Amigos del Libro Rioplatense, 1934.

El hombre que habló en la Sorbona. Buenos Aires: Manuel Gleizer, 1926.

The Jewish Gauchos of the Pampas. Trans. Prudencio de Pereda. New York: Abelard-Schuman, 1955. Rev. ed. Albuquerque: U of New Mexico P, 1998.

La jofaina maravillosa: Agenda cervantina. Buenos Aires: Biblioteca Argentina de Buenas Ediciones Literarias, 1922.

Nuestro Señor Don Quijote. Buenos Aires: Coni, 1913.

Nuestros escritores: Roberto J. Payró. Buenos Aires: J. Menéndez, 1925.

Pequeñas prosas. Buenos Aires: Manuel Gleizer, 1926.

El pino y la palmera. Buenos Aires: Sociedad Hebraica Argentina, 1952.

El problema judío. Buenos Aires: Macabí, 1945. Reprinted as *El pino y la palmera,* 1952.

Retorno de Don Quixote. Prologue Jorge Luis Borges. Buenos Aires: Sudamerica, 1951.

MARGO GLANTZ

Borrones y borradores. México, D.F.: Universidad Autónoma Nacional de México/ El Equilibrista, 1992.

De la amorosa inclinación a enredarse en cabellos. México, D.F.: Océano, 1984.

El día de tu boda. México, D.F.: SEP, 1982.

Doscientos ballenas azules. México, D.F.: La Máquina de Escribir, 1979.

Erosiones. Toluca: Universidad Autónoma del Estado de México, 1984.

Esquince de cintura: Ensayos sobre narrativa mexicana del siglo XX. México, D.F.: Consejo Nacional para la Cultura y las Artes, 1994.

The Family Tree. Trans. Susan Bassnett. London: Serpent's Tail, 1990.

Del fistol a la linterna: Homenaje a José Tomás de Cuellar y Manuel Payno en el centenerio de su muerte. Mexico, D.F.: UNAM, 1997.

Las genealogías. México, D.F.: M. Casillas, 1981.

Intervención y pretexto. México, D.F.: Universidad Nacional Autónoma de México, 1980.

La lengua en la mano. México, D.F.: Premià, 1983.

Las mil y una calorías (novela dietética). México, D.F.: Premià, 1978.

No pronunciarás. México, D.F.: Premià, 1980.

Onda y escritura en México. México, D.F.: Siglo XXI, 1971.

Repeticiones: Ensayos sobre literatura mexicana. Xalapa: Universidad Veracruzana, 1979.

Sor Juana Inés de la Cruz ¿Hagiografía o autobiografía? México, D.F.: Grijalbo, 1995.

Syndrome de naufragios. México, D.F.: Joaquín Mortiz, 1984.

ISAAC GOLDEMBERG

De Chepén a La Habana. With José Kozer. New York: Editorial Bayú-Menoráh, 1973.

"Crónicas/genealogías/cronologías." 1985.

The Fragmented Life of Don Jacobo Lerner. Trans. Roberto S. Picciotto. New York: Persea, 1976. Albuquerque: U of New Mexico P, 1998.

El gran libro de América Judía. San Juan: Editorial de la Universidad de Puerto Rico, 1998.

Hombre de paso/Just Passing Through. Trans. David Unger and Isaac Goldemberg. Hanover, NH: Point of Contact/Ediciones del Norte, 1981.

"On Being a Writer in Peru and Other Places." Trans. David Unger. *Lives on the Line: The Testimony of Contemporary Latin American Writers.* Ed. and introd. Doris Meyer. Berkeley: U of California P, 1988. 300–305.

Play by Play. New York: Persea Books, 1985.

Play by Play. Trans. Hardie St. Martin. Hanover, NH: Ediciones del Norte, 1983.

Tiempo al tiempo. Hanover, NH: Ediciones del Norte, 1984.

Tiempo de silencio. Colección de Poesía Hispanoamericana. Palencia, Spain: Colón, 1969.

La vida al contado. Hanover, NH: Ediciones del Norte, 1992.

La vida a plazos de Don Jacobo Lerner. Lima: Libre 1, 1980.

JOSÉ KOZER

Antología breve. Santo Domingo, Dominican Republic: Luna Cabeza Caliente, 1981.

The Ark Upon the Number. Trans. Ammeil Alcalay. Merrick, NY: Cross-Cultural Communications, 1982.

Bajo este cien. México, D.F.: Fondo de Cultura Económica, 1983.

Carece de causa. Buenos Aires: Ultimo Reino, 1988.

De Chepén a La Habana. With Isaac Goldemberg. New York: Bayú-Menoráh, 1973.

El carillón de los muertos. Buenos Aires: Ultimo Reino, 1987.

Díptico de la restitución. Madrid: Ediciones del Tapir, 1986.

De donde oscilan los seres en sus proporciones. La Laguna, Tenerife, Canary Islands: H.A. Editor, 1990.

Este judío de números y letras. Tenerife, Canary Islands: Nuestro Arte, 1975.

La garza sin sombras. Barcelona: Ediciones Libres del Mall, 1985.

Jarrón de abreviaturas. México, D.F.: Premià, 1980.

Nueva poesía hispanoamericana en Estados Unidos. San Salvador: Nueva Cultura, 1971.
Nueve láminas (glorieta) y otros poemas. Iztapalapa, México, D.F.: Universidad Autónoma Metropolitana, 1984.
Padres y otras profesiones. New York: Antiediciones Villa Miseria, 1972.
Las plagas. New York: Exilio, 1971.
Poemas de Guadalupe. Buenos Aires: Ediciones por la Poesía, 1973.
La rueca de los semblantes. León, Spain: Instituto Fray Bernardino de Sahagún, 1980.
Stet. New York: Junction C. Forthcoming.
Trazas del lirondo. Iztapalapa, México: Universidad Autónoma Metropolitana, 1993.
Y así tomaron posesión en las ciudades. Barcelona: Ambito Literario, 1978.

ALCINA LUBITCH DOMECQ

"Bottles." *Tropical Synagogues: Short Stories by Jewish Latin-American Authors.* Ed. Ilan Stavans. New York: Holmes & Meier, 1994. 159–61.
El espejo de espejo; o, La noble sonrisa del perro. México, D.F.: Joaquín Mortiz, 1983.
Intoxicada. México, D.F.: Joaquín Mortiz, 1984.
"It Just Isn't Right [On Being a Freak]." Trans. Ilan Stavans. *Albany Review* 4 (Summer 1990): 54–61.
Stories and essays in English in more than thirty magazines and anthologies, including the *American Voice*, the *Albany Review, Out of the Mirrored Garden: New Fiction by Latin American Women* (New York: Anchor, 1996), and *The Oxford Book of Jewish Stories* (New York: Oxford University Press, 1998).

ANGELINA MUÑIZ-HUBERMAN

"El campanero de Stephenholmer." *Hispamérica* 22.66 (1993): 63–68.
Castillos en la tierra (seudomemorias). México, D.F.: Hora Actual, 1995.
"Ciudad de oro amurallado." *Noaj* 3.3–4 (1989): 43–46.
Cuerpo entero. México, D.F.: Universidad Nacional Autónoma de México, 1991.
"De las tinieblas a la luz: La historia de la literatura judeomexicana." *La Jornada Semanal* (Mexico) 285 (November 1994): 32–35.
Dulcinea encantada. México, D.F.: Joaquín Mortiz, 1992.
Enclosed Garden. Trans. Lois Parkinson Zamora. Pittsburgh: Latin American Literary Review Press, 1988.
La guerra del unicornio. México, D.F.: Artifice Ediciones, 1983.
Huerto cerrado, huerto sellado. México, D.F.: Oasis, 1985.

"Inland." Trans. Terry Seymour. *Icarus* 6 (Spring 1992): 107–15.

"In the Name of His Name." Trans. Lois Parkinson Zamora. *Tropical Synagogues: Short Stories by Jewish Latin-American Authors.* Ed. Ilan Stavans. New York: Holmes & Meier, 1994. 189–92.

La lengua florida: Antología sefardí. México, D.F.: Fondo de Cultura Económica, 1989.

El libro de Miriam y Primicias. México, D.F.: Universidad Autónoma Metropolitana, 1990.

De magias y prodigios: Transmutaciones. México, D.F.: Fondo de Cultura Económica, 1987.

La memoria del aire. México, D.F.: Universidad Autónoma de México, 1995.

El mercader de Tudela. México, D.F.: Fondo de Cultura Económica, 1998.

Morada interior. México, D.F.: Joaquín Mortiz, 1972.

Narrativa relativa. México, D.F.: Universidad Nacional Autónoma de México, 1992.

Las raíces y las ramas: Fuentes y derivaciones de la Cábala hispanohebrea. México, D.F.: Fondo de Cultura Económica, 1993.

"Rising Mournful from the Earth." Trans. Lois Parkinson Zamora. *Contemporary Women Authors of Latin America.* 2 vols. Ed. Doris Meyer and Margarie Olmos. Brooklyn: Brooklyn College Press, 1983. 2:212–14.

La sal en el rostro. México, D.F.: Molinos de Viento/UNAM, 1998.

Serpientes y escaleras. México, D.F.: Universidad Nacional Autónoma de México, 1991.

"Testimonio de una obra en torno al exilio y promisión." *Noaj* 6.7–8 (1992): 25–28.

Tierra adentro. México, D.F.: Joaquín Mortiz, 1977.

Vilano al viento. México, D.F.: Universidad Autónoma de México, 1982.

Las voces de la mística en Ramón Xirau. México, D.F.: Universidad Nacional Autónoma de México, 1995.

MOACYR SCLIAR

Amante da madonna & outras historias. Porto Alegre: Mercado Aberto, 1997.

O anão no televisor: Contos. Porto Alegre: RBS/Globo, 1979.

A balada do falso messias. São Paulo: Atica, 1976.

The Ballad of the False Messiah. Trans. Eloah F. Giacomelli. New York: Ballantine, 1987.

Os calavos de Repæblica. São Paulo: FTD, 1989.

Caminhos da esperança: A presença judaica no Rio Grande do Sul/Pathways of Hope: The Jewish Presence in Rio Grande do Sul. Porto Alegre: Instituto Cultural Judaico Marc Chagall, 1991.

No caminho dos sonhos. São Paulo: FTD, 1988.

O carnaval dos animais. Porto Alegre: Movimento, 1976.

The Carnival of the Animals. Trans. Eloah F. Giacomelli. New York: Ballantine, 1986.

Cavalos e obeliscos. Porto Alegre: Mercado Aberto, 1981.

Cenas da vida minúscula. Porto Alegre: L&PM, 1991.

Cenas médicas: Pequena introdução da medicina. Porto Alegre: Editora da Universidade, Universidade Federal do Rio Grande do Sul, 1987.

The Centaur in the Garden. Trans. Eloah F. Giacomelli. New York: Ballantine, 1985.

O centauro no jardim: Romance. Rio de Janeiro: Nova Fronteira, 1980.

O ciclo das águas. Porto Alegre: Globo, 1976.

The Complete Short Stories. Albuquerque: U of New Mexico P, 1998.

A condição judiaca: Das Tábuas da Lei à mesa de cozinha. Porto Alegre: L&PM, 1985.

Contos reunidos. São Paulo: Companhia das Letras, 1995.

[Dez] 10 contos escolhidos. Brasília: Horizonte Editora/ Instituto Nacional do Livro/Fundação Nacional Pro-Memória, 1984.

Doutor Miragem. Porto Alegre: L&PM, 1978.

Os dueses de Raquel. Rio de Janeiro: Expressão e Cultura, 1978.

Del Edén al diván. Buenos Aires: Shalom, 1991.

Do Edén ao divã: Humor judaico. With Eliahu Toker and Patricia Finzi. São Paulo: Shalom, 1990.

The Enigmatic Eye. Trans. Eloah F. Giacomelli. New York: Ballantine, 1989.

A estranha nação de Rafael Mendes. Porto Alegre: L&PM, 1983.

O exercito de um homem só: Novela. Rio de Janeiro: Expressão e Cultura, 1973.

A festa no castelo. Porto Alegre: L&PM, 1982.

The Gods of Raquel. Trans. Eloah F. Giacomelli. New York: Ballantine, 1986.

A guerra no Bom Fim. Porto Alegre: L&PM, 1981.

Histórias da terra trémula. São Paulo: Vertente, 1977.

Histórias de médico em formação. Porto Alegre: Editora Difusão de Cultura, 1962.

"Inside My Dirty Head—The Holocaust." Trans. Eloah F. Giacomelli. *Tropical Synagogues: Short Stories by Jewish Latin-American Authors.* Ed. Ilan Stavans. New York: Holmes & Meier, 1994. 113–16.

Introdução à práctica amorosa. São Paulo: Scipione, 1988.

Do mágico ao social: A trajetória da saúde pública. Porto Alegre: L&PM, 1987.

A majestade do Xingu. São Paulo: Companhia das Letras, 1997.

A massagista japonesa. Porto Alegre: L&PM, 1984.

Mauricio: A trajetóra, o cenário histórico, a dimensão humana de um pioneiro da communicação do Brasil. [On Mauricio Sirotsky Sobrhino.] Porto Alegre: Sulina, 1991.

Max e os felinos. 1982.

Max and the Cats. Trans. Eloah F. Giacomelli. New York: Ballantine, 1989.

Os melhores contos de Moacyr Scliar. Sel. Regina Zilberman. São Paulo: Global, 1984.

Mês de cães danados. Porto Alegre: L&PM, 1977.

Os mistérios de Porto Alegre: Coletânea de crônicas publicadas em Zero Hora. Porto Alegre: Gaúcha Gráfica/Editora Jornalística, 1976.

O olho enigmatico. Rio de Janeiro: Guanabara, 1986.

The One-Man Army. Trans. Eloah F. Giacomelli. New York: Ballantine, 1986.

O orelha de van Gogh: Contos. São Paulo: Companhia das Letras, 1989.

Um país chamado infância. Porto Alegre: Sulina, 1989.

A paixão transformada: Historia da medicina na literatura. São Paulo: Companhia das Letras, 1996.

Pega pra kapput! With Josué Guimarães, Luis F. Veríssimo, and Edgar Vasques. Porto Alegre: L&PM, 1978.

Se eu fosse Rothschild: Citações que marcaram a trajetoria do povo judeu. Porto Alegre: L&PM, 1993.

Um sonho no caroço do abacate. São Paulo: Global, 1995.

Sonhos topicais. São Paulo: Companhia das Letras, 1992.

The Strange Nation of Rafael Mendes. Trans. Eloah F. Giacomelli. New York: Harmony Books, 1987.

O tio que flutava. São Paulo: Atica, 1990.

Os voluntários. Porto Alegre: L&PM, 1980.

The Volunteers. Trans. Eloah F. Giacomelli. New York: Ballantine, 1988.

ILAN STAVANS

"América Latina y su pluma judía." Revista Hispánica Moderna 63.1 (1990): 114–17.

Anti-Heroes: Mexico and Its Detective Novel. Trans. Jesse Lytle and Jennifer Mattson. Madison, NJ: Farleigh Dickenson P, 1997.

Anti-héroes: México y su novela policial. México, D.F.: Joaquín Mortiz, 1993.

Antología de cuentos de misterio y terror. México, D.F.: Editorial Porrúa, 1993.

"An Appointment with Héctor Belascoarán Shayne, Mexican Private Eye." Preview: Latin American Arts and Literature 42 (1990): 5–9.

Art and Anger: Essays on Politics and the Imagination. Albuquerque: U of New Mexico P, 1996.

Bandido: Oscar "Zeta" Acosta & the Chicano Experience. New York: HarperCollins, 1996.

The Collected Stories: Calvert Casey, John Polk, Ilan Stavans. Durham: Duke UP, 1998.

"The Death of Yankos." *Calypso* 1.1 (1989): 42–46. Also in *Tropical Synagogues: Short Stories by Jewish Latin-American Authors*. Ed. Ilan Stavans. New York: Holmes & Meier, 1994. 193–98.

Growing Up Latino: Memoirs and Stories. Coedited with Harold Augenbraum. Boston: Houghton Mifflin, 1993.

"A Heaven Without Crows." Trans. David Unger. *Michigan Quarterly Review* 32.3 (1993): 380–85.

The Hispanic Condition: Reflections on Culture and Identity in America. New York: HarperCollins, 1994.

Imagining Columbus: The Literary Voyage. New York: Twayne-Macmillan, 1993.

"In the Margins of Time." *Present Tense* 15.2 (1988): 24–30.

"Jewish Writers in Latin America." *Midstream* 34.6 (1986): 51–53.

Julio Cortázar: A Study of the Short Fiction. New York: Twayne, 1996.

"The Left-handed Pianist." Trans. Harry Morales. *TriQuarterly* 82.2 (1994): 76–80.

"Letter to a German Friend." *Midstream* 36.3 (April 1990): 30–32.

"Lost in Translation." *Massachusetts Review* 34.4 (Winter 1993–94): 489–502.

Manual del (im)perfecto reseñista. México, D.F.: UAM, 1989.

Masterworks of Latin American Short Fiction: Eight Novelas. Introd. New York: HarperCollins, 1996.

New World: Young Latino Writers. New York: Delta, 1997.

The One-Handed Pianist and Other Stories. Albuquerque: U of New Mexico P, 1996. Translations from *Talia y el cielo* and *La pianista manca*.

The Oxford Book of Jewish Short Stories. New York: Oxford UP, 1998.

The Oxford Book of Latin American Essays. New York: Oxford UP, 1997.

La pianista manca. Caracas: Alfadil, 1992.

La pluma mágica. Ed. with Flora H. Schiminovich. Boston: Heinle & Heinle, 1994.

La pluma y la máscara. México, D.F.: Fondo de Cultura Económica, 1993.

Prontuario. México, D.F.: Joaquín Mortiz, 1992.

The Riddle of Cantinflas: Essays on Hispanic Popular Culture. Albuquerque: U of New Mexico P, 1998.

"Sam Spade Otra Vez." *Nation* 255.6 (1992): 214–15.

Sentimental Songs/La poesía cursi. [Trans. of Felipe Alfau.] Philadelphia: Dalkey Archives Press, 1992.

Talia y el cielo, o el libro de los ensueños. With Zuri Balkoff. México, D.F.: Plaza y Valdés, 1989.

Tropical Synagogues: Short Stories by Jewish Latin-American Authors. New York: Holmes & Meier, 1994.

The Urban Muse: Stories on the American City. New York: Doubleday, 1997.

Vals triste. One-act play. West Bank Stage, Off-Broadway, 1992.

MARIO SZICHMAN

A las 20:25, la señora entró en la immortalidad. Hanover, NH: Ediciones del Norte, 1981.

At 8:25 Evita Became Immortal. Trans. Roberto Picciotto. Hanover, NH: Ediciones del Norte, 1983.

"Botín de guerra." *Noaj* 4.5 (1990): 28–32.

Crónica falsa. Buenos Aires: Jorge Alvarez, 1969.

"Cuidado con las imitaciones." *Hispamérica* 24.72 (1995):77–85.

Los judíos del Mar Dulce. Buenos Aires and Caracas: Galerna/Síntesis 2000, 1971.

Miguel Otero Silva: Mitología de una generación frustrada. Caracas: Universidad Central de Venezuela, 1975.

"La terca fundación de Buenos Aires." *Noaj* 1 (1987): 11–13.

Uslar: Cultura y dependencia. Caracas: Vadell Hermanos, 1975.

La verdadura crónica falsa. Buenos Aires: Centro Editor de América Latina, 1972.